Ancient Christian Texts

Commentaries on Romans, 1–2 Corinthians, and Hebrews

Cyril of Alexandria

TRANSLATED BY

David R. Maxwell

EDITED BY

Joel C. Elowsky

ivp
Academic
An imprint of InterVarsity Press
Downers Grove, Illinois

InterVarsity Press
P.O. Box 1400, Downers Grove, IL 60515-1426
ivpress.com
email@ivpress.com

InterVarsity Press® is the book-publishing division of InterVarsity Christian Fellowship/USA®, a movement of students and faculty active on campus at hundreds of universities, colleges, and schools of nursing in the United States of America, and a member movement of the International Fellowship of Evangelical Students. For information about local and regional activities, visit intervarsity.org.

The publisher cannot verify the accuracy or functionality of website URLs used in this book beyond the date of publication.

Design: Cindy Kiple
Interior design: Daniel van Loon
Image: Saints Peter and Paul by Crivelli, Carlo at Accademia, Venice/Art Resource, NY

ISBN 978-0-8308-2918-7 (print)
ISBN 978-0-8308-8727-9 (digital)

Printed in the United States of America ♾

InterVarsity Press is committed to ecological stewardship and to the conservation of natural resources in all our operations. This book was printed using sustainably sourced paper.

Library of Congress Cataloging-in-Publication Data
A catalog record for this book is available from the Library of Congress.

P 25 24 23 22 21 20 19 18 17 16 15 14 13 12 11 10 9 8 7 6 5 4 3 2 1
Y 42 41 40 39 38 37 36 35 34 33 32 31 30 29 28 27 26 25 24 23 22

CONTENTS

ABBREVIATIONS

Cod. Coisl.	Codex Coislinianus
Cod. Pantokrator.	Codex Athous Pantokratoros
Cod. Vat. Gr.	Codex Vaticanus Graecus
Cod. Vat. Syr.	Codex Vaticanus Syriacus
GCS	Der Griechischen Christlichen Schriftsteller der ersten drei Jahrhunderte
PG	Patrologia Graeca
PL	Patrologia Latina
PTS	Patristische Texte und Studien

GENERAL INTRODUCTION

Ancient Christian Texts (hereafter ACT) presents the full text of ancient Christian commentaries on Scripture that have remained so unnoticed that they have not yet been translated into English.

The patristic period (AD 95–750) is the time of the fathers of the church, when the exegesis of Scripture texts was in its primitive formation. This period spans from Clement of Rome to John of Damascus, embracing seven centuries of biblical interpretation, from the end of the New Testament to the mid-eighth century, including the Venerable Bede.

This series extends but does not reduplicate texts of the Ancient Christian Commentary on Scripture (ACCS). It presents full-length translations of texts that appear only as brief extracts in the ACCS. The ACCS began years ago authorizing full-length translations of key patristic texts on Scripture in order to provide fresh sources of valuable commentary that previously were not available in English. It is from these translations that the ACT series has emerged.

A multiyear project such as this requires a well-defined objective. The task is straightforward: *to introduce full-length translations of key texts of early Christian teaching, homilies and commentaries on a particular book of Scripture.* These are seminal documents that have decisively shaped the entire subsequent history of biblical exegesis, but in our time have been largely ignored.

To carry out this mission each volume of the Ancient Christian Texts series has four aspirations:

1. To show the approach of one of the early Christian writers in dealing with the problems of understanding, reading and conveying the meaning of a particular book of Scripture.

2. To make more fully available the whole argument of the ancient Christian interpreter of Scripture to all who wish to think with the early church about a particular canonical text.

3. To broaden the base of the biblical studies, Christian teaching and preaching to include classical Christian exegesis.

4. To stimulate Christian historical, biblical, theological and pastoral scholarship toward deeper inquiry into early classic practitioners of scriptural interpretation.

For Whom Is This Series Designed?

We have selected and translated these texts primarily for general and nonprofessional use by an audience of persons who study the Bible regularly.

In varied cultural settings around the world, contemporary readers are asking how they might grasp the meaning of sacred texts under the instruction of the great minds of the ancient church. They often study books of the Bible verse by verse, book by book, in groups and workshops, sometimes with a modern commentary in hand. But many who study the Bible intensively hunger to have available as well the thoughts of a reliable classic Christian commentator on this same text. This series will give the modern commentators a classical text for comparison and amplification. Readers will judge for themselves as to how valuable or complementary are their insights and guidance.

The classic texts we are translating were originally written for anyone (lay or clergy, believers or seekers) who wished to reflect and meditate with the great minds of the early church. They sought to illuminate the plain sense, theological wisdom, and moral and spiritual meaning of an individual book of Scripture. They were not written for an academic audience, but for a community of faith shaped by the sacred text.

Yet in serving this general audience, the editors remain determined not to neglect the rigorous requirements and needs of academic readers who until recently have had few full translations available to them in the history of exegesis. So this series is designed also to serve public libraries, universities, academic classes, homiletic preparation and historical interests worldwide in Christian scholarship and interpretation.

Hence our expected audience is not limited to the highly technical and specialized scholarly field of patristic studies, with its strong bent toward detailed word studies and explorations of cultural contexts. Though all of our editors and translators are patristic and linguistic scholars, they also are scholars who search for the meanings and implications of the texts. The audience is not primarily the university scholar concentrating on the study of the history of the transmission of the text or those with highly focused interests in textual morphology or historical-critical issues. If we succeed in serving our wider readers practically and well, we hope to serve as well college and seminary courses in Bible, church history, historical theology, hermeneutics and homiletics. These texts have not until now been available to these classes.

Readiness for Classic Spiritual Formation

Today global Christians are being steadily drawn toward these biblical and patristic sources for daily meditation and spiritual formation. They are on the outlook for primary classic sources of spiritual formation and biblical interpretation, presented in accessible form and grounded in reliable scholarship.

These crucial texts have had an extended epoch of sustained influence on Scripture interpretation, but virtually no influence in the modern period. They also deserve a hearing among modern readers and scholars. There is a growing awareness of the speculative excesses and spiritual and homiletic limitations of much post-Enlightenment criticism. Meanwhile the motifs, methods and approaches of ancient exegetes have remained unfamiliar not only to historians but to otherwise highly literate biblical scholars, trained exhaustively in the methods of historical and scientific criticism.

It is ironic that our times, which claim to be so fully furnished with historical insight and research methods, have neglected these texts more than scholars in previous centuries who could read them in their original languages.

This series provides indisputable evidence of the modern neglect of classic Christian exegesis: it remains a fact that extensive and once authoritative classic commentaries on Scripture still remain untranslated into any modern language. Even in China such a high level of neglect has not befallen classic Buddhist, Taoist and Confucian commentaries.

Ecumenical Scholarship

This series, like its two companion series, the ACCS and Ancient Christian Doctrine (ACD), is an expression of unceasing ecumenical efforts that have enjoyed the wide cooperation of distinguished scholars of many differing academic communities. Under this classic textual umbrella, it has brought together in common spirit Christians who have long distanced themselves from each other by competing church memories. But all of these traditions have an equal right to appeal to the early history of Christian exegesis. All of these traditions can, without a sacrifice of principle or intellect, come together to study texts common to them all. This is its ecumenical significance.

This series of translations is respectful of a distinctively theological reading of Scripture that cannot be reduced to historical, philosophical, scientific or sociological insights or methods alone. It takes seriously the venerable tradition of ecumenical reflection concerning the premises of revelation, providence, apostolicity, canon and consensuality. A high respect is here granted, despite modern assumptions, to uniquely Christian theological forms of reasoning, such as classical consensual christological and triune reasoning, as distinguishing premises of classic Christian textual interpretation. These cannot be acquired by empirical methods alone. This approach does not pit theology against critical theory; instead, it incorporates critical historical methods and brings them into coordinate accountability within its larger purpose of listening to Scripture.

The internationally diverse character of our editors and translators corresponds with the global range of our audience, which bridges many major communions of Christianity. We have sought to bring together a distinguished international network of Protestant, Catholic and Orthodox scholars, editors and translators of the highest quality and reputation to accomplish this design.

But why just now at this historical moment is this need for patristic wisdom felt particularly by so many readers of Scripture? Part of the reason is that these readers have been longer deprived of significant contact with many of these vital sources of classic Christian exegesis.

The Ancient Commentary Tradition

This series focuses on texts that comment on Scripture and teach its meaning. We define a commentary in its plain-sense definition as a series of illustrative or explanatory notes on any work of enduring significance. The word *commentary* is an Anglicized form of the Latin *commentarius* (or "annotation" or "memoranda" on a subject, text or series of events). In its theological meaning it is a work that explains, analyzes or expounds a biblical book or portion of Scripture. Tertullian, Origen, John Chrysostom, Jerome, Augustine and Clement of Alexandria all revealed their familiarity with both the secular and religious commentators available to them as they unpacked the meanings of the sacred text at hand.

The commentary in ancient times typically began with a general introduction covering such questions as authorship, date, purpose and audience. It commented as needed on grammatical or lexical problems in the text and provided explanations of difficulties in the text. It typically moved verse by verse through a Scripture text, seeking to make its meaning clear and its import understood.

The general Western literary genre of commentary has been definitively shaped by the history of early Christian commentaries on Scripture. It is from Origen, Hilary, the *Opus imperfectum in Matthaeum,* John Chrysostom and Cyril of Alexandria that we learn what a commentary is—far more so than in the case of classic medical, philosophical or poetic commentaries. It leaves too much unsaid simply to assume that the Christian biblical commentary took a previously extant literary genre and reshaped it for Christian texts. Rather it is more accurate to say that *the Western literary genre of the commentary (and especially the biblical commentary) has patristic commentaries as its decisive pattern and prototype.*

It is only in the last two centuries, since the development of modern historicist methods of criticism, that modern writers have sought more strictly to delimit the definition of a commentary so as to include only certain limited interests focusing largely on historical-critical method, philological and grammatical observations, literary analysis, and socio-political or economic circumstances impinging on the text. While respecting all these approaches, the ACT editors do not hesitate to use the classic word *commentary* to define more broadly the genre of this series. These are commentaries in their classic sense.

The ACT editors freely take the assumption that the Christian canon is to be respected as the church's sacred text. The reading and preaching of Scripture are vital to religious life. The central hope of this endeavor is that it might contribute in some small way to the revitalization of religious faith and community through a renewed discovery of the earliest readings of the church's Scriptures.

An Appeal to Allow the Text to Speak for Itself

This prompts two appeals:

1. For those who begin by assuming as normative for a commentary only the norms considered typical for modern expressions of what a commentary is, we ask: please allow the ancient commentators to define *commentarius* according to their own lights. Those who assume the preemptive authority and truthfulness of modern critical methods alone will always tend to view the classic Christian exegetes as dated, quaint, premodern, hence inadequate, and in some instances comic or even mean-spirited, prejudiced, unjust and oppressive. So in the interest of hermeneutical fairness, it is recommended that the modern reader not impose upon ancient Christian exegetes modern assumptions about valid readings of Scripture. The ancient Christian writers constantly challenge these unspoken, hidden and indeed often camouflaged assumptions that have become commonplace in our time.

We leave it to others to discuss the merits of ancient versus modern methods of exegesis. But even this cannot be done honestly without a serious examination of the texts of ancient exegesis. Ancient commentaries may be disqualified as commentaries by modern standards. But they remain commentaries by the standards of those who anteceded and formed the basis of the modern commentary.

The attempt to read a Scripture text while ruling out all theological and moral assumptions—as well as ecclesial, sacramental and dogmatic assumptions that have prevailed generally in the community of faith out of which it emerged—is a very thin enterprise indeed. Those who tendentiously may read a single page of patristic exegesis, gasp and toss it away because it does not conform adequately to the canons of modern exegesis and historicist commentary are surely not exhibiting a valid model for critical inquiry today.

2. In ancient Christian exegesis, chains of biblical references were often very important in thinking about the text in relation to the whole testimony of sacred Scripture, by the analogy of faith, comparing text with text, on the premise that *scripturam ex scriptura explicandam esse*. When ancient exegesis weaves many Scripture texts together, it does not limit its focus to a single text as much modern exegesis prefers, but constantly relates them to other texts, by analogy, intensively using typological reasoning, as did the rabbinic tradition.

Since the principle prevails in ancient Christian exegesis that each text is illumined by other texts and by the whole narrative of the history of revelation, we find in patristic comments on a given text many other subtexts interwoven in order to illumine that text. In these ways the models of exegesis often do not correspond with modern commentary assumptions, which tend to resist or rule out chains of scriptural reference. We implore the reader not to force the assumptions of twentieth-century hermeneutics upon the ancient Christian writers, who themselves knew nothing of what we now call hermeneutics.

The Complementarity of Research Methods in This Series

The Ancient Christian Texts series will employ several interrelated methods of research, which the editors and translators seek to bring together in a working integration. Principal among these methods are the following:

1. The editors, translators and annotators will bring to bear the best resources of *textual criticism* in preparation for their volumes. This series is not intended to produce a new critical edition of the original-language text. The best urtext in the original language will be used. Significant variants in the earliest manuscript sources of the text may be commented upon as needed in the annotations. But it will be assumed that the editors and translators will be familiar with the textual ambiguities of a particular text and be able to state their conclusions about significant differences among scholars. Since we are working with ancient texts that have, in some cases, problematic or ambiguous passages, we are obliged to employ all methods of historical, philological and textual inquiry appropriate to the study of ancient texts. To that end, we will appeal to the most reliable text-critical scholarship of both biblical and patristic studies. We will assume that our editors and translators have reviewed the international literature of textual critics regarding their text so as to provide the reader with a translation of the most authoritative and reliable form of the ancient text. We will leave it to the volume editors and translators, under the supervision of the general editors, to make these assessments. This will include the challenge of considering which variants within the biblical text itself might impinge upon the patristic text, and which forms or stemma of the biblical text the patristic writer was employing. The annotator will supply explanatory footnotes where these textual challenges may raise potential confusions for the reader.

2. Our editors and translators will seek to understand the *historical context* (including socioeconomic, political and psychological aspects as needed) of the text. These understandings are often vital to right discernment of the writer's intention. Yet we do not see our primary mission as that of discussing in detail these contexts. They are to be factored into the translation and commented on as needed in the annotations, but are not to become the primary focus of this series. Our central interest is less in the social location of the text or the philological history of particular words than in authorial intent and accurate translation. Assuming a proper social-historical contextualization of the text, the main focus of this series will be upon a dispassionate and fair translation and analysis of the text itself.

3. The main task is to set forth the meaning of the biblical text itself as understood by the patristic writer. The intention of our volume editors and translators is to help the reader see clearly into the meanings that patristic commentators have discovered in the biblical text. *Exegesis* in its classic sense implies an effort to explain, interpret and comment on a text, its meaning, its sources and its connections with other texts. It implies

a close reading of the text, using whatever linguistic, historical, literary or theological resources are available to explain the text. It is contrasted with *eisegesis,* which implies that interpreters have imposed their own personal opinions or assumptions on the text. The patristic writers actively practiced intratextual exegesis, which seeks to define and identify the exact wording of the text, its grammatical structure and the interconnectedness of its parts. They also practiced extratextual exegesis, seeking to discern the geographical, historical or cultural context in which the text was written. Our editors and annotators will also be attentive as needed to the ways in which the ancient Christian writer described his own interpreting process or hermeneutic assumptions.

4. The underlying philosophy of translation that we employ in this series is, like the Ancient Christian Commentary on Scripture, termed *dynamic equivalency.* We wish to avoid the pitfalls of either too loose a paraphrase or too rigid a literal translation. We seek language that is literary but not purely literal. Whenever possible we have opted for the metaphors and terms that are normally in use in everyday English-speaking culture. Our purpose is to allow the ancient Christian writers to speak for themselves to ordinary readers in the present generation. We want to make it easier for the Bible reader to gain ready access to the deepest reflection of the ancient Christian community of faith on a particular book of Scripture. We seek a thought-for-thought translation rather than a formal equivalence or word-for-word style. This requires the words to be first translated accurately and then rendered in understandable idiom. We seek to present the same thoughts, feelings, connotations and effects of the original text in everyday English language. We have used vocabulary and language structures commonly used by the average person. We do not leave the quality of translation only to the primary translator, but pass it through several levels of editorial review before confirming it.

The Function of the ACT Introductions, Annotations and Translations

In writing the introduction for a particular volume of the ACT series, the translator or volume editor will discuss, where possible, the opinion of the writer regarding authorship of the text, the importance of the biblical book for other patristic interpreters, the availability or paucity of patristic comment, any salient points of debate between the Fathers, and any special challenges involved in translating and editing the particular volume. The introduction affords the opportunity to frame the entire commentary in a manner that will help the general reader understand the nature and significance of patristic comment on the biblical text under consideration and to help readers find their critical bearings so as to read and use the commentary in an informed way.

The footnotes will assist the reader with obscurities and potential confusions. In the annotations the volume editors have identified Scripture allusions and historical references embedded within the texts. Their purpose is to help the reader move easily from passage to passage without losing a sense of the whole.

The ACT general editors seek to be circumspect and meticulous in commissioning volume editors and translators. We strive for a high level of consistency and literary quality throughout the course of this series. We have sought out as volume editors and translators those patristic and biblical scholars who are thoroughly familiar with their original language sources, who are informed historically, and who are sympathetic to the needs of ordinary nonprofessional readers who may not have professional language skills.

Thomas C. Oden, Gerald L. Bray, and Michael Glerup, Series Editors

INTRODUCTION TO CYRIL OF ALEXANDRIA'S COMMENTARIES ON ROMANS, 1-2 CORINTHIANS, AND HEBREWS

David R. Maxwell

Cyril of Alexandria saw himself first of all as an interpreter of Scripture. Though he is best known for his dogmatic and polemical writings against Nestorius, this reputation does not actually correspond to the weight of his literary output. His exegetical writings make up seven out of his ten volumes in Migne's Patrologia series.[1] Some of the works, such as the *Commentary on Isaiah* and the *Commentary on John*, are massive.

Perhaps part of the reason his exegetical writings have been overlooked is that they have not been readily available in English. This state of affairs is now changing. Since the turn of the millennium, new English translations have been published of Cyril's commentaries on Isaiah, the Minor Prophets, and John, as well as his *Glaphyra*, which is a commentary on the Pentateuch.[2] The current volume seeks to continue this trend.

Of course, Cyril's contribution to the Christology of the early and contemporary church is undeniable, and it is no surprise that Cyril is often read with that set of issues in mind. However, his biblical commentaries reveal a full-bodied theology that includes a well-developed soteriology, a clear vision of the Christian life, and an intense concern for pastoral care, not to mention an encyclopedic knowledge of the Scriptures. With the increasing accessibility of Cyril's biblical commentaries in English, readers will be able to gain a deeper and more balanced appreciation for the theologian considered by the ancients to be the "seal of the fathers."

This volume presents, for the first time in English, a translation of Cyril's commentaries on Romans, 1 Corinthians, 2 Corinthians, and Hebrews, which are extant in fragmentary form. Despite the fact that we lack the full commentaries, the fragments we do possess are significant enough in their length and wide-ranging enough in their content that

[1]Cyril's works are contained in Patrologia Graeca 68-77.

[2]St. Cyril of Alexandria, *Commentary on the Twelve Prophets*, trans. Robert Charles Hill, 3 vols., Fathers of the Church (Washington, DC: Catholic University of America Press, 2007–2013); St. Cyril of Alexandria, *Glaphyra on the Pentateuch*, trans. Nicholas P. Lunn, 2 vols., Fathers of the Church (Washington, DC: Catholic University of America Press, 2018–2019); Cyril of Alexandria, *Commentary on John*, trans. David R. Maxwell, 2 vols., Ancient Christian Texts (Downers Grove, IL: IVP Academic, 2013–2015).

the editors of this series thought they were worth making available. An Armenian translation of Cyril's complete commentary on Hebrews has recently been discovered as well, but that is not included in the present volume.[3]

The State of the Text

Since the remains of these commentaries are fragmentary, a few comments on the state of the text are in order. The fragments appear in various catenae (literally "chains"), which are lists of quotations of church fathers. Catenae were used for pedagogical purposes in the ancient world, not only in the field of theology, but also in philosophy, medicine, law, and education.[4] The catenae that concern us here were used to elucidate Scripture. They presented a verse from Scripture, called a lemma, under which they listed quotations from various church fathers commenting on that passage. InterVarsity Press's Ancient Christian Commentary on Scripture series would be a modern example of this genre.

The comments from Cyril were collected from these lists in the nineteenth century by P. E. Pusey and published in a critical edition.[5] Pusey drew mainly on two medieval manuscripts for the material on Romans: the Codex Vaticanus Graecus 762 (tenth/eleventh centuries), edited by Angelo Mai,[6] and the Codex Monacensis (eleventh century), edited by J. A. Cramer.[7] The material on 1 and 2 Corinthians comes primarily from the same Codex Vaticanus Graecus 762 along with the Codex Athous Pantokratoros 28 (ninth/tenth centuries).[8] For Hebrews, the bulk of the material comes from the *Niketae Catena* (perhaps thirteenth century), edited by Mai[9] and the Codex Parisiensis 238 (perhaps twelfth or thirteenth century), edited by Cramer. In addition, there are a few Syriac fragments from the Codex Syriacus 12155.[10] Some Syriac fragments are from Cyril's commentary, while others are from homilies. Since the present volume is devoted to Cyril's biblical commentaries, only the fragments from the commentary are included here.

Pusey's text serves as the basis for the translation of Cyril's commentaries on Romans, 2 Corinthians, and Hebrews in this volume. In the body of the commentary proper I have included in bolded brackets the page numbers that correspond to the Pusey text. I have done the same for the *Commentary on 1 Corinthians*, where we have a recent critical

[3]Cyril of Alexandria, *Commentary on the Letter to Hebrews*, Armenian text compiled by Hakob Keoseyan, ed. Khachik Grigoryan (Yerevan, Armenia: Ankyunacar Publishing, 2020). A subsequent volume will contain both the Armenian text and an English translation: Cyril of Alexandria, *Commentary on the Letter to Hebrews*, Armenian text compiled by Hakob Keoseyan, trans. Khachik Grigoryan, ed. Diana Tsaghikyan (Yerevan, Armenia: Ankyunacar Publishing, forthcoming).

[4]William R. S. Lamb, *The Catena in Marcum: A Byzantine Anthology of Early Commentary on Mark* (Leiden: Brill, 2012), 91-108.

[5]P. E. Pusey, *Sancti Patris Nostri Cyrilli Archiepiscopi Alexandrini in D. Joannis Evangelium Accedunt Fragmenta Varia Necnon Tractatus ad Tiberium Diaconum Duo*, vol. 3 (Oxford, 1872; repr., Brussels: Culture et Civilisation, 1965). Though this is volume 3 of a subsection of Pusey's series, it is actually volume 5 of the entire series. Therefore, it is hereafter cited as "Pusey 5."

[6]Angelo Mai, *Bibliotheca Nova Patrum* (Rome, 1845), 3:1-47. It may also be found in Migne's Patrologia Graeca 74:773-856.

[7]J. A. Cramer, *Catenae Graecorum Patrum in Novum Testamentum*, vol. 4 (Oxford, 1844).

[8]Pusey 5:vii.

[9]Mai, *Bibliotheca Nova Patrum* 3:107-27.

[10]Pusey 5:vii, 362.

edition by Konrad Zawadzki.[11] Where the two main source manuscripts cover the same material, Zawadzki lays them out side by side so that the reader can compare them. I have adopted the same layout for the *Commentary on 1 Corinthians* because it helps the reader to gain a sense for how much variation there is between different catenae.

The fact that there is variation raises the question of how confident we can be that the quotations ascribed to Cyril actually represent his words. It is possible that the catenist edited the quotations. It is also possible that some of the quotes attributed to Cyril really come from different authors. Pusey tried to verify the authenticity of the quotes as much as possible when he produced his critical edition, and he did eliminate about a dozen passages from the Munich catena on Romans that he found to come from other writings of Cyril or other authors such as Chrysostom, Theodoret, and Photius.[12]

The best way to determine whether a given catena manuscript accurately transmits texts is to examine fragments that are from a work that has elsewhere been preserved in its entirety. In his 1926 study *Die Pauluskatenen*, Karl Staab did exactly that for Codex Vaticanus Graecus 762, which is the most important manuscript for the material in this volume. Staab compared the fragments of Theodore of Mopsuestia and John Chrysostom in the catena to the complete commentaries of both fathers, which we have from independent sources. Staab reports that in Theodore there are extraordinarily few textual variations between the catena fragment and the complete commentary, while in Chrysostom there are more.[13] He further notes that in Chrysostom there are a few instances where the text of the source is almost completely lost in the catena fragment. Staab suggests that the rhetorical form of Chrysostom's homilies may not fit very well with the more exegetical aims of the catena and that this may explain the emendations.[14] Despite the variance in the Chrysostom material, Staab concludes that Codex Vaticanus 762 is a reliable witness to the original commentaries: "We may from all these arguments conclude with certainty *that the author of our catena is always accurate in reproducing the thought of his source documents and almost always accurate in reproducing their form*."[15]

If we compare the two main manuscripts for the *Commentary on 1 Corinthians*, we see that Staab's conclusion seems to hold, even if he is a bit optimistic about reproducing the exact wording. Often the two provide almost identical quotations, but there are also cases where the quotations have fairly significant variation in wording. The following comment, on 1 Corinthians 10:1-5, illustrates how much variation there can be:

---

[11]Konrad Zawadzki, *Der Kommentar Cyrills von Alexandrien Zum 1. Korintherbrief: Einleitung, Kritischer Text, Übersetzung, Einzelanalyse* (Leuven: Peeters, 2015).

[12]C. H. Turner, "Patristic Commentaries," in *A Dictionary of the Bible*, extra vol., ed. James Hastings (Edinburgh: T&T Clark, 1927), 515 n. †.

[13]Karl Staab, *Die Pauluskatenen nach den Handschriftlichen Quellen untersucht* (Rome: Verlag des Päpstlichen Bibelinstituts, 1926), 31.

[14]Staab, *Die Pauluskatenen*, 31.

[15]"Wir dürfen aus all diesen Argumenten mit Gewissheit schliessen, *das unser Kettenschmied die Gedanken seiner Quellenschriften immer, ihre Form fast immer treu wiedergibt*" (Staab, *Die Pauluskatenen*, 32 [emphasis original]).

(Cod. Vat. Gr. 762)	(Cod. Pantokrator. 28)
And what happened to the ancients after that? How did they offend God? They were profaned at Shittim, they worshiped idols, and they were consecrated to the Baal of Peor.[16] Since they were entangled with idol worshipers and associated with them and took part in the table of idols, they fell into apostasy and danced in a chorus with women, "and the people entangled itself with a harlot," as the prophet says.[17] That is what it means that they "rose up to revel."[18] Therefore, it is dangerous to associate with the wicked and with unbelievers.	And what happened to the ancients after that? How did they offend God? They were profaned, they worshiped idols, and they were consecrated to the Baal of Peor. Notice how they who were baptized in the cloud and the sea and who ate the bread from heaven and drank the spiritual drink nevertheless entangled themselves with idolatry. Since they associated with idolaters and took part in the table of idolatry, they quickly became distracted and fell into apostasy and worshiped the Baal of Peor. Therefore, it is dangerous to live with the wicked and with unbelievers.

In places, the two versions match verbatim. In others, there is variation in the wording and even the details that are included. Codex Vaticanus Graecus 762 mentions Shittim and quotes Hosea 4:14, while Codex Pantokratoros 28 does not. Nevertheless, the sense of the passage is clearly the same in both manuscripts.

In light of these variations, it seems that we can have a fair degree of confidence that the catenae supply us with an accurate representation of Cyril's thought, but we must be mindful of the fact that the catenists may have edited the citations, so that the precise wording may not always be Cyril's. In this regard, it may be good to take Robert Devreesse's advice: "One should study a collection for what it *is*, without worrying about what it *could* yield."[19]

Another question one might ask about the text is whether Cyril wrote complete verse-by-verse commentaries, or whether the catenae drew their quotations from letters, homilies, or some other writings of Cyril. Here we do have enough evidence to conclude that Cyril wrote continuous commentaries on these books. Some of the citations include references to book and chapter divisions within the original commentaries. The Codex Pantokratoros 28, for example, specifies the *tomus* and *logos* of Cyril's commentary on 2 Corinthians for many of the fragments it preserves,[20] while it and other catenae manuscripts refer to internal divisions in the commentary on 1 Corinthians which indicate that it was divided into seven books.[21] Cyril's commentary on 2 Corinthians was also cited in the acts of the Second Council of Nicaea (787).[22] For Romans, the evidence is simply the sheer number of fragments that appear in the Cramer and Mai catenae.[23] For Hebrews, not only do we have evidence in ancient authors (Theodoret, Leontius, Facundus, and others) that Cyril had written a commentary on that book,[24] but we now have an Armenian translation of the complete work.

[16]Cf. Num 25:1-3.
[17]Hos 4:14.
[18]Ex 32:6; cf. 1 Cor 10:7.
[19]Robert Devreesse, "Chaines Exégetiques Grècques," in *Dictionnaire de la Bible*, supplement (Paris: Letouzey, 1928), 1098, cited in Lamb, *Catena in Marcum*, 47.
[20]Turner, "Patristic Commentaries," 515.
[21]Zawadzki, *Der Kommentar Cyrills*, 62-64.
[22]Turner, "Patristic Commentaries," 515.
[23]Turner, "Patristic Commentaries," 515.
[24]Turner, "Patristic Commentaries," 515.

The Dates of Cyril's Commentaries

Given that Cyril did write complete commentaries on these books, the next question is, When? The framework for dating Cyril's writings was established by Georges Jouassard in 1945. Jouassard argues that there are two turning points in Cyril's life that are critical for identifying the date of any given writing. The first is the year 424, when he first becomes engaged with the Arian controversy. Cyril's festal letters provide the evidence for this date. Before 424, these letters were concerned primarily with the Christian life, and his main opponents were the pagans and the Jews. The letter of 424, however, shows a sudden preoccupation with the Arians, which suggests that he began to be engaged with them in 423, as he prepared the letter.[25] Therefore, writings that engage the Arians were likely written after 423. The second turning point is the year 428, when Nestorius becomes patriarch of Constantinople, initiating the outbreak of the Nestorian controversy. Consequently, writings that engage this controversy were likely written in 428 or later. In view of this timeline, it is helpful, therefore, to pay attention to the main opponents Cyril engages in his commentaries to get a sense of the date of their composition.

The main opponents in view in the Romans commentary are the Jews, the Origenists, and the pagans. In the case of the Origenists, he is concerned primarily with one issue: the Origenist claim that souls were embodied because of a sin they committed in a preembodied state.[26] In the case of the pagans, the main issue is their view of fate, which would make reward and punishment meaningless. His main argument against the Jews is that they worship types and not realities, and that they fail to realize Christ is God by nature.

This constellation of opponents suggests a date before 424. However, in those passages where he faults the Jews for not recognizing the divinity of Christ, it is possible that he may have the Arians in mind as well. For example, Cyril distinguishes the sense in which Jesus is the Son of God from the sense in which we are sons of God,[27] and he criticizes the Jews for failing to recognize that Christ is "God by nature."[28] These are both polemics that could be directed against the Arians. If that is what he had in mind, then the *Commentary on Romans* could have been written in 424 or later. On the other hand, he does not constantly bring up Arian issues or mention them by name, as he does in other anti-Arian commentaries like the *Commentary on John*. He seems more engaged by the themes of Christian life and proper typological understanding of the Old Testament. For that reason, I am inclined to offer the tentative suggestion that the *Commentary on Romans* should be dated 424 or earlier.

[25]See Georges Jouassard, "L'activité littéraire de Saint Cyrille d'Alexandrie jusqu'a 428," in *Mélanges E. Podechard* (Lyon: Facultés catholiques, 1945), 168-69.

[26]See his comments on Rom 6:6.

[27]Cyril, *Commentary on Romans* 1:3.

[28]Cyril, *Commentary on Romans* 10:2.

The *Commentary on 1 Corinthians*, on the other hand, engages not only the Arian controversy but the Nestorian controversy as well. The term *theotokos* appears in the commentary along with other christological formulations that point to an anti-Nestorian context.[29] The appearance of the term *theotokos* is significant because it appears frequently in Cyril's writings composed after 428[30] but rarely in those written before that date.[31] This fact is not definitive, however, because the term was used by Cyril's predecessors well before the outbreak of the Nestorian controversy.[32] Therefore, the appearance of other themes and terminology from the Nestorian controversy is helpful for confirming a date after 428. If that reasoning is sound, then the *Commentary on 2 Corinthians* may also be dated after 428. In that work, Cyril refers to Mary as *theotokos* and rejects the description of Christ as *theophoros*,[33] both terms that figure prominently in the Nestorian controversy.

The *Commentary on Hebrews* shows both an anti-Arian and an anti-Nestorian concern. It does not mention Nestorius, but it does cite Theodore of Mopsuestia, though without mentioning his name.[34] It does not discuss the term *theotokos*, but it does discuss the mode of union, insisting that it is hypostatic and not according to good pleasure. This commentary is the only one of Cyril's exegetical works to use the phrase "hypostatic union."[35] This suggests that the commentary was written after the outbreak of the Nestorian controversy in 428. Since Cyril's *Commentary on Hebrews* is referred to in a letter of Alexander of Hierapolis to Acacius of Beroea, written in about 432, the commentary must have been written before that date.[36]

Cyril's Exegesis

When Cyril comments on a biblical text, he is primarily trying to clear up questions that arise when reading that text, whether those questions arise from the text itself or from heretical interpretations of the text current in Cyril's day. In some cases, that means establishing the punctuation. Texts in Cyril's day had little or no punctuation, so if he thinks a verse should be read as a question, he sometimes makes that explicit.[37] If he

[29]For a more detailed description of the evidence, see Zawadzki, *Der Kommentar Cyrills*, 37-60. Zawadzki concludes that the *Commentary on 1 Corinthians* was written between 433 and 438.

[30]J. Mahé, "La date du Commentaire de saint Cyrille d'Alexandrie sur l'évangelie selon saint Jean," *Bulletin de littérature ecclésiastique* 8 (1907): 43-44.

[31]It does appear in the following early works, but the texts are sometimes uncertain: *Expositio in Psalmos* (PG 69:1117B), *Fragmentum in Canticum Canticorum* (PG 69:1292C), *Commentarium in Isaiam Prophetam* (PG 70:1036D).

[32]Origen, *Fragmentum 80 in Lucam* 4 (GCS 49); Athanasius, *Expositio in Psalmos* (PG 27:373); Didymus the Blind, *Fragmenta in Psalmos* 693A, 15 (PTS 16:69); cited in Zawadzki, *Der Kommentar Cyrills*, 40n56.

[33]Cyril, *Commentary on 2 Corinthians* 1:1 and 2:14. Cf. Zawadzki, *Der Kommentar Cyrills*, 60n96.

[34]Paul M. Parvis, "The Commentary on Hebrews and the Contra Theodorum of Cyril of Alexandria," *Journal of Theological Studies*, n.s. 26, no. 2 (October 1975): 416.

[35]Henry Chadwick, "Eucharist and Christology in the Nestorian Controversy," *Journal of Theological Studies* n.s. 2 (1951): 146, cited in Parvis, "Commentary on Hebrews," 418.

[36]Parvis, "Commentary on Hebrews," 417.

[37]E.g., Cyril, *Commentary on 1 Corinthians* 6:2b-3.

thinks words or phrases are unclear, he will clarify them. For example, when St. Paul asks, "Where is the one who is wise? Where is the scribe? Where is the debater of this age" (1 Cor 1:20), Cyril describes the people he thinks the terms *wise*, *scribe*, and *debater* refer to.[38]

Paraphrase is another tool that Cyril brings to bear on the text. Sometimes he simply restates the point of the text in a slightly expanded form. Other times he places the text in a larger narrative to help the reader make sense of it. An example of the latter would be his comment on Romans 3:5-8, in which St. Paul responds to the objection that God is not just in his judgments. Cyril provides the background for the objection by explaining that when the Israelites returned from the Babylonian captivity, they made excuses for not rebuilding the temple, and God chastised them for it. In return, they began to consider other races who did not serve God to be better off than they were. This is what Cyril thinks gives rise to the bitter sentiment that God is unjust when he imposes his wrath (Rom 3:5) and the cynical exhortation, "Let us do evil that good may result" (Rom 3:8).[39]

Very often, Cyril tries to envision and then respond to questions that may arise in the mind of the reader or from one of his opponents. Sometimes the question stems from a tension in the biblical text itself, as when Cyril raises the question of how to reconcile Paul's statement that Abraham was not justified by works (Rom 4:2) with James's statement that he was (Jas 2:24).[40] Other times Cyril imagines how one of his opponents would interpret the passage and then he offers an explanation to guard against such an interpretation. For example, when Paul says that Christ was "raised from the dead by the glory of the Father" (Rom 6:4), Cyril wants to make sure that the reader does not infer from this that Christ lacked strength.[41]

One point that Cyril is always keen to make is that Christ fulfills the Old Testament. This is what he thinks the statement "Christ is the end of the law" (Rom 10:4) means.[42] Therefore, he makes numerous connections between the Old Testament and its fulfillment in Christ. For example, Satan is the spiritual Pharaoh, and Christ rescued us from the slavery of demonic oppression through baptism, which was prefigured by the crossing of the Red Sea.[43] The veil over Moses' face, mentioned in 2 Corinthians 3:13, indicates that the Old Testament presents the mystery of Christ in shadows, while the New Testament changes the types into truth.[44]

Overall, Cyril's goal is to help the reader understand the text. He certainly has doctrinal points he wants to make, but he spends most of his time and effort unpacking the

[38]Cyril, *Commentary on 1 Corinthians* 1:20.
[39]Cyril, *Commentary on Romans* 3:5-8.
[40]Cyril, *Commentary on Romans* 4:2.
[41]Cyril, *Commentary on Romans* 6:3-4.
[42]Cyril, *Commentary on Romans* 10:4, *Commentary on 2 Corinthians* 3:13.
[43]Cyril, *Commentary on 1 Corinthians* 10:1-5.
[44]Cyril, *Commentary on 2 Corinthians* 3:18.

Scriptures and understanding them on their own terms. There are a few terms that I have chosen to transliterate so that the reader may more easily follow Cyril's thinking as he does so. The term *prosopon* means "person," but it can also mean "mask" or "character" (in a drama). Cyril consistently fights against the notion that the union of human and divine in Christ is a union of *prosopon* because that term is too superficial. It says that Christ has one outward appearance, or mask, but says nothing about his interior constitution. Cyril prefers to say that the union is hypostatic, since that term signifies that the union takes place on an ontological level. *Oikonomia* means "management" or "arrangement." In Cyril and other patristic authors, it usually refers to God's plan of salvation generally or to the incarnation specifically. The opposite of *oikonomia* is *theologia*, which refers to discourse about God's nature, considered apart from creation or salvation. When Cyril uses these words in their technical sense, I have transliterated them.

Cyril's Audience

From the foregoing, we may infer that Cyril expects his readers to be engaged in the task of biblical interpretation. The most likely candidates for that would be the bishops and presbyters under Cyril's supervision. They are the ones charged with preaching and teaching the faith. They are the likely audience for Cyril's *Commentary on John*,[45] and there are indications that the same may be true for the commentaries in the present volume.

On a number of occasions, Cyril stops to consider how the simple or less educated might interpret a passage.[46] Presumably, the readers themselves would have a fair degree of education in order to read the commentaries in the first place. The implication seems to be not that Cyril thinks his readers lack education, but that he envisions them teaching people who are not highly educated. This would certainly be the case if bishops and presbyters are his intended audience.

One passage even suggests that Cyril's readers are presiding at the Eucharist. It is his discussion of speaking in tongues in the *Commentary on 1 Corinthians*. There Cyril explains that the churches have the custom of the presider summing up the people's prayers in the service. The problem, though, is that some of the presiders are offering this summary in tongues so that no one can understand what they are saying. In response to this abuse, Cyril turns to the reader and says, "*We* must do everything for the sake of building up and benefiting the brothers,"[47] indicating that among his readers might be one of the presiders or preachers. If this analysis is correct, it suggests that Cyril views his own task as well as that of his readers to be centered on the interpretation of Scripture.

---

[45]Cyril, *Commentary on John* (Maxwell 1:xvii-xix).

[46]Cf. Cyril, *Commentary on Romans* 7:15 and 9:1.

[47]Cyril, *Commentary on 1 Corinthians* 14:16-17 (emphasis added).

The Narrative of Salvation in Cyril's New Testament Commentaries

In order to understand how Cyril's individual exegetical decisions fit into the larger whole of his theology, it is helpful to have a sense for the way he tells the story of salvation. Here I will present what I take to be the broad contours of that story as Cyril expresses it in his New Testament commentaries.

The key verse that anchors the whole story is Genesis 2:7, God "breathed into his nostrils the breath of life; and the man became a living being." This is the point at which Adam was sealed in the divine image by the Holy Spirit and received life.[48] Because creation has no life on its own but is alive only by participation in God,[49] the gift of life elevates Adam beyond his nature and in a sense divinizes him.[50] Genesis 2:7, then, describes the original human condition to which salvation is a return. Key themes in Cyril's description of salvation, such restoration of the divine image, sharing in the divine life, and justification, are established by this verse.

What humanity gained in Genesis 2:7, however, it lost in Genesis 3:19, when God responded to Adam's sin with the words, "Earth you are, and to earth you will return."[51] For Cyril, this verse imposes the ultimate calamity on the human race. It has two aspects: a juridical one and an ontological one. First, it is juridical because it is a sentence or a curse[52] against the human race. Cyril refers to it as the "ancient charges" that Christ needed to overcome on our behalf.[53] Second, this verse has an ontological aspect in that it imposes death on the human race, thus effacing the divine image and stripping it of the Holy Spirit and participation in divine life. Both of these aspects need to be addressed in order for humanity to be saved. Cyril says, "We possess calamity from Adam's transgression in that we bear the *curse* and *death*."[54]

Christ comes as the second Adam, the new head of the human race, to set things right. He addresses both aspects of Genesis 3:19. His death on the cross is a sacrifice to pay for sins, which addresses the sentence declared against us.[55] The term that captures the juridical aspect of salvation is the Pauline term "justification," which Cyril defines as the "dropping of the ancient charges,"[56] referring to the charges expressed in Genesis 3:19. On the ontological side, various events in Christ's life return humanity to its original condition of Genesis 2:7, in which humanity shares in divine life. The incarnation

[48]Cyril, *Commentary on John* 1:32-33 (Maxwell 1:81), 7:39 (Maxwell 1:311).

[49]Cyril, *Commentary on John* 1:4 (Maxwell 1:33).

[50]Cyril, *Commentary on John* 14:20 (Maxwell 2:186, see especially n267).

[51]Translated from the Septuagint, which is the wording Cyril consistently uses.

[52]Cyril, *Commentary on John* 1:29 (Maxwell 1:76), 8:28 (Maxwell 1:342), 13:29 (Maxwell 2:132), 17:18-19 (Maxwell 2:299), 20:15 (Maxwell 2:359).

[53]Cyril, *Commentary on 1 Corinthians* 15:17, *Commentary on Romans* 4:2.

[54]Cyril, *Commentary on Hebrews* 1:1 (emphasis added).

[55]Cyril, *Commentary on John* 19:19 (Maxwell 2:345); Cyril, *Commentary on Hebrews* 2:17.

[56]Cyril, *Commentary on Romans* 4:2. Cf. Cyril, *Commentary on John* 13:29 (Maxwell 2:132), where Cyril explicitly connects justification with the dissolution of Gen 3:19.

overcomes the curse of death by uniting human nature with the Word.[57] Christ's reception of the Holy Spirit at his baptism reestablishes the presence of the Spirit in the human race as originally given in Genesis 2:7.[58] Christ's death and resurrection defeat death, thus rolling back the curse of Genesis 3:19.[59] This ontological aspect of salvation corresponds to the idea of *theosis*, though Cyril generally describes that process in nontechnical language rather than using the term *theosis*.

Of these two aspects, the sharing in divine life tends to receive most of the attention in scholarship.[60] However, the juridical aspect is also quite prominent in Cyril's New Testament commentaries.[61] This is true not only in the *Commentary on Romans*, in which Cyril's discussion of justification is prompted by its presence in Paul's text, but in the *Commentary on John* as well. There he refers to justification some sixteen times throughout the entire breadth of the commentary. This suggests that justification is an important soteriological category for Cyril, which he brings to bear on passages even when the passage itself does not contain the term. In fact, Cyril frequently mentions participation in divine life side by side with justification or righteousness. For example, in his *Commentary on John* he states, "We are justified through faith and rendered sharers in the divine nature by participation in the Holy Spirit."[62] Both aspects should be understood as two sides of the same coin. They both entail the reversal of the curse of Genesis 3:19 and the return of humanity to its original state in Genesis 2:7.[63]

Other Themes in Cyril's New Testament Commentaries

Beyond the narrative of salvation, Cyril also covers a number of other themes throughout these commentaries. He mentions baptism, marriage, virginity, slavery, the relation between male and female, speaking in tongues, and prophesying, to name a few. There are more-extended discussions of topics such as election, the Christian life, and the resurrection of the body.

Cyril's discussion of election focuses on distinguishing it from a more fatalistic pagan view. His concern is that fate would render any notion of reward and punishment meaningless. To counter that, he insists that humans have free will, and he rejects any interpretation of election that would violate it. Instead, he argues that God chooses to show

[57]Cyril, *Commentary on John* 1:14 (Maxwell 1:63).

[58]Cyril, *Commentary on John* 1:32-33 (Maxwell 1:81-82).

[59]Cyril, *Commentary on 1 Corinthians* 15:20-23, *Commentary on 2 Corinthians* 5:3.

[60]This has been particularly emphasized by Daniel A. Keating, *The Appropriation of Divine Life in Cyril of Alexandria* (Oxford: Oxford University Press, 2004).

[61]This aspect has been highlighted by Lars Koen in *The Saving Passion: Incarnational and Soteriological Thought in Cyril of Alexandria's Commentary on the Gospel According to St. John* (Stockholm: Almquist & Wiksell International, 1991), 108.

[62]Cyril, *Commentary on* John 14:4 (Maxwell 2:148). Similar connections occur in *Commentary on Romans* 5:11, 8:9; Cyril, *Commentary on 1 Corinthians* 15:20-23; Cyril, *Commentary on John* 5:24 (Maxwell 1:155), and 10:10 (Maxwell 2:61).

[63]For a discussion of the relation between *theosis* and justification in Cyril, see David R. Maxwell, "Justification in the Early Church," *Concordia Journal* 44, no. 3 (Summer 2018): 25-40.

mercy on those whom he foresaw would be deserving of it.[64] When St. Paul says, "So it depends not on human will or exertion, but on God who shows mercy" (Rom 9:16), Cyril claims that Paul is not stating his own position but reporting the "ignorant response" of his opponents![65]

Cyril describes the Christian life primarily as a battle against the passions. He describes Adam as being created free from "alien impulses,"[66] but Adam's fall debilitates the human race so that the flesh is now "disposed to pleasure because of its natural impulses."[67] These "natural impulses" seem to be biological drives that arise from the body and drag down the soul.

Not all natural impulses are sinful, however. Cyril at one point notes that God implanted certain impulses in the human race to lead us to himself.[68] He also recognizes that in the incarnation, Christ has natural impulses as well, though only those that are free from the taint of sin, such as hunger, thirst, or weariness.[69]

However, Cyril normally portrays natural impulses as something to be overcome. Christians overcome them first and foremost by being "crucified with Christ." This frees them from the ancient curse, and it also does away with the "body of sin"—that is, the carnal impulses that drag the mind down into sin.[70] Cyril does not think it is possible to overcome passions completely in this life,[71] but he does think that Christ's death and resurrection provide the Christian with a unique power to resist these natural impulses. He also sees the practice of asceticism as an aid in this endeavor.[72]

Cyril's discussion of the resurrection in his comments on 1 Corinthians 15 picks up some of the main themes in his account of salvation and of the Christian life. There he emphasizes the soteriological significance of Christ's resurrection, noting that it both justifies us (Rom 4:25) and overcomes death.[73] He also raises the question of what kind of body humans will have at the resurrection on the last day. After rejecting the Origenist notion that souls preexist bodies,[74] he interprets Paul's term "spiritual body" (1 Cor 15:44) to mean not an incorporeal body but a body that is free from a "carnal earthly mind."[75] Thus Cyril's view of the resurrection is consistent with his vision of the Christian life as a battle against the passions as well as being opposed to the Origenist notion that humans were originally meant to be incorporeal.

[64]Cyril, *Commentary on Romans* 9:14-24.
[65]Cyril, *Commentary on Romans* 9:14-24.
[66]Cyril, *Commentary on Romans* 5:18.
[67]Cyril, *Commentary on Romans* 6:6.
[68]Cyril, *Commentary on Romans* 5:20.
[69]Cyril, *Commentary on Romans* 6:6.
[70]Cyril, *Commentary on Romans* 6:6 and 7:24-25.
[71]Cyril, *Commentary on John* 7:24 (Maxwell 1:288).
[72]Cyril, *Commentary on 2 Corinthians* 4:16.
[73]Cyril, *Commentary on 1 Corinthians* 15:20-23.
[74]Cyril, *Commentary on 1 Corinthians* 15:35-38.
[75]Cyril, *Commentary on 1 Corinthians* 15:44-45.

When it comes to Christology, Cyril's particular emphasis in a given writing depends on which opponents he has in mind. It turns out that Christology is not a major emphasis in the fragments in this volume the way it is in his *Commentary on John*, for instance. The most extended discussion of Christology in this volume is in his *Commentary on 2 Corinthians*. There he engages both the Arians and the Nestorians, though his primary concern seems to be the Arians. Since his Christology has received so much attention, I will not dwell on it here. I will simply observe that his Christology coheres with his construal of the narrative of salvation. Overturning God's verdict and restoring human participation in God's life are acts that only God can do. If the Savior is less than God, as the Arians claim, or if he operates independently from God, as the Nestorians claim, then the reversal of the curse of Genesis 3:19 does not take place. This is why it is important to affirm that "he who is from holy Mary, *theotokos*, is himself God by nature."[76]

The commentaries in this volume provide a glimpse of Cyril's larger theological vision. They challenge the stereotype that Cyril's contribution is limited to christological questions. In these fragments, Cyril shows himself to be a biblical commentator who strives for a close reading of the text, even down to the level of punctuation. That close reading, in turn, gives rise not only to his Christology but also to a set of issues that span the theology and practice of the church.

[76]Cyril, *Commentary on 2 Corinthians* 1:1.

COMMENTARY ON THE EPISTLE TO THE ROMANS (FRAGMENTS)

[174]*

1:3 Concerning his Son, who originated from the seed of David according to [175] the flesh.

And he says that he who has originated "from the seed of David according to the flesh" was declared to be the Son of God "in power according to the Spirit of holiness by resurrection from the dead." Now we too were declared to be sons—not "in power," but by having a share of grace. We are considered worthy of our calling and gain that possession only by the will of God the Father.[1] This would not be the case with Emmanuel, however. Far from it! Even though he originated "from the seed of David according to the flesh" and like one of us is considered to be son of God on account of his human nature, he is nevertheless the natural Son "in power" and in truth. Through him, we too are made sons. If indeed it is true to say this (since we are enriched by his Spirit through holy baptism), **[176]** then—then!—do we say without reproach, "Abba! Father!"[2] Therefore, as images are related to the archetype, so also we who are sons by adoption are related to him who is attested to be from the Father by nature, "in power," and truly.

1:20 His eternal power and divine nature.

How is his "eternal power" recognized through the creation? Creatures have a corruptible nature. Since they have been brought into being and called into existence in time, their creator will surely be incorruptible and eternal. That is why they will have no excuse on the day of judgment.

3:3-4 Will their unfaithfulness nullify the faithfulness of God?

Those who were foreknown and who received the law as a teacher and have the promises about Christ were more honored than the others. In fact, they have been separated from the others and called ahead of them. As the Savior said, "I was sent only to the lost sheep of the house of Israel."[3] They have become the firstfruits of those who are saved through faith. Now if some of them have fallen away from the faith due to their own madness, he is saying, God would not on that account be less than truthful, would he? So the Father sent the Son from heaven, but not everyone believed in him. But just because some became insolent and faithless, will that make God untrue? "By no means! Although everyone is a liar, let God be proved true." Instead of thinking and claiming that the truth is on our side, let us indict every person, as it were, with the charge

*The numbers in bold brackets refer to the page numbers in P. E. Pusey, *Sancti Patris Nostri Cyrilli Archiepiscopi Alexandrini in D. Joannis Evangelium Accedunt Fragmenta Varia Necnon Tractatus ad Tiberium Diaconum Duo*, vol. 3 (Oxford, 1872; repr., Brussels: Culture et Civilisation, 1965). Though this is volume 3 of a subsection of Pusey's series, it is actually volume 5 of the entire series. Therefore, it is hereafter cited as "Pusey 5."

[1]This is an anti-Arian concern. Arius wanted to classify Jesus as a "son" of God by grace or will. For Cyril, that classification is appropriate for us, but not for Christ.

[2]Rom 8:15.

[3]Mt 15:24.

of lying. The divine nature is completely free of turning and change,[4] but human nature has been shaken to the core and everyone is, at least potentially, [177] a liar. Sometimes the sin of lying overcomes the human mind and human nature contracts this disease, as it were. It is not right, however, to think or say such a thing about almighty God. The charge, then, must be true that human nature, or more specifically the human mind, can succumb to lying. Even the blessed David says somewhere: "I said in my amazement, 'Everyone is a liar!'"[5] The same statement about God and us could be made in the case of all other attributes as well. For example, when it comes to righteousness, one could say (and not without reason), "Although everyone is unrighteous, let God be proved righteous."

3:5-8 If our unrighteousness confirms the righteousness of God. . . .

The pretext for such a slanderous statement came about as follows. After the return from Babylon, the Israelites were commanded by Cyrus to rebuild the temple and to offer prayers and sacrifices, but they were lazy. They made excuses because of their poverty and the hardship of their captivity. Therefore, they were chastised with a punishment commensurate with the crime: famine and drought. But they were very upset by these calamities. They began to consider other races, who did not serve God, to be blessed because those races lived their lives in happiness. They even began to say that the other peoples were better off than they were. For example, the prophet Malachi said to them, "'You have spoken harsh words against me,' says the Lord. Yet you say, 'How have we spoken against you?' You have said, 'It is vain to serve God. What do we profit by keeping his command or by walking as suppliants before the Lord Almighty? Now we count aliens happy, and those who practice lawlessness are fortified. They oppose God, yet they are delivered.' Those who feared the Lord said these things [178] to each other, and the Lord paid attention and listened to them."[6] That is why, he says, some thought that the Jews were saying, "Let us do evil that good may result." And indeed their condemnation is deserved, he says, whether it is the condemnation of those who allege these things about the Jews or those who actually dare to say, "Let us do evil that good may result."

3:21-25 But now, apart from law, the righteousness of God has been disclosed.

I know that it is written concerning some that "both of them were righteous, walking blamelessly in the commandments and regulations of Christ."[7] Moreover, the blessed Paul said that he "was blameless as to the righteousness of the law."[8] Yet he who was blameless in these matters had not yet accomplished what would make him glorious and renowned. Indeed, the blessed Paul himself went on to say that he counted all things related to the law to be "loss" and he considered them the same as "rubbish." Instead, he would seek the "surpassing value of knowing Christ."[9] Furthermore, the law condemns transgressors. Somewhere else he says, "If there is glory in the ministry of condemnation, how much more does the ministry of righteousness abound in glory!"[10] Since the demands of the law are very great, even the most scrupulous keeper of the law must stumble at some points and become a transgressor of the law. Yes, the divinely inspired disciples have explicitly confessed that the law is truly burdensome. They said, "Now

[4]Cf. Jas 1:17.
[5]Ps 116:11 (Ps 115:1 LXX).

[6]Mal 3:13-16.
[7]Lk 1:6, referring to Zechariah and Elizabeth.
[8]Phil 3:6.
[9]Phil 3:8.
[10]2 Cor 3:9.

therefore why are you putting God to the test by placing on the neck of the disciples a yoke that neither our fathers nor we have been able to bear?"[11] So when the Greeks were under sin because they did not know the Creator and the Jews were under sin because they were guilty of transgressing the law, everyone on earth needed Christ, who justifies. For we have been justified "not because of any works of righteousness that we had done, but according to his great [179] mercy."[12] After all, he was the same one who said long ago through the voice of the prophets, "I am he who blots out your transgressions, and I will not remember them."[13] And so justifying grace rushes to everyone alike (I mean Jews and Greeks) because "all have sinned and fall short of the glory of God." The "glory of God" may reasonably be understood as neither knowing sin nor being of such a nature that you sin. The entire originate creation is surely inferior to the glories of the divine nature. Even some of the angels fell, after all. Yet God the Father was pleased "to gather up all things in Christ,"[14] who justifies "freely by his grace." God put him forward as a "propitiation by his blood, through faith." Since he has offered his own blood in exchange for the life of all, he has saved the life of those under heaven, and he has rendered God the Father in heaven propitious and favorable toward us.

3:27 Then what becomes of boasting? It is excluded.

Who on earth can boast, and what will they boast about, since all have become useless and have left the straight road and there is no one at all who does good? That is why he says that boasting is "excluded"; that is, it is cast off and taken away and has no place among us. And how is it excluded? We have become rich with the remission of our former sins since we are justified freely by the mercy and grace that are in Christ.

3:31 Do we then overthrow the law by faith?

The God of the universe said to the divinely inspired Moses, "I will raise up for them a prophet like you from among their brothers; I will put my word in his mouth, and he will speak to them just as I command. Anyone who does not heed the words that [180] the prophet shall speak in my name, I will take vengeance[15] on him."[16] So when we believe his word, how could we not also be upholding the law through faith? Now Emmanuel was designated a prophet because of his humanity since, like Moses, he is a mediator between God and human beings.[17] Furthermore, the law was in shadows, but it labors to give birth to the form of the truth. The truth does not take away the types, but gives them more clarity.

4:2 For if Abraham was justified by works, he has something to boast about, but not before God.

I suppose it is inevitable, someone has remarked, that those who busy themselves with this statement about our forefather Abraham would say the following: One of the holy disciples said somewhere that apart from works, faith is dead.[18] He then adds, "Do you want to be shown, you senseless person, that faith apart from works is dead? Was not our father Abraham justified by works when he

[11]Acts 15:10.

[12]Titus 3:5.

[13]Is 43:25. Cyril's citations of Titus 3:5 and Is 43:25 in this context indicates that he understands justification to refer to salvation (Is 43:25) and the forgiveness of sins (Titus 3:5).

[14]Eph 1:10.

[15]ἐκδικήσω. This word is from the same root as "justify" (δικαιόω).

[16]Deut 18:18-19.

[17]1 Tim 2:5.

[18]Jas 2:17.

offered his son Isaac on the altar?"[19] So do the Spirit-bearers contradict one another? What shall we say to this? When he had already reached old age, the God of the universe astonishingly promised him a son. God also said that the seed that would come from him would rival the countless multitude of stars. [**181**] Since Abraham honored the one who made the promise by ascribing to him the power to accomplish all things, thus bearing witness to God, Abraham was justified before God and received a reward commensurate with an attitude of such devotion to God: the dropping of the ancient charges.[20] At the proper time, God made the prophecy concerning Isaac into a training exercise for the righteous man. And even there he was faithful and devoted to God since he placed nothing ahead of love for God. Rather, as the Savior's disciple says, "Faith was active along with his works, and faith was confirmed by the works."[21] The marvelous Paul himself said somewhere concerning our forefather Abraham, "By faith he, when put to the test, offered up Isaac. He who had received the promise offered up his only begotten, of whom it was said, 'It is through Isaac that your seed shall be named for you.' He reasoned that God is able even to raise someone from the dead."[22] Therefore, though it may perhaps be said that he was justified by works because he offered up Isaac when he was tested, yet even this is a clear proof of the firmness of his faith.

5:11 But more than that, we even boast in God.

Our Lord Jesus Christ highlighted the truly remarkable love that God the Father showed us by citing the completion of his *oikonomia* in the flesh and his suffering of the cross, saying somewhere, "For God so loved the world that he gave his only begotten Son, so that everyone who believes in him may not perish but may have eternal life."[23] After all, he actually gave his very own Son for us, and we have been redeemed and freed from death and sin. "The Word became flesh and lived in us"[24] for no other reason than to endure death in the flesh and so to triumph over the rulers and authorities[25] and to neutralize the one who "holds the power [**182**] of death, that is," Satan,[26] and to take away corruptibility and with it to remove sin, which tyrannizes us. In this way he also canceled that ancient curse, which human nature endured in Adam as the firstfruits of our race and our original root. When Adam transgressed the command, he gave offense to the Creator. That is how he became both cursed and subject to death. But the Lord of the universe had mercy on those who had utterly perished. The Son came down from heaven. He removed the charges, justifying the ungodly by faith. As God, he forged human nature to make it incorruptible and raised it to its original condition. Whatever is in Christ is a "new creation"[27] because he has established himself as the new root and has become the second Adam. Now that does not mean he is the reason for God's wrath, as Adam was, or the reason that those born of him turned away

[19]Jas 2:20-21. A summary of Cyril's discussion of Paul and James is also found in some catenae on the Catholic Epistles in comments on Jas 2:20. See Pusey 5:180n11.

[20]"Ancient charges" refers to the curse in Gen 3:19: "You are dust, and to dust you will return." See Cyril's comments on Rom 5:11 below.

[21]Jas 2:22.

[22]Heb 11:17-19.

[23]Jn 3:16. Most modern English translations render μονογενῆ as "only" rather than "only begotten" on the grounds that it is from γίνομαι (come into being), not γεννάω (beget). However, in the fourth and fifth centuries, it was commonly understood to entail begetting. The meaning of the Son's status as "only begotten" was a key issue in the Arian controversy.

[24]Jn 1:14. In his *Commentary on John*, Cyril makes clear that he understands John's phrase ἐν ἡμῖν to mean "in us" (i.e., in the flesh) rather than "among us." See Cyril of Alexandria, *Commentary on John* 1:14 (trans. David R. Maxwell, 2 vols., Ancient Christian Texts [Downers Grove, IL: IVP Academic, 2013–2015], 1:63).

[25]Cf. Eph 6:12.

[26]Heb 2:14.

[27]2 Cor 5:17.

from above; rather, he is the benefactor and bestower of kinship with God through sanctification and incorruptibility and the righteousness that is by faith. The wise Paul explains this to us in the words of the passage at hand. "Just as through one man," he says, "sin came into the world and death through sin, so also death spread to all people because all have sinned."[28] So death entered through sin, as I said, in the man who was formed first, in the source of our race. Then the entire race was subsequently plundered. And when the serpent, the inventor of sin, prevailed in Adam by the ways of wickedness, he gained access to the human mind. "For all have turned aside, together they have become worthless."[29] Indeed, when we turned away from the face of the all-holy God because the human mind diligently occupied itself with "evil from its youth,"[30] we began to live a life even more devoid of reason,[31] and "death prevailed and swallowed [us] up,"[32] as the prophet says, and Hades "enlarged its appetite and opened its mouth without ceasing."[33] When we became imitators of the transgression in Adam, **[183]** in accordance with which "all sinned,"[34] we were subject to the same penalty as he was. But the earth under heaven did not remain without aid. Sin was taken away. Satan fell. Death was brought to nothing.

5:13 Sin was indeed in the world before the law.

The law given through Moses accused the weakness of the fallen, as I said. It did not destroy sin. Rather, it worked wrath.[35] After all, it was necessary that the transgressors undergo the punishments prescribed by the law. Indeed, where there is any kind of transgression, there is surely also sin. And if sin is the patron of death, we must surely say that death is strengthened right along with it, since death sprang from it. Likewise, when sin is abolished, death is surely torn down and destroyed, just like its mother. So "sin was in the world before the law." But when the law was laid down, the accusation of transgression against the fallen was intensified. Now that the law is abrogated, however, the charge of transgression has ceased as well. And since sin has ceased, as I said, death has ceased along with it.

5:14 Yet death exercised dominion from Adam to Moses . . .

But if this is so, someone might ask, How did death obtain control over the inhabitants of the earth even before the law? Even though some are not guilty of transgressing the law (since of course the law was not yet given), yet they too were subject to decay "in the likeness of the transgression of Adam." I suppose it is as though he were to say this: Just like death attacked Adam, it attacked the entire race that came from him, as when a plant suffers damage to its root, the branches that spring from it inevitably wither. He is saying that Adam is actually a type of the one who is to come **[184]** (that is, Christ), even though he was already present back then accomplishing the mystery of his *oikonomia* in the flesh. Perhaps someone might reply, How then can he call him "the one who is to come"? After he introduces the first man to us and recalls the time of his transgression, he then refers to Christ as the last Adam who would come later. He was foreordained by the will and foreknowledge of God the Father to be the Savior and Redeemer. He then appeared in his own time, which the Lord chose. This is the end time and the sunset of the present age, as it

[28]Rom 5:12.
[29]Rom 3:12; Ps 14:3; 53:3 (Ps 52:4 LXX).
[30]Gen 8:21.
[31]ἀλογώτερον.
[32]Is 25:8 (LXX).
[33]Is 5:14.
[34]Rom 5:12.
[35]Rom 4:15.

were. After introducing the second in the pattern of the first, he all but interrogates the hearer, uttering the next sentence as a question with a question mark:[36]

5:15 But is not the trespass just like the free gift?

It is as though he were to say, We have been condemned to death by the transgression of Adam, since the entire nature of humanity experienced this in him. Indeed, he was the firstfruits of our race. In Christ, however, we blossomed once more into life. Adam was the type of the one who is to come (that is, Christ), and Christ brought us grace commensurate with the debilitation of those who came before. So, he says, did I miss the truth when I said this? Did I stray from what is fair to say? Is not the trespass just like the free gift? Death conquered through one man. Will life be too weak to conquer through one man even though it is surely true to say, "For if the many died through the one man's trespass, much more surely have the grace of God and the free gift in the grace of the one man, Jesus Christ, abounded for the many"? After all, in his love for humanity the Creator will hardly allow death to conquer through the one man while life through the one man sits idle. No. Grace will trump wrath. **[185]**

5:16 And is not the free gift like the effect that came through the one man's sin?

He elevates his subject matter, as it were, and his thoughts to what is especially fitting for God. If, he says, the condemnation of Adam that came from one man (or rather "through the one man") spread to everyone in his likeness—since he was the root of our race, as I said, which suffered corruption—how could it not be both pleasing to God and credible to us that by one act of righteousness, the many are fittingly justified from many trespasses? Shouldn't God choose to save rather than to destroy? Adam was condemned and the power of Moses' curse prevailed, which subjected the inhabitants of the earth to decay. In the same way, now that Christ the second Adam has been justified, justification will surely come to us by that original road. Now when we say that Christ was justified, that does not mean that he was ever unrighteous, as if he reached righteousness by advancing toward the better. No, he was the first and only man on earth who "committed no sin, and no deceit was found in his mouth."[37]

5:17 If, because of the one man's trespass, death exercised dominion through that one man . . .

See once more how he considers justifying grace to be more formidable than the condemning curse. He is saying that no one could sensibly claim that death through the one man overpowers the inhabitants of the earth while life lacks that strength. After all, when people have grace through Christ and the free gift of righteousness that comes from the generosity from above, they will "much more surely" shake off the power of death and reign with Christ, who gives life to all. **[186]**

5:18-19 Therefore, just as one man's trespass led to condemnation for all . . .

The divinely inspired Paul adds a kind of conclusion to the foregoing thoughts when he says, "Therefore, just as one man's trespass," and what follows. We have all been condemned in Adam, as I said before, and when the curse of death came about, the result spread to all as

[36] The Greek text of the New Testament that Cyril had contained little or no punctuation. When Cyril thinks a verse should be construed as a question, he sometimes makes that explicit, as he does here.

[37] 1 Pet 2:22.

from an original root. But we have also been justified and have blossomed again into life when Christ was justified for us. Our forefather neglected the command he had been given. He offended God and suffered the consequences of divine wrath. Indeed, he fell into decay. That is when sin rushed into human nature. And that is how "the many were made sinners," which refers to everyone on earth. Now someone might say: Yes, Adam fell. He disregarded the divine command, and he was condemned to decay and death. But how were "the many made sinners" because of him? Why does his fall affect us? Why have we been condemned with him when we were not even born yet? On the contrary, God says, "Fathers will not be put to death for their children," nor children for their fathers,[38] and, "It is the soul who sins that shall die."[39] What defense could we make for our position? It is indeed the soul who sins that shall die. Nevertheless, we have become sinners through Adam's disobedience in the following way. He was created in incorruption and life. He lived a holy life in luxurious paradise. His mind completely and continually enjoyed the vision of God. His body was calm and untroubled, since all shameful pleasure was at rest. There was no tumult of alien impulses in him. When he fell under sin, however, and sank into decay, then pleasures and impurities rushed into the nature of the flesh, and a savage law sprang up in our members. **[187]** So our nature contracted sin "through the disobedience of the one man" (that is, Adam). That is how "the many were made sinners"—not because they transgressed along with Adam (since they did not yet exist), but because they were of his nature, which had fallen under the law of sin. Just as human nature was enfeebled with decay in Adam through his disobedience (and that is how the passions entered into it), so also it has been freed once again in Christ. He was obedient to God the Father and "committed no sin."[40]

5:20 But the law came in, that the trespass may multiply.

I suppose someone may reasonably make the following argument, he says. Adam was the "type of the one who was to come."[41] Just as we were made sinners in him because of his transgression, so also we have been justified in Christ through his obedience. Therefore, justification in Christ had to dawn on the inhabitants of the earth even if no one seized it. What need or necessity was there, then, for the laws of Moses? Paul is all but rising up against such an objection when he adds, "But the law came in, that the trespass may multiply." He says it "came in" meaning that it interposed itself between the condemnation in Adam and the justification in Christ. So what need should we understand there to be for the entrance of the law? You may hear him stating it explicitly: "that the trespass may multiply." What are you saying, Paul? Was the law a patron of sin? Did trespass multiply through it? By no means. It was necessary to open up the way for mystagogy. David said, "They have all gone astray, they are all alike useless; there is no one who does good, no, not one."[42] All people on earth had corrupted their ways after the transgression of Adam.[43] And they were punished like this: they all endured the flood as their common penalty—each in their own time throughout their regions and cities. Even though there was no law, **[188]** God guided human nature to the knowledge of the good by natural impulses.[44] God had mercy on the

[38]Deut 24:16.
[39]Ezek 18:4.

[40]1 Pet 2:22.
[41]Rom 5:14.
[42]Ps 14:3 (Ps 13:3 LXX).
[43]Cf. Gen 6:12.
[44]ἐξ ἐμφύτων κινημάτων. Elsewhere, Cyril uses this same phrase to describe the impulses that lead to sin. Cf. his comments on Rom 6:6.

miserable inhabitants of the earth and graciously planned to free them in Christ from the sin that ruled over them. He quite rightly thought it was necessary to start by showing the inhabitants of the earth that they were desperately ill so that the righteousness in Christ may be seen as having a most necessary entrance into the world. After all, we do not say that someone who is already righteous is justified, but only one who is guilty of sins. Otherwise, why did he have to show ahead of time that the inhabitants of the earth needed the grace that is in Christ? "Law came in, that the trespass may multiply," that is, in order that the trespass might be utterly clear in those under the law, which is to say that no one is able to be justified because of the weakness of our nature, but all are subject, as it were, to the charge of transgression. So the law was established as a sort of cross-examination of the weakness of all to show that the human condition stands in need of one thing: Christ's healing. That is why it says, "But where sin increased, grace abounded all the more." Grace had to be shown to be that much better than the law, which condemns.

6:3-4 Do you not know that all of us who have been baptized into Christ Jesus. . . .

Of course, we have been baptized in the name of the Father and of the Son and of the Holy Spirit, but if one were to say that we have been baptized "into Christ Jesus," that person would not be wrong. The Father is distinguished from the Son particularly by the names and hypostases and differences of *prosopa,* each with his own properties. And the Spirit is distinguished from both. The Father is the Father and not the Son. The Son, in turn, is from him by nature. He is not the Father. And the Holy Spirit is properly the Spirit. But since the Son is in the Father and the Father is in the Son and the Holy Spirit is in both because of the identity of essence, **[189]** anyone who names one makes reference to all of them. Therefore, someone who names Christ will not forget about the Father or the Spirit. When Jesus became human and endured death for the life of all, the blessed Paul could not help but spread abroad the most important point of the mystagogy before us. After all, he had to name the one who suffered. That is the sense in which he says, "All of us who have been baptized into Christ Jesus were baptized into his death." When we offered an honest appeal to Christ from a good conscience,[45] as it were, and by faith we accepted that he died for us and was buried and rose again, we had the forgiveness of sins through holy baptism. We also experienced the death of sin and we died, in a manner of speaking, with the one who died for us because our earthly members were put to death. Christ "died to sin, once for all; but the life he lives, he lives to God."[46] Because of this, we ourselves undergo the same death as he did and we are for all practical purposes buried with him. We were buried with Christ in the sense that we bear his death in our own bodies. What then do we gain from this? He makes this clear when he says, "so that, just as Christ was raised from the dead by the glory of the Father, so we too might walk in newness of life." We who were buried with him, as it were, must also be spiritually raised with him. And if being buried with Christ means dying to sin, it should surely be clear that being raised with him ought to be understood to be nothing else than living in righteousness.

Now when he maintains that Christ was raised "by the glory of the Father," that does not mean Christ lacked strength. After all, he is the Lord of powers. No, it is customary for both Christ and his disciples to attribute acts that transcend human nature to the nature that is above all. Therefore, even if God the Father may be said to raise him, **[190]** we do not

[45] Cf. 1 Pet 3:21.

[46] Rom 6:10.

exclude the Son from any of the Father's actions. After all, if "all things came into being through him,"[47] how could anyone doubt that the Father worked the resurrection through the Son and through the Son's holy body? In fact, the Son showed himself to be active in the resurrection when he said to the Jews, "Destroy this temple, and in three days I will raise it up."[48] Notice how he is said to raise his own temple, even though God the Father is said to resurrect him. Since he himself is the life-giving Power of God the Father, he gave life to his own temple.

6:5 For if we have been planted with the likeness of his death . . .

The divinely inspired Paul says that those who are buried with Christ should expect to be raised with him as well. And the word "planted" seems to suggest that we have the same spiritual shape and form. Emmanuel gave his life for us and died according to the flesh. But how are we who are baptized buried with him? Do we re-experience the death of the flesh with him? No. How then are we "planted with the likeness of his death"? Come! Come! Let us explain it. Christ died according to the flesh in order to destroy the sin of the world. We too die, but not according to the flesh. How then? We die "to sin" as it is written[49]—that is, we render sin inactive and inoperative in ourselves by putting to death "whatever is earthly: fornication, impurity, passion, evil desire, and greed."[50] So we are "planted" not only with Christ's death according to the flesh **[191]** but also with "the likeness of his death." This should be understood to refer to his death for sins, but not for his own—far from it! God is blameless and is far removed from even the ability to sin. Rather he died, as I said, for the sin of the world. "The death he died, he died to sin, once for all."[51] Therefore, "we have been planted with the likeness of his death." We will surely also be planted with and have the same form of resurrection as his. We will live in Christ. Our flesh will return to life, and we will live in a different manner when we offer our soul to him and are transformed to holiness and glorious citizenship in the Holy Spirit.

6:6 We know that our old man . . .

We must now investigate these questions in detail: What is our "old man"? What is "the body of sin" that is done away with? How are we "crucified with Christ"? Now perhaps some will suppose that "body of sin" refers to the earthly flesh as if it were given to the human soul as a punishment for sin committed before bodies existed. Some people hold and express this view, you know. But we should reject this Greek opinion as untrue. The phrases "body of sin" and "our old man" refer to our earthly body, which is subject to the necessity of decay because of its oldness, so to speak, in Adam. In fact, we were condemned in him, the first man. And the love of pleasure debilitated us as well, since the flesh is naturally disposed to pleasure because of its natural impulses.[52] How then has it been crucified with Christ? The Only Begotten became human and clothed himself in earthly flesh. This flesh had fallen into death, as I said, because of the oldness in Adam. It also gave birth in itself, as it were, to incitement toward sin from its natural impulses.[53] **[192]** The law of sin is silent, however, in the holy and utterly pure flesh of Christ. We maintain that no alien human passions move around in him except those whose impulses are harmless. I am referring to hunger and thirst and weariness and as many of our experiences as the law

[47]Jn 1:3.
[48]Jn 2:19.
[49]Rom 6:2.
[50]Col 3:5.

[51]Rom 6:10.
[52]ἐξ ἐμφύτων κινημάτων. Earlier, Cyril uses this same phrase to describe the natural impulses by which God leads the Gentiles toward the good. Cf. his comments on Rom 5:20.
[53]ἐξ ἐμφύτων κινημάτων. See previous footnote.

of nature observes blamelessly. Yet even though the law of sin may not be stirred in Christ since it is lulled to sleep by the power and activity of the Word, who controls it, nevertheless, when we investigate the nature of the flesh in itself, we will find that it is no different from our own, even though it happens to be in Christ. We were crucified with him since his flesh was crucified, and it contains our entire nature in itself. Just as in Adam our entire nature certainly succumbed to the curse when he was cursed, so also we are said to be raised with Christ and seated with him in the heavenly places.[54] Emmanuel is above us as God, but since he became like us, he has been raised and sits with God the Father as one of us. The "old man" has therefore been "crucified with him" since the power of that ancient curse was dissolved through the resurrection, and "the body of sin" has been done away with. Now "body of sin" surely does not refer to the flesh but to the natural ferocity of the impulses within the flesh that always drag the mind down to more shameful thoughts and throw it into the dirt and mud of earthly pleasures. How could anyone doubt that in Christ this too has been set right for human nature? Paul clearly states, "For God has done what the law, weakened by the flesh, could not do: by sending his own Son in the likeness of sinful flesh, and to deal with sin, he condemned sin in the flesh."[55] So do you see how the "body of sin" is done away with? The sting of sin has been condemned in the flesh. **[193]** It has been put to death first in Christ, and so grace has come from and through him to us.

7:1 Do you not know, brothers? For I am speaking to those who know the law.

He shows that seeking to be under the law is a completely untenable position. He exhorts and urges them instead to thirst for grace (that is, for righteousness in Christ) through faith with their whole mind. He just stated that the baptized have been buried with him so that they might die to sin and live to God in righteousness. He said, "Therefore, do not let sin exercise dominion in your mortal bodies, to make you obey their passions. No longer present your members to sin as instruments of wickedness, but present yourselves to God as those who have been brought from death to life, and present your members to God as instruments of righteousness. For sin will have no dominion over you, since you are not under law but under grace."[56] Observe how he commands them to come out from the shadow of the law and to rush to be under the grace that is in Christ. But the Spirit Bearer was not unaware that some would surely say (or rather argue) that the fathers strayed from the straight road and from life. The law did not help them at all, and the glory of their way of life has vanished. So if seeking to be under the law is wrong, yet that was the ancients' goal in life, how could it not be true to say that they strayed from what is right? So he who has Christ in himself enters the fray. He shrewdly pretends to want to talk with those who live under the law. He takes the conversation through various turns so that they realize that when the moment arrives that calls them to faith, they must have no desire to remain in the ancient customs. He says this: "Do you not know, brothers—for I am speaking to those who know the law—that the law is binding on a person while that person is still alive?" This general definition **[194]** applies to all laws and to people who live under those laws. For all who are subject to the rule of kings, the laws define what may and may not be done. They are in force for people as long as they are alive. But whenever those under the law depart from their bodily life, they strip off the authority of the law along with their life.

[54]Eph 2:6.
[55]Rom 8:3.
[56]Rom 6:12-14.

After all, if they have stopped transgressing, then the law will surely do nothing to them. Therefore, it is true that "the law is binding on a person while that person is still alive." Next we must say what the purpose of the statement is. It introduces two beneficial points. The first is that we who are buried with Christ through baptism, who have died to sin, are now beyond the authority of the law since we have been transformed to a different life. The other is that those who lived before the advent of Christ, who had not undergone death in Christ, were still alive to sin. So the law had power over them as living people, just like the husband of a wife. A woman who is "bound to her husband" is not unaccountable for intercourse with someone else as long as the one she lawfully lives with is still alive. But if her husband dies, he says, she will be exempt from penalty if she should decide to do this lawfully. In the same way, I think, those who do not yet possess the mortification of sin in Christ but are alive, as it were, to sin are reasonably under the law since "the law is binding on a person as long as that person is alive." But those who are now under the grace of Christ have through that grace died to sin and have been put to death in the flesh (this is, in the passions of the flesh). Since the designation *living in the world* no longer applies to them, their life, which is beyond the reach of the law, would be rendered unimpeachable. As I said, they have been put to death "through the body of Christ"[57] and they have died to the law, being justified through faith.

7:5 While we were in the flesh, our sinful passions by the law were at work in us . . .[58]

He calls the carnal mind "flesh." As he also says **[195]** elsewhere, "Those who are in the flesh cannot please God."[59] Surely he does not entrust these things to anyone but those whom he is leading into the mysteries. So we must investigate carefully what he intends to communicate. When we used to live carnally, he says, and our earthly mind dominated us, the passions of the flesh were at work in us by the law "to bear fruit for death." "What?" someone might ask. "The passions of the flesh were introduced through the law? In that case, how shall we rescue the law from accusation?" How then do we reply to this? The passions of the flesh are not stirred up in us by the law. Rather, they are born from natural pleasure, and they capture the weak mind. He makes this clear to us when he says, "What the flesh desires is opposed to the Spirit, and what the Spirit desires is opposed to the flesh; for these are opposed to each other."[60] Now here he omits the law and says that the flesh opposes the Spirit without putting anything in between them. Therefore, it is not by the law that the passions of the flesh are stirred up in us, but by nature. And, incredibly, the passions oppose the will of the law, as Paul himself says somewhere: "The mind of the flesh is hostile to God; it does not submit to God's law—indeed it cannot."[61] Now if the mind of the flesh wars against the law, how is it not insane to think that the law stirs into action what is so opposed to it? So what is Paul saying? He is speaking to those who have been buried with Christ through baptism as having died to sin and having already attained the mortification of the passions. For them it would be proper to proceed without the law, at least in the sense that they have been freed from the passions that the law condemns. But since we still retain the mind of the flesh, those things that are identified and condemned as passions "by the law," he says, "were at work in us." We are

[57]Rom 7:4.

[58]I have preserved the Greek word order here, even though it is awkward in English, to make Cyril's argument more intelligible. He understands the passage to mean, "Our sinful passions [identified and condemned as sinful] by the law were at work in us."

[59]Rom 8:8.

[60]Gal 5:17.

[61]Rom 8:7.

accountable to the law so long as sin still lives in us. [196]

7:6 But now we are discharged from the law, dead to that which held us captive.

We were accountable to the law, he says, because sin subjected us to it. But if we died "to that which held us captive"—that is, sin—then surely the law will be inactive right along with it. After all, the law was decreed by God because of sin in order to accuse transgressors. So those who have died to sin are outside the scope of the law. We have come to belong to another, and we will serve him "in the new way of the Spirit and not in the old way of the letter."

7:7 What then should we say? That the law is sin?

Notice how skillfully he crafts his words concerning the law. Earlier he said, "While we were in the flesh, our sinful passions by the law were at work in us." But now that statement is freed from any suspicion. An impartial judge would have replied: Is the law then the author of sin? If it is true that the passions of the flesh are at work in us through the law, how could the law not be understood as the originator of sin? What do you say to that, O expounder of the mysteries? He is keen to answer. He denies that the law is the father of sin and instead lays the blame on human nature for being weak and for being convicted by the judgments of the law. He makes that point in this way: "What then should we say? That the law is sin? By no means! Yet, I would not have known sin except through the law." Look at the sobriety! He did not say, "I would not have *had* sin except through the law," but rather, "I would not have *known* sin." The law, therefore, is not a pretext for sin, but a revealer of it. It lays sin bare for those who do not know it. It does this not so that they may commit sin once they learn it [197]—they were surely committing sin even before they knew it, as the psalm says, "No one is righteous, not even one"[62]—but so that once they realize what is wrong, they may progress to what is better. It seems to me that something similar came about for the ancients through the command of Moses. As an example, say that there is a broad road leading somewhere. Now toss a large boulder in the middle of it and dig pits in it too, if you will. Now, say there are some people walking on the road in the dark of night, constantly stumbling against what lay in the middle of the road and even accidently falling into the pits. Then in this state of affairs someone took a torch and set it on a tripod to illuminate the surroundings for the people there to prevent them from further stumbling and to deliver and free them from harm. Was the light then to blame since it revealed the danger? Wouldn't we rather say that it brings them the greatest possible profit since it makes them safer? I think this is obvious to everyone. So when we sinners, who stumble into the greatest possible charges, learn our sin through the law, it would not be reasonable for us to think or say that the law is sin—far from it! Rather, the law is a revealer of sin, as I have explained.

7:7-8 I would not have known what it is to covet if the law had not said, "You shall not covet." But sin, seizing an opportunity in the commandment, produced in me all kinds of covetousness.

He also brings up the weakness of our nature. Though the law was given for our benefit, it had unintended consequences, just as the light of the sun has for those with diseased eyes. So when he says that the commandment somehow became an "opportunity" for covetousness, no one should think that he is blaming the law.

[62]Ps 14:3 (Ps 13:3 LXX).

No, [**198**] he is crying out against our weakness. Those who were being pushed toward evil by this weakness needed to be stopped by the law. You see, the human mind is sick with a love of vanity that always leads to covetousness. Now those who covet live as they wish without being troubled. But those who beat back their covetous desire experience a fierce onslaught of passions. No one covets what they already have. Rather, they covet what they are prevented from having. So since the law prevents us from having what is harmful, it becomes the occasion for the weak to covet that very thing all the more.

7:8-11 Apart from the law, sin is dead.

If the law that condemns the way of wickedness were to be without force, he says, then sin would be powerless. That is because sin is all but provoked into becoming strong through the law, while the sting of pleasure will be more sluggish when no one is commanding anything. It is all but blunted and put under a spell by broad permissiveness. Where there is no opposition at all, contentiousness surely remains idle. So sin is dead when the law does not issue commands. The expounder of the mysteries says that he once was alive "apart from the law," but then, when "the commandment came," he states that sin revived and he died.

He frames his discussion of these matters to be about his own situation, but I think he intends to communicate something like this: It is common knowledge that those who transgress in ignorance are subject to penalty, but those who transgress knowingly will receive a harsher punishment. The Savior confirms this when he says that the one who knew his master's will and did not do it will be beaten with many blows, but the one who did not [**199**] know and did not do it will be beaten with few blows.[63] And so, as everyone knows, it is better to transgress in ignorance than to transgress with knowledge of the law. If someone comes under the law after living life outside the law and then chooses to ignore its commands, that person is convicted of the charge of sin and falls under judgment. Then—then!—he will mourn his laziness and all but cry out against the severity of the law, saying, "I was once alive apart from the law, but when the commandment came, sin revived and I died." Now if sin is truly "dead apart from the law," how can one credibly suppose that sin is somehow brought to life by the same law that unmasks it or that the law starts it breathing, as it were, even though sin was in us before (albeit formerly unrecognized)? We were not righteous, of course. But just as sin was dead because there happened to be no condemning law, so also we were alive because we had an excuse based on our ignorance. "For where there is no law, there is no transgression,"[64] as he says. So when the commandment arrived, sin came back to life, as it were, and death was restored and therefore also punishment for those who fell into transgression out of weakness. And what is the result of this? What happens is contrary to our hope and expectation. The "commandment," he says, which was given for life, "proved to be death." It is like the light from the sun's rays. That light injures anyone with an eye disease, even though light is intrinsically pleasant and highly desirable. The light itself is surely not to blame. Rather, the harm that it inflicts should be considered an indictment of the illness of those who suffered. In the same way, I think, he is saying that the commandment gives an opportunity for sin to deceive people and drag them down to death. Or perhaps someone might take it in a different sense and say [**200**] that the intense desire for pleasure always strives against the demands of the law. A wicked way of life resists goodness and

[63]Lk 12:47-48.

[64]Rom 4:15.

generally drives it out. Sometimes it drags off the mind and casts it down into transgression, subjecting it to the penalties of the law. So the law is actually the occasion for the battle. In this sense, the wise Paul says that he was deceived by the commandment and put to death through it since it all but killed him by stirring up his desires into opposition to it in the way I just described.

7:12 So the law is holy, and the commandment is holy and just and good.

"The law is holy, and the commandment is holy and just and good." That is because when anyone chooses to keep the law, it shows them to be holy and just and good so that they are unimpeachable by any charge of transgression. This, however, is unattainable. "For who can detect their errors?" as it is written.[65]

7:13 Did what is good, then, bring death to me?

The law is holy, and the commandment is holy and good. So how could he say, "And the very commandment that was given for life proved to be death to me"? Is it the case then, tell me, that what was good became the patron of destruction? "By no means!" he says. I lay no blame on the law for this. Rather, I rise, as it were, to accuse sin. It so subdues human nature and overpowers our mind that the very law that was given for our salvation [201] and life, the commandment that was truly holy and good, became the occasion for death for those who were subject to it. How did that happen? Well, if the penalty always catches up with the transgressors and we have reached such a state of weakness that we are always caught in transgression, then this is clearly how the saving law, which is holy and good, somehow seems to have turned into the cords of sin and a way to death for those under sin. He then immediately adds, "that through the commandment, sin might become sinful beyond measure." When those who do not know their master's will are caught in sin, it will certainly result in punishment. They did sin, after all, even though they were ignorant. Yet they have a certain defense, which I think is not implausible. They can reasonably bring up their ignorance as a defense. For those under the law, however, it would surely be futile to claim that they did not know their master's will. So if someone is openly caught living a life of sin, the charge against them will not be one of ignorance but of madness and ultimately of irreverence toward the Most High. That is how he could say that sin became "sinful beyond measure." After all, those who sin in ignorance are sinful, but they are not "sinful beyond measure," nor are they called that.

7:14 For we know that the law is spiritual.

He says that the law is "spiritual" because it makes those who follow it spiritual. [202] Being spiritual means that one does not live according to the flesh but rather inclines away from it and toward the will to follow what the Spirit wants. The blessed David said, "The law of the Lord is blameless, converting souls. The testimony of the Lord is faithful, instructing infants. The fear of the Lord is pure, abiding forever."[66] So he says that the law is blameless because it makes people blameless, and the testimony is faithful because it renders them faithful, and the fear is pure because it purifies. You should conclude from this that the law is called spiritual in the same sense: because it makes those who follow it spiritual. Even though it is in the shadows, it still has the semblance of truth. What then is Paul saying? He insists that "the law is spiritual," but he blames human nature for being utterly

[65] Ps 19:12 (Ps 18:13 LXX).

[66] Ps 19:7, 9 (Ps 18:8, 10 LXX).

infected with sin. And he tries to convince us that precisely because the law is spiritual, it is a heavy burden for human nature. If the law is spiritual, he is saying, why, tell me, am I "of the flesh," that is, ruled by the mind of the flesh? Do you see how he posits such a great conflict of wills within us? We should understand the will of the Spirit to be one thing and the will of the flesh another.[67] They are opposed to each other and irreconcilable. They cannot agree. So if a person is "of the flesh," and the law is "spiritual," how could it even be bearable for those who are so sick with sin? It is quite reasonable that if he is "of the flesh," we should consider him to be like a captive or a household slave.

7:15 I do not understand my own actions.

Some of the less educated will probably think that he means to support a Greek myth that they have learned to espouse (I know not how) as they were "deceiving others and being deceived."[68] **[203]** First they invent fate and fortune in line with their own ideas. Then they attribute power over our affairs to these nonexistent concepts. In so doing, they rob humanity of what is most characteristic of it: the destiny to live life freely and to have a voluntary inclination—not subject to fate—to whatever deeds we may choose. By necessity, as it were, they lead people astray with their definitions and decrees, and in the process they do immeasurable harm to people in this life. In their view if someone were to proceed to do something wrong, that person would not have the power, even if they wanted to, to escape the decree of fate. And no one could reasonably find fault with them even if they witnessed the transgression. After all, if someone were caught committing an act that was forced on them against their will, they would certainly be excused from blame and punishment. On the other hand, it would be entirely unreasonable to praise anyone for being good and decent. Why should they be praised if they were brought into that condition not willingly but by the decree of another, or rather by fortune imposing invincible necessity on them?

Therefore, it is completely tone deaf to claim that he who leads us into the noblest of teachings is drawing on obtuse Greek arguments, or to imagine that our steward of divine mysteries is following their foolishness when he happens to say, "I do not understand my own actions. For I do not do what I want, but I do the very thing I hate." If anyone were at all to claim—much less choose to think—that he attributes authority over our affairs to fate and fortune, one could reasonably reply: If our actions are controlled by unyielding and indomitable necessity and we do not rule over them, but instead we yield control to others and are constrained by their will, how is it that Paul wrote, "Do you not know, brothers—for I am speaking to those who know the law—that the law rules over a person as long as that person **[204]** is alive?"[69] The law, then, rules over the path of the living. It has no authority whatsoever over the dead. It was not meant for them. How could it be? No, it was meant for those who are still living their life in the body. It crowns the honorable with praises and condemns the impure. So how could the lawgiver be a holy judge if he punishes those who were forced to fall into sin against their will by fortune? Or rather, why did he decree the law at all? The law imposes a just penalty on those who have control over whatever they decide to do. This occurs in the case of those who, though they are able to devote their mind to honor through good works, instead treasure what is shameful and exchange the better for what is condemned by the law. However, for

[67]Cf. Gal 5:17.
[68]2 Tim 3:13.
[69]Rom 7:1.

those who have the yoke of necessity on their necks and who are turned wherever their masters may decide, it seems to me that the divine law is superfluous. Indeed, he who knows all things surely would not have imposed the yoke of the law on us—the law that teaches us what pleases him and leads us to the better—if he knew that we would be caught in the snare of fate! Now let our opponents either say that God did not realize this, or (if they choose to think rightly) let them shudder to heap the charge of ignorance on his ineffable glory. They do say that God has given laws and they will even admit openly that he has decreed punishments for the transgressors. So I suppose he certainly knows that people live their lives with their own free will, and by their own free inclinations can direct themselves to wherever they wish, with no one to hinder them. That is why the divinely inspired Paul said that "the law rules over a person as long as that person is alive."[70] Now he does not say this on the assumption that the human mind is subject to the will of others. Rather, he is carefully **[205]** discussing the passions of the human nature. He is in effect digging up the infirmities of the mind, in a subtle way, and charging the body with an innate love of pleasure, as he masterfully dons the character of one who is still sick with love of the flesh. Although he has been crucified to the world and the world to him and he is truly admirable for that, nevertheless he thought it wise not to focus on his own gift but to address the important topic of the weakness of those who have not yet become like him. So when you hear him say, "I do not understand my own actions," you should think of the worst sinners, who imagine that they truly live the best life of all and that nothing could match the delight and vanity of this world. They loathe virtuous behavior and pride themselves on running riot with their excessive pleasures. I think Paul is talking about them when he says somewhere, "Their minds are set on earthly things. Their god is their belly, and their glory is in their shame."[71] When they commit some evil deed that they are especially fond of, it would make sense for them to say, "I do not understand my own actions." So let them hear, "Wake up, you drunkards, from your wine!"[72] Just as winebibbers and drunkards are robbed of their mental faculties by the experience and do not know what they are doing when they are drinking, so also those whose minds are infected by fleshly lust and the most shameful pleasures do not know what they are doing at the time either. So Paul is explaining to us the disease of the human heart when he says, "I do not understand my own actions." But there may be someone whose heart is quite tender, so to speak, because of the accusations of their conscience. They may regret the fact that they sin but are still overcome by sinful pleasure and proceed against their will, as it were, to the transgression. It would make sense for them to say, **[206]** "I do not do what I want, but I do the very thing I hate." How often do people admire self-control and indeed take care to protect it at first? But then they are conquered by the goads of filthy pleasure, and their mind squats down to what is inferior. They commit sin but afterward are filled with remorse. It would be fitting and altogether reasonable for these people, who were unwillingly afflicted by disease, to turn around and say, "But in fact it is no longer I that do it, but sin that dwells within me."[73]

7:16 Now if I do what I do not want, I agree that the law is good.

Once again he devotes careful attention to the nature of the body and examines the power of

[70]Rom 7:1.

[71]Phil 3:19.
[72]Joel 1:5.
[73]Rom 7:17.

the maladies that naturally dwell therein. That is because the appetites, which lead to all manner of passion, and the sins of the hedonistic life have the flesh as their source. The Savior's disciple confirms this point for us when he says, "Those conflicts and disputes among you, where do they come from? Do they not come from your cravings that are at war within you?"[74]

7:18 I can will what is right, but I cannot do it.

"I can will what is right," he says, "but I cannot do it." . . . As proof that the flesh is guilty of the dreadful birth of sin within, he skillfully concedes the presence of the good in us, though not the ability to bring it to fruition. Indeed, he is forced to turn away against his will into a state of mind he did not want. So **[207]** as far as his own resolve is concerned, he would not have sinned. And since he was subject to inescapable compulsion, it would be reasonable to place the blame not on him, but on the compulsion. Thus he says, "Now if I do what I do not want, it is no longer I that do it, but sin that dwells within me."

Now someone might say: If some heathen barbarians lay waste to a city or countryside and then capture some of the inhabitants at the point of a spear and impose the yoke of slavery on them, the victims would yield to the laws of their conquerors just as they would be forced to yield to their chains. Would they then deserve blame or indictment because they do not rise above the compulsion or disregard the power of their tyrants and eagerly pursue what they themselves want? No, I do not think anyone could reasonably blame them for that. They cannot stop being slaves, after all, and they submit to their circumstances against their will, as I said. They are distraught because they have been deprived of their freedom. Indeed, they have been overcome by force by people more powerful than they. So they are not slaves by their own choice. But if this is a fair representation, then we should conclude that the human mind is exonerated from the charge against the infirmities of the flesh. However, it was the fault of his mind, he says, that he did what he did not want, since the mind itself holds the reins of his will. Therefore, we should conclude that the mind is superior to the power of sin and not ruled by it. But if the nature of the flesh is unbearable and impossible to oppose, rising up with untamable pleasure against the mind, and the law is a rather ineffective aid (for it does not have the power to kill sin), then one could not justly bring a charge against the mind for not doing the better but giving free reign to disgraceful acts, even if it should perhaps hold the reins of our will.

7:21 So I find the law to be with me when I want to do good, telling me that evil lies close at hand.

Now notice how wisely and skillfully he accepts the **[208]** law, not because it has the power to blunt the sting of sin, nor because it can kill sin in us, but simply because it supplies the mind with knowledge of one's circumstances. If, as it seems to me, he is saying that "evil lies close at hand" because it dwells in the flesh but the law forbids it, then the law grants aid and serves as an advisor, though it is not a redeemer. It is surely necessary for those who are sick with sin not only to recognize that they ought to do better but also to have the power to accomplish what is good in the eyes of the law. Even in the case of those who want to distinguish themselves in combat, the mere knowledge of tactics by itself is not enough to accomplish this. But if they were to possess strength as well, then such people would achieve fame and notoriety, though just barely. Therefore, if the law teaches the art of the

[74]Jas 4:1.

good but does not render any aid to those who are captured by sin to loosen sin's grip, then the law is good because it is a teacher, but it would still be unreasonable to consider it equal to the grace of Christ. He is able both to teach us and to make us stronger than evil.

7:22 For I delight in the law of God in my inmost self.

As I have already said, the mind thirsts to be free and wants to be delivered from what is harmful. And so it crowns the law with the highest honors because it introduces a person to what is best. But the nature of the flesh drags it into alien pleasures as the law of sin wars against it and presses hard on it. He uses the term "law of sin" to refer to natural impulse[75] and whatever else one might call the passions of fleshly desire, just as he of course uses the term "law of my mind" to describe his inclination and will toward the good.[76] **[209]**

7:24-25 Wretched man that I am! Who will rescue me from this body of death? Thanks be to God through Jesus Christ our Lord!

Up to this point, he is bemoaning the flesh and inveighing against it. Because of the sickness it contains, he even refers to the law of sin as the "body of death" that comes from the earth and is devoted to pleasure. He says that he is seeking someone who can free him from such evils so that he may at the right moment introduce to us the Redeemer, that is, Christ, to whom he also ascribes all grace. We have been redeemed by him not from the flesh, but from the death of the flesh. This happens not by us dying, but by us being freed from death in our members, that is, from the savage pleasure in our members. That is because Christ made us superior to pleasure and sin.

[75]τὸ ἔμφυτον κίνημα.

[76]Rom 7:23.

7:25–8:1 So then, with my mind I am a slave to the law of God, but with my flesh I am a slave to the law of sin. There is therefore now no condemnation for those who are in Christ Jesus, those who walk not according to the flesh, but according to the spirit.

The apostle's discourse has grown very long as he minutely investigates everything inside us along with the kinds of assaults that the human mind usually endures in its conflict with evil. He states that the mind is sometimes reluctant, as it were, to do good because it is tyrannized by the passions of the flesh. It wanders all about and is disgraced by its weakness. But it cannot cast off this involuntary sin, since pleasure mounts a fearsome attack. It is too weak to stand up against this pleasure, and it finds no help at all from the law to do so. Therefore, the divinely inspired Paul is telling the truth when he states that "with my mind I am a slave to the law of God, but with my flesh I am a slave to the law of sin." I think that means the same thing as what he said before: "I can will what is right, but I cannot do it."[77] **[210]** Now in ancient times, as I have said, it was within our ability, as far as the mind and its will were concerned, to choose to serve the divine law. But the flesh interposed its own will, as it were, and forced the mind into sin. Therefore, there was "condemnation" for those who wanted to do good but were still unable to because they were tyrannized by the passions. But in Christ that which condemns—that is, the assault of the fleshly impulses—has come to an end.

8:2 For the law of the spirit of life in Christ Jesus . . .

In order to provide a detailed explanation of the meaning of this passage, I need to make the following comments. Just as he calls the fleshly

[77]Rom 7:18.

will the "law of sin and death" that carries us off to every kind of wickedness, so also he calls the spiritual will the "law of the spirit of life," that is, the inclination of the mind toward the good. Indeed, "the one who sows to the flesh will reap corruption from the flesh, but the one who sows to the spirit will reap eternal life from the spirit."[78] Now the "law of the spirit of life"—that is, the will of the mind that carries us to life—was in us in ancient times, since in our mind we were slaves to God's law.[79] But our weaker part fell sick, as I said, and resisted the law. Our mind was overcome by the desires of the flesh and was condemned by the law. Yet when it had cast off its illness, it was strengthened by Christ. He sealed us in the Holy Spirit and clothed us with "power from on high."[80] By this we have been redeemed. We were no longer under the yoke of evil, but we were called, as I said, to the dignity of freedom. So "the law of the spirit of life," that is, the will of the mind that inclines toward doing good and that carries us into life—when it was enriched by the grace of Christ and delivered from that ancient malady—[211] it disregarded the evil effects of sin, gained mastery over the law of the flesh, and "set me free," he says. That law certainly did not grant freedom of itself. Rather, it became the agent of the freedom that comes to us through Christ. Just as those who are under the law of sin must be utterly entangled in the snare of death, so also those who have been released from sin and freed by Christ must also be released from death, be superior to decay, and live a life of sanctification.

8:3 The powerlessness of the law, weakened by the flesh.

The mystagogue is admirable and exceedingly detailed in his contemplation, but he also says that he is "untrained in speech."[81] For this reason we may say without any embarrassment that there is a little bit missing from the words he composes here. They do not quite give us a full explanation.[82] He should have said that the powerlessness of the law, weakened by the flesh, "was destroyed," perhaps, or "ceased." Then he could have provided the explanation and joined it to the manner of destruction by adding, "God, by sending his Son in the likeness of sinful flesh and for sin, destroyed sin in the flesh," and so on.[83] So since that is what these words mean, at least according to their inner intent, come let us examine how Christ heals and how "the powerlessness of the law" ceases, as well as what "the powerlessness of the law" refers to in the first place and what kind of law is meant. The Theologian[84] goes into great detail in this passage. He accepts the law of God as profitable—I mean both the law of the letter and the law of the spirit, according to which we have a good will, even though we may not perhaps have the ability [212] to carry it out. He said, "I can will what is right, but I cannot do it."[85] That is because sin is violent, and the law of the flesh drags the mind down, even against its will, to the flesh's level. In the phrase *powerlessness of the law,* I think it would be reasonable to take "law" in the same way, as referring to the law of the letter by Moses, as I just said, and also to the natural law in us, by which even the Gentiles by nature do the works of the law and are a law unto themselves, even though they do not have the written law.[86] "For they show that the work of the law is

[78]Gal 6:8.

[79]Cf. Cyril's comments on Rom 7:25 above.

[80]Lk 24:49.

[81]2 Cor 11:6.

[82]Rom 8:3-4 reads as follows: "The powerlessness of the law, weakened by the flesh—God, by sending his Son in the likeness of sinful flesh and for sin, destroyed sin in the flesh." It is difficult to see how the first clause relates to the rest of the sentence, which is why Cyril says something is missing.

[83]Rom 8:3.

[84]The early church sometimes referred to the apostle John as the Theologian. Here Cyril gives that title to Paul as well.

[85]Rom 7:18.

[86]Rom 2:14.

written on their hearts," as it is written.[87] And now it is time to investigate what kind of "powerlessness" is in both. The law of the letter was a teacher of good conduct and an instructor of the best behavior, but it justified absolutely no one. The natural law in us, which he also calls the law "of the spirit," inclined toward the good, but it is far less powerful than the law that summons us to the worse. So Christ brought to an end the "powerlessness," that is, the weakness, both of the law of the letter and of the natural law. That is because when the flesh has been mortified in a sense, in that the pleasure inherent in us has been taken away, the law of the spirit or of the mind will not be weak at all. Come, let us discuss, as far as possible, how the sin in us has been mortified. The Word of God, with the approval of God the Father, came to be in the "likeness of sinful flesh" in order to "condemn sin in the flesh." He became a human being and condescended to empty himself, and his body is the same form and nature as ours. How could anyone doubt that? The exception is that the bodies of all the others would be called "sinful flesh" because their infirmity naturally brings forth alien pleasures, but no one would say that the body of Christ is "sinful flesh." By no means! Rather, it is the "likeness of sinful flesh"—that is, **[213]** it is like our bodies, but it is not sick with fleshly impurity. That divine temple[88] was holy from the womb. Now when it comes to the definition and inner constitution of his nature, no one would shrink from saying that since his body was flesh, it would have contained in itself the natural impulses[89] that are proper to the flesh. But since the Word who sanctifies all creation dwelt in it, the power of sin has been condemned so that the restoration may extend to us as well. That is because we participate in him both spiritually and corporeally. When Christ dwells in us through the Holy Spirit and through the Mystical Blessing,[90] then the law of sin is completely condemned in us. Now "the powerlessness of the law, weakened by the flesh," was truly ended by Christ when he condemned and abolished "sin in the flesh, so that the just requirements of the law might be fulfilled in us." The just requirements of the law (that is, the force of the law's decrees, which is that the will should focus on virtue) are fulfilled when the law in us is no longer weakened in any way, as I said, by the tyranny of natural pleasures. Therefore, "the just requirements of the law" are fulfilled in us when we "walk not according to the flesh," but rather will to live spiritually.[91]

8:6-7 The mind of the flesh is death, but the mind of the spirit is life and peace.

He calls the mind of the flesh "death," and rightly so, while he calls the mind of the spirit "life and peace." The love of the flesh is truly the patron of death, but choosing to live spiritually is the patron of eternal life and blessings from above. If "the mind of the flesh is hostile to God" since **[214]** it does not allow itself to submit to the divine laws, "indeed it cannot," how will foul and impure pleasure "please God"? Surely the mind that is cleansed of filth and passions, as far as is possible for human nature, is the one that is reconciled with God.

8:8-9 And those who are in the flesh cannot please God. But you are not in the flesh; you are in the spirit, since the Spirit of God dwells in you.

When earthly pleasure gains mastery over the human mind, a person is in the flesh since they

[87]Rom 2:15.
[88]Jesus refers to his body as a "temple" in Jn 2:19-21.
[89]ἔμφυτον κίνημα.
[90]"Blessing" (εὐλογία) is the way Cyril normally refers to the Eucharist.
[91]Rom 8:4.

think about fleshly concerns. Such a person cannot please God. But when the mind is enriched by the grace of Christ and full of power from above and seething with the Spirit and striving for virtue, such a person is not "in the flesh" but "in the spirit" and easily accomplishes great things for God.

8:9 Anyone who does not have the Spirit of Christ does not belong to him.

Anyone who is in the spirit is also in righteousness and life since the body of sin has all but died and all alien pleasure has been extinguished. After all, it is impossible for righteousness and unrighteousness or for sanctification and impurity to exist in the same person at the same time. We take the phrase "the spirit is life" to refer to the human spirit that is given life by the grace of the Holy Spirit and enriched with righteousness by communion with the Holy Spirit. That is how we are "participants of the divine nature"[92] since Christ dwells in us through the Holy Spirit.

8:11 If the Spirit of him who raised Jesus from the dead dwells in you . . .

Our Lord Jesus Christ was raised from the dead by the **[215]** Father as life was brought about in his body through the Holy Spirit, who is his. After all, he shows that he himself brought his own temple back to life when he says to the Jews, "Destroy this temple, and in three days I will raise it up."[93] Therefore, even though he is said to be raised by the Father, he is the one who does the raising through the Holy Spirit. All God-befitting actions are carried out by the Father through the Son in the Spirit. That is how Christ will raise our bodies from the dead as well.

[92]2 Pet 1:4.
[93]Jn 2:19.

8:14-15 For all who are led by the Spirit of God are children of God.

Those who live by the spirit are also the ones who are led by the Spirit because they have been sealed by the Holy Spirit. They have been delivered from the slavery of the law and the letter and transferred to freedom. The Spirit of adoption bears witness that they are children of God and they cry out in the same Spirit of adoption, "Abba! Father!"

8:17 If, in fact, we suffer with him so that we may also be glorified with him.

The good is not accomplished without effort, but effort holds great hopes for the saints. That is because they are promised no earthly reward, but eternal glory and participation in realities beyond thought and understanding. Those who fix their gaze above earthly matters are worthy of the highest rewards. And those who have labored with courage and endurance will enjoy crowns of incomparable dignity. Our efforts toward virtue fall short in comparison with those honors. I am referring to the glory of the saints, since at that time "the righteous will shine like the sun,"[94] and they will attain honor and glory and incorruptibility as their bodies are transfigured, just as Christ was transfigured on the mountain. **[216]**

8:19 For the creation waits with eager longing for the revealing of the children of God.

Hope is the "eager longing." It is the expectation and observation of the outcome of events. However, creation waits for the revealing of the children of God not in the sense that it knows what is going to happen. How could it? Rather, by the ineffable plan of

[94]Mt 13:43.

God, who directs all things toward what is better, creation will arrive at this end. When the children of God, that is, those who achieve a God-pleasing life, are remolded, as it were, from dishonor to glory and from decay to incorruption, then creation itself will surely also be changed for the better. The divinely inspired Peter leaves us no doubt on this point when he says, "We look for new heavens and a new earth and his promises."[95]

8:20-22 For the creation was subjected to futility.

Here he uses the word "futility" to refer to those who live in futility, that is, in a fleshly mind. It could quite rightly be said of them, "Humanity was like futility."[96] In fact, they even "resembled senseless beasts and became like them."[97] The life of such people truly is "futility." And creation is subject to them, though certainly not by its own will. How can that be? How can we make this claim? After all, the tangible and visible creation knows nothing at all of our affairs since it is not rational. But if one were to grant creation some ability to understand, he is saying, it would not bear such disgraceful slavery, **[217]** nor would it be willing to be subjected to and to serve those who decree that it live its life without that which it ought to live for—namely, the good. But it is subject "in hope," he says, referring to the saints and elect who will be saved at that time. God imposed this yoke and reserved creation, so to speak, for the "freedom" that is found in subjection to the saints and those who love him, so that creation may serve only his children and be subject to the needs of the elect. Creation is practically at wits' end as it labors and is distressed. And if it had any ability to understand our affairs, it would probably wail (except that it yields to the divine will) as it somehow awaits "the revealing," as it says, "of the children of God."

8:23 And not only the creation, but we ourselves, who have the firstfruits of the Spirit, groan inwardly while we wait for adoption.

He takes what naturally occurs in us as proof of his statement. "We ourselves," he says, "who have the firstfruits of the Spirit" are weighed down and "groan inwardly while we wait for adoption, the redemption of our bodies." It is true that "a perishable body weighs down the soul, and this earthly tent burdens the thoughtful mind."[98] Once the Holy Spirit is within us and he transforms us to desire virtue, the love of the flesh is removed, as it were, along with the law that attacked our members and incited alien pleasures and set itself up as an implacable foe. This is how we understand the words "we groan for the redemption of our bodies, for adoption." We do not thirst for the removal of our bodies, and we reject the idea that this is what redemption is. Rather, we look forward to there being **[218]** a "spiritual body,"[99] that is, a mind that has completely put off what is carnal and earthly along with the sting of sin. We maintain that this is what the spiritual body is.

If the grace of adoption includes "the redemption of our bodies," then certain people should stop criticizing the resurrection. They should not be so stupid as to say that the flesh is destroyed and completely disappears when it is laid into the ground and that it arises as something else: a sort of spiritual entity, ethereal and airy (since that is what they think "spiritual" means).

[95]2 Pet 3:13.
[96]Ps 144:4 (Ps 143:4 LXX).
[97]Ps 49:12 (Ps 48:13 LXX).
[98]Wis 9:15.
[99]1 Cor 15:44.

8:24 For in hope we were saved.

We believe that our bodies are going to be superior to death and decay. But this lies in store for us in hope. It is not yet present, but it will surely and definitively happen. We wait for it with patient endurance so that we may gain such a majestic gift.

8:26 Likewise, the spirit helps us in our weakness. . . . But that very spirit intercedes for us with sighs too deep for words.

With sighs too deep for words, the spirit—namely, our spirit—intercedes for us. Sometimes we sigh as we eagerly make our supplications before God. And even this we learn from the Holy Spirit since he is wise, just like the Son. Now since it says, "We do not know how to pray as we ought," let us investigate that. Christ has already taught us how we ought to pray. He stated explicitly, **[219]** "Pray this way: Our Father in heaven, hallowed be your name. Your kingdom come. Your will be done, on earth as it is in heaven," and the rest.[100] Now since we know how we ought to make our petitions, what could be the meaning, tell me, of the apostle's words? What could Paul's statement be aiming at? Well, we define prayer as making a request for good things, and above all for those things that promote the glory of God and that result in our good conduct and our living a life that is truly pleasing. "We ourselves, who have the firstfruits of the Spirit, groan inwardly while we wait for adoption, the redemption of our bodies."[101] This passage is what the words "we do not know how to pray as we ought" refer to. After all, if "no eye has seen, nor ear heard, nor the human heart conceived what God has prepared for those who love him,"[102] what shall we ask for when we approach him? How could we know that which we have not seen, or rather that which exceeds the mind and remains incomprehensible to human hearts? What kind of redemption of the body will take place? What will the renovation be like? How is the body transformed to incorruption and glory? Only the craftsman of these things could know. Furthermore, the Savior's disciple somewhere said to certain people who did not know how to pray as they ought, "You ask and do not receive, because you ask wrongly, in order to spend what you get on your pleasures."[103] It would be quite proper and reasonable to say to people in that condition, "We do not know how to pray as we ought." **[220]** "With sighs too deep for words" we pray in the spirit for things that we believe will happen in the future, but we do not at all know how.

8:28 We know that all things work together for good for those who love God, who are called according to purpose.

"All things work together for good for those who love God, who are called according to purpose." But who are those called according to purpose? And what does "according to purpose" mean? Well, "according to purpose" means "according to will." According to whose will are they called? Is it the will of the one who called them or the will of those who are called? Every desire that leads us to righteousness comes to us from God the Father. Christ said somewhere, "No one can come to me unless drawn by the Father who sent me."[104] Yet in this case, one would not fall short of a fitting statement if one were to say that people are called according to purpose—both the purpose of him who called them and their own purpose.

[100]Mt 6:9-10.
[101]Rom 6:23.
[102]1 Cor 2:9.
[103]Jas 4:3.
[104]Jn 6:44.

8:29 For those whom he foreknew, he also predestined to be conformed . . .

Many people, he says, are called according to purpose. But not all are elect. The only ones who receive this honor are those whom he foreknew would be conformed "to the image of his Son." And the blessed Paul himself clarifies what "the image of his Son" means when he says, "Just as we have borne the image of the man of dust, we will also bear the image of the man of heaven."[105] Those who disregard carnal desires are the ones who imitate the image of Christ, that is, **[221]** life and conduct characterized by sanctification. Just as we say that the image of the man of dust, that is, Adam, is a life of disobedience and sin, so also we say that the image of the man of heaven, that is, Christ, is sanctification, righteousness, and obedience. So as many as he foreknew would ultimately be conformed to the life of Christ and would be imitators of him (as far as it is possible for human nature), these he also called.

8:30 And those whom he predestined he also called; and those whom he called he also justified; and those whom he justified he also glorified.

As a consequence of their unbelief, some people are captured by ignorance and do not consider it unreasonable to say: If those whom he foreknew according to purpose and predestined are the ones who are called, then it is no surprise that we do not believe. After all, we were neither called nor foreknown. To them we reply: The one who held a wedding banquet for his son sent his servants to gather the invited[106] guests, but they were not willing to come. After them, those who were invited according to his own purpose entered, and thus the wedding hall was filled with guests.[107] Clearly, nothing prevented those who wanted to from coming. Foreknowledge does no harm to anyone, nor does it benefit anyone. This account teaches us that they were not foreknown who by their unbelief insulted the God who invited them. Others were invited and came to the wedding, yet they were not elect, nor justified, nor glorified. Why not? They were wearing clothes that were not appropriate for a wedding.[108] Elsewhere we find that our Lord Jesus Christ himself has clearly stated, **[222]** "Come to me, all you that are weary and carrying heavy burdens, and I will give you rest."[109] See, here he was calling all people to himself. No one is without a share of the grace of being called. When he says "all," he is excluding absolutely no one.

8:31-32 What then are we to say about these things? If God is for us, who is against us? He who did not withhold his own Son . . .

All things work together for those who have chosen to do good, since God defends them. He who did not spare his natural Son so that he might save those who were in danger and free them from their danger, "will he not with him also give us everything else?"

8:33-34 Who will bring any charge against God's elect? It is God who justifies. Who is to condemn?

Swiftly and in good order, Paul refuses to allow the mind of those who are called to fall into helplessness. Rather, he teaches that they will be freed from the ancient sins and they will be justified as God wills it. All sin involves transgression of the divine law and condemns the frivolous offender, yet since the Lord of the

[105]1 Cor 15:49.
[106]The word for "invited" is the same as the word for "called."
[107]Mt 22:1-10.
[108]Mt 22:11-14.
[109]Mt 11:28.

law himself accepts the sinner, "who is to condemn?" **[223]**

9:1-5 I am speaking the truth in Christ—I am not lying; my conscience confirms it.

At the beginning, God chose Israel. More specifically, he called Israel the "firstborn."[110] But they grew proud and insolent and what is more, they killed the Lord. Thus they perished since they were rejected and cast out. They utterly fell away from their relationship with God, and they were ranked behind the Gentiles. They were clearly estranged from the hope of their fathers. Since the blessed Paul was appointed as a servant of the divine gospel, he proclaimed Jesus to the Gentiles, incessantly repeating that those descended from Israel have fallen away and maintaining that those who were once in darkness and worshiped demons are now called according to the purpose and foreknowledge of God. So that the simple may not think that he is pouncing on those of his own race and laughing at those who fell, he makes a much-needed defense against this idea by saying, "I am speaking the truth in Christ—I am not lying," and so on. Now one should be sorry for those who habitually practice such perversity that they fall away from love toward God and ultimately endure harsh penalties for that. It would not be unreasonable to shed a tear for them out of love for one another. But he has complete love for them. Indeed, wanting to be "accursed and cut off from Christ" for them is beyond the measure of love. No one in their right mind would choose to offend God for the salvation of others and to disregard their own life to obtain this benefit for others. **[224]**

What then is he saying when he offers his own life in exchange for the salvation of the Jews? His statement is hyperbolical and indicates perfect love. "For I could wish," he says, "that I myself were accursed and cut off from Christ for the sake of my own people." It is as if he were to say: If Israel could be saved by my offending Christ, I myself would choose to do so. I who said to those justified by faith, "For I decided to know nothing among you except Jesus Christ, and him crucified,"[111]—I who proclaim to everyone, "Who will separate us from the love of Christ? Will hardship, or distress, or persecution, or famine, or nakedness, or peril, or sword?"—I myself would choose to endure such a terrible evil and to go to my destruction, one in the place of all. These are the words of someone trying to net the Jews for faith and throw off the oppression of their ignorance. Some of the Jews thought that the divinely inspired Paul suffered a stroke, as it were, when he opposed the laws of Moses. That is why he writes to the believers and says, "For if we are beside ourselves, it is for God; if we are in our right mind, it is for you."[112] Therefore, I, at least, would eagerly choose to be "accursed and cut off from Christ," he says, in order to save my blood relatives. Then he adds another point as if to show that the reason for his grief for them is not unfitting, at least when it comes to its ability to create such a disposition in him. He does not want anyone to think he is saying something difficult or absurd when he offers his life in exchange for the life of others. So he says first, "They are Israelites, and to them belong the adoption, the glory, the covenants, the giving of the law, the worship, and the promises." And "from them, according to the flesh, comes Christ himself." Now if there were some in ancient times who did not recognize him who is truly God by nature, if the law of Moses had not served as an arbiter of their relationship with him, **[225]** if they had not sprung from the root of the holy fathers and been established as the heirs of

[110]Ex 4:22.

[111]1 Cor 2:2.

[112]2 Cor 5:13.

their nobility, if they had not been the first to practice the worship of God and possess the rich hope of the promise, one could have grieved over them more moderately. But since their fathers and the rest veered off to an unexpected destination and they completely missed their hope, even though matters were proceeding under fair winds, as it were, isn't the outcome for these poor people truly terrible?

9:6-9 It is not as though the word of God had failed.

This statement is precise. He is in no way saying that the word of God lied or that it could fall short of the truth. Everyone agrees that the God of the universe did promise to Abraham in ancient times that he would be the father of many.[113] He also says, "I will make your offspring as numerous as the stars of heaven."[114] Accordingly, Abraham had to be made the father not only of the Israelites. One nation came from him, but there are multitudes throughout the world who are considered children of Abraham since they are born of the promise[115] and they "follow the example of his faith before he was circumcised," as it is written.[116] As the blessed Paul himself says somewhere, "The promise that he would inherit the world did not come to Abraham through the law but through the righteousness of faith. If it is the adherents of the law who are to be the heirs," he says, "faith is null and the promise is void."[117] So since the descendants of Abraham are reckoned to be in Isaac, according to the promise (since the words of the promise say, "About this time I will return, and Sarah shall have a son"[118]), it should be clear that the children of the flesh are not the ones who would always and everywhere be considered children of God. Rather the children of the promise (those who are children by faith) are the ones who would have [226] this glory for themselves.

9:10 Not only, but also Rebecca when she had conceived children by one husband, our father Isaac.

We must realize that the meaning of this statement is not at all complete. Rather, the statement is detached and is missing a brief introduction, which needs to be supplied so that the passage does not limp. What I mean is this. He just showed Isaac being given to Abraham by a promise so that it is certainly not the children of the flesh who should be considered Abraham's descendants, but we should call him the father of his descendants by faith and by the promise. Then he refers to Rebecca and her circumstances and says, "Not only," that is, My statement pertains not only to the birth of Isaac, "but also Rebecca, when she had conceived children by one husband, our father Isaac." We also need to add something else, perhaps that this should be taken as evidence or assurance, or rather as a type or an image of the calling and grace of election and foreknowledge. If something like this were added, it would have seemed right to make this statement right after it. But if it is omitted, I do not know how he could go straight to the words and deeds pertaining to the birth of Isaac's descendants.

9:14-24 What then are we to say? Is there injustice on God's part? By no means. . . . Until he called us not from the Jews only but also from the Gentiles.

It is likely that some critics will think [227] Jacob and Esau received their lots by an arbitrary inclination of God's will and that the

113Gen 17:4.
114Gen 22:17.
115Gal 4:23.
116Rom 4:12.
117Rom 4:13-14.
118Gen 18:10.

one was loved by grace, as God willed it, and the other was hated. The apostle has to get rid of this idea as deadly, so he tries to argue the case for the decree from above, which seems to contradict his words like some kind of opponent. If, he says, even before the infants did anything and before they attempted any deeds, one was deemed worthy of love and the other was hated and enslaved to the younger, then perhaps God was unjust, he says. How is this not deranged? If Jacob were not a good man and Esau were not an evil one, perhaps one could reasonably make the case that God's foreknowledge was in error and that his decrees about both of them were the result of a random choice and an unstable will. But since Esau was exceedingly foolish and Jacob was wise, God's foreknowledge did absolutely no wrong when it bestowed ahead of time love on the good man and condemnation on the man who was not good. After all, it is not a terrible thing that God is long-suffering and that he holds off until the works are accomplished so that each of them may be revealed by his deeds. Since the mystery of the grace of election and of the gift of foreknowledge had to be prefigured in a type, God, who masterfully arranged these things for us, seized the moment, as it were. At the birth of the children, he showed that Isaac was the one and only son of Abraham, and so he would be the father of countless nations who would be called by the promise and in faith. Now if he happened to choose them on the basis of his knowledge, or rather if he chose those on whom it was fitting to show mercy, then he shows mercy **[228]** as God, as he somewhere said to Moses, "I will have mercy on whom I will have mercy, and I will have compassion on whom I have compassion."[119] Surely that fact is immune from all criticism, isn't it? But I think the apostle distinctly foresees that some people would probably think that the will of God makes some good and others disobedient. So he needs to state their ignorant response: "So it depends not on human will or exertion, but on God who shows mercy." If Esau was hated even before he did anything wrong and Jacob was honored even before he came into being and God has mercy on whom he has mercy, is it not a valid conclusion that all our actions depend on the will of God, since the one who strives or wills (that is, that one who intends to do good) accomplishes nothing?

Then he piles onto this the argument that can support this opinion: "For the Scripture says to Pharaoh, 'I have raised you up for the very purpose of showing my power in you.'" After that, he adds a kind of conclusion to the whole argument: "So then he has mercy on whomever he chooses, and he hardens the heart of whomever he chooses. You will say to me then, 'Why then does he still find fault? For who can resist his will?'" What kind of defense, then, does he have? This is quite obscure, and perhaps he even seems to come to the aid of their argument. Nevertheless, one may find sufficient proof for his defense in the fact that none of his statements exceed the bounds of what is fitting for God. God distributes to each person what is proper to that person.[120] He has mercy and compassion on those for whom appropriate mercy would be fitting, and he imposes punishment on the sinner, but not with his wrath immediately following on the heels of the accusation. Rather, great patience intervenes so that some even think that God is neglecting the inhabitants of the earth. Then Paul replies and opposes those who make this argument, **[229]** and in so doing, he dissipates the force of the argument regarding the characters who were cited, I mean Esau and Pharaoh. He says, as if addressing each of the aforementioned men,

[119]Ex 33:19.

[120]Cyril seems to be using Cicero's definition of justice in *De natura deorum* 3.38: "Justice attributes to each person what belongs to that person" (*iustitia . . . suum cuique tribuit*).

"But who indeed are you, O man, to argue with God? Will what is molded say to the one who molds it, 'Why have you made me like that?'" He shows with a clear example that it is very difficult to criticize God's judgment. Those who choose to think reasonably would leave it to the all-knowing God to judge every matter in the way he himself knows best. They would not doubt in the least that whatever he wills to do is holy as he fashions the circumstances of each person by his authority, whatever those circumstances may be. Therefore, Paul vehemently accuses those who apply their mind to God's will to determine whether it is good or not. They must rather imitate that which is molded by the hand of the potter, he says, and endure in silence whatever comes from God. "Will what is molded say to the one who molds it, 'Why have you made me like that?'"

But perhaps some will also raise this objection: If God, like a potter, molds however he wants so that he makes "one vessel for honor and another for dishonor," how could that fact not utterly persuade us to think that whatever exists anywhere and everywhere exists just as he made it? So one person is created "for honor"[121] and has been allotted that kind of nature, but another has been created, or rather hardened, in order to proclaim God's name "in all the earth." What charge remains then against those who stumble? After all, they were created that way.

One may respond to this by saying that no one can claim that the meaning of this sentence indicates that there are differences of natures among ourselves. It does not say that some people are created savage or hardened or that they are created as vessels "of honor" and "of dishonor." Nor does it ascribe such a nature to them **[230]** at all. Rather, it convinces us to think people are formed as the kind of pottery vessel that is "for honor" or "for dishonor." We learn the point of the example from the words of the prophet. By reading the words of Jeremiah, one may learn in what sense some are molded, as by a potter, "for honor" and others "for dishonor" and for what kind of dishonor. It is written: "Arise and go down to the potter's house, and there you will hear my words. So I went down to the potter's house, and behold, he was making a vessel on the stones. And the vessel that he was making with his hands fell, so he made it into a different vessel, as it pleased him to make it. And the word of the Lord came to me," it says, "saying, 'Can I not do with you, O house of Israel, just as this potter has done? Behold, just like the clay in the potter's hand, so are you in my hand. If I declare at one point concerning a nation or kingdom to destroy it, and that nation turns from all their wicked ways, then I will repent of the evils that I had planned to inflict upon them. And if I declare at one point concerning a nation or kingdom to rebuild it and plant it, and they do evil before me by not listening to my voice, then I will repent of the good that I had said I would do to them.'"[122] Do you see how some are molded for honor and others for dishonor? They are not allotted a nature that is created that way, but they receive a fitting reward that is commensurate with their deeds. Therefore, if the Creator of the universe punishes the one who leaves the good paths for the disgraceful ones and crowns with honor the one who leaves disgraceful behavior for the better, how is it not true **[231]** to say that no one is evil by nature (or more specifically, no one is molded by him that way), but rather they became vessels of dishonor because even though they had decided to please God, they fell ill due to their voluntary inclination to evil?

But it says that he hardened Pharaoh's heart. And furthermore, God said to him, "I have raised you up for the very purpose of

[121]Pusey's text actually has "dishonor" (ἀτιμίαν), but the context seems to indicate that this is a typographical error.

[122]Jer 18:2-10.

showing my power in you." So if he hardens some people and raises them up to be "vessels of wrath" and they are said to be "prepared for destruction," "why does he still find fault? For who can resist his will?" How could someone hardened by him become good?

What then could I say in response to this? To know the truth, it is sufficient to maintain and think that God could never be the creator of anything bad. "Everything that he made is very good."[123] Now if they contend that the Egyptian is not human and has not received the same nature as we have, let them prove it and we will be silent. But if he is like us, either let them openly condemn God's statement for failing to distinguish between what is good and what is not, or if they shrink back from this, then let them admit that what God brought into being was good. In this way they will reject their utterly rash opinion. The statement addressed to Pharaoh, "I have raised you up for this very purpose," does not mean, "I have made or created you," but rather, "I have called you to will to oppose me." And this happened not at the beginning of his existence, but when Moses was sent to redeem Israel. The all-wise Paul explains clearly to us the reason why [232] when he says, "God desiring to show his wrath," and so on. The whole earth went astray in ancient times. Some worshiped the creation, while others fabricated their own seeming worship. Only Abraham was called to the knowledge of God, and so his descendants grew up with the worship of God.

Now when they went down into Egypt, they spent a long time there. They slipped into error and worshiped the gods of that country. But God remembered his promises to their fathers, and Moses was chosen for a mission to free Israel from slavery. Yet it was necessary both for those whom Moses called to worship and for everyone on earth to learn that the God of the Hebrews has been revealed after a long time. Not only that, but they also needed spectacular miracles to establish them in faith toward him and in the conviction that he is not mute and impotent like the other gods, but rather he directs all things, and his wrath falls on those who resist his will. Yet it was also necessary that once God decided to do miracles, he be seen to arrive at them in an appropriate way. So Pharaoh was raised up in opposition to him according to God's design and he was hardened against God's power. But he was not punished unjustly since he was an unholy idolater who oppressed Israel with clay and brickmaking and rewarded them with punishment. Therefore, it was appropriate for God to make him a "vessel of wrath" and to prepare him for destruction—that is, he reached such a level of wicked behavior that he was finally a vessel of wrath and destruction. God used him as a demonstration of his power so that he may proclaim his name in all the earth and so that once Pharaoh had suffered, he may be seen to [233] have deserved it. He deserved to suffer on account of his prior sins even if he did not offend subsequently. Therefore, let us be done with all blaming and nonsense directed against God. After all, "desiring to show his wrath and make known his power, he endured with much patience the vessels of wrath that are made for destruction" in order to help the "vessels of mercy," that is, those who receive mercy through faith, since we have been called "not from the Jews only but also from the Gentiles."

9:25 As indeed he says in Hosea.

But we who were worshipers of idols, who did not know him who is truly God by nature, were not his people. Yet we received mercy through faith and became his subjects. We have been called by grace, and we have been justified and sanctified through Christ.

[123]Gen 1:31.

9:27 Though the number of the children of Israel were like the sand of the sea.

So even though Israel were many, like the sand, "only the remnant will be saved." The remnant are those who have been justified by faith in Christ. And this happens when God has mercy on them.

9:28 For he kept his word decisive and brief.

He saved them, it says, as he "kept his word decisive and brief." That means that when he revealed the gospel proclamation to us, the message was noble, brief, and if I may put it this way, abridged. The Law and the Prophets used many cycles of words, and they barely managed to set before us in writing the meaning of what they had to say. [234] But the gospel proclamation is simple and its message is brief.

9:31 But Israel pursued the law of righteousness.

Now when he gives the reason that not all the Jews have been saved, he immediately weaves wonder into his discourse. O strange fact! he exclaims. The multitude in error, who have no intention whatsoever to do good, have been justified. But Israel, even though they are led to righteousness by the law of Moses, have missed their hope entirely and have been left without a share in this gift. So what is the reason for this? It is clear. They did not attain the salvation that is by faith. They did not attain the righteousness that is in Christ. Instead, they thought it was sufficient for them to boast in shadows.

9:33 A stumbling block.

Of course, we do not say that this was the reason Christ was placed in Israel. But since God foreknew what would happen, he needed to announce it ahead of time. An occasion for stumbling would be laid in the foundation of Zion, and some who lacked understanding would trip over it because of unbelief. It was beneficial for him to make this prediction, and he did so not that they might fall, but that by knowing ahead of time they might overcome the evil. Therefore, Christ was placed there as a precious stone. For those who stumble from unbelief, their loss is ruinous, but for those who have believed, their profit is life and righteousness.

10:2 I testify about them.

He testifies about their "zeal" for God, but he criticizes them for erring. They should have marveled at Christ for being God by nature because of what [235] he did. But they said, "It is not for a good work that we are going to stone you, but for blasphemy, because you, though only a human being, are making yourself God,"[124] or other things like this. They did not know the righteousness of God, that is, Christ, or the righteousness that is through faith in him. They thought they were defending the law of Moses, but they remained in unbelief. They did not seek the Son who can make you free,[125] who justifies the ungodly,[126] who in his plan of salvation put an end to the arduous righteousness of the law to free them from being crushed and vexed.

10:4 Christ is the end of the law.

The law was introduced beforehand to guide the ancients to the mystery of Christ and to give them a glimpse of the truth in figures. So we declare Christ to be the fulfillment of the law and the prophets, and we are quite right to do so. Wouldn't the truth reasonably be

[124]Jn 10:33.
[125]Jn 8:36.
[126]Rom 4:5.

understood to be the fulfillment of every unclear figure? Indeed, how could anyone doubt it? Therefore, the passing from shadows to truth abrogates the laws of Moses, but it also clarifies their meaning.

When these matters ultimately reach the truth and types and figures are transformed into what is better, we do not say the law has been destroyed, but rather that it has been fulfilled at the right time, when the truth, that is, Christ, shone on us. After all, Christ is the end[127] of the Law and the Prophets. He would not have lied when he said, "I have come not to abolish the law, but to fulfill it."[128] Just as the introduction of many colors at the right moment does not in the least remove the outlines prefigured in a picture but brings them into sharper focus, so in the same way we say that the shadows of the law are not overturned but are rather fulfilled on the way to the truth. **[236]**

10:5 Moses writes concerning the righteousness that comes from the law . . .

"Moses writes concerning the righteousness that comes from the law," he says, "that 'the person who does these things will live by them.'"[129] But there is absolutely no one who can keep it blamelessly. "For who can detect their errors?"[130] Therefore, justifying grace is superior and frees us from the accusation of the law.

10:6 But the righteousness that comes from faith says . . .

He beneficially defines how our faith should be, if it is to be blameless before God and to believe that everything he does is exceedingly good. All doubt must be completely rejected along with the willful wavering of feeble hesitancy. Perhaps one of the greatest causes of stumbling is to be bent on busying ourselves with matters that are beyond all thought and that transcend our mind. After all, how could the ineffable works of God be clear to us? Indeed, what eye of the heart could ever be so strong that it could gaze on God? And more to the point, even if someone were to choose to speak about and relate matters that are far above us, how could that person understand them? Our Lord Jesus Christ once discoursed with Nicodemus about the spiritual rebirth and said to him, "Truly, truly I tell you, no one can see the kingdom of God without being born again."[131] [He then adds the rest].[132] But since he understood nothing at all, then—then!—Christ completely separated the coarseness of human thinking from the subtlety of his own thoughts and said, "If I have told you about earthly things **[237]** and you do not believe, how can you believe if I tell you about heavenly things?"[133] To this he added, "Truly, truly I tell you, we speak of what we know and testify to what we have seen; yet you do not receive our testimony."[134] Therefore, matters that are above us cannot be examined. If it is true that "what is at hand we find with labor," as it is written,[135] would we not have to think that in matters that transcend reason, faith is what we need the most, unaccompanied by investigation or the undertaking of vain inquiry? After all, it is clear that such matters are honored by prudence.

---

[127]The word for "end" (τέλος) here and in the text of Rom 10:4 can also mean "goal" or "fulfillment," which is how Cyril construes it.

[128]Mt 5:17.

[129]Lev 18:5.

[130]Ps 19:12 (Ps 18:13 LXX).

[131]Jn 3:3, 5.

[132]This fragment comes from Nicephorus of Constantinople, who reports Cyril's comments in his own *Apologeticus Major*. Cf. Pusey 5:236n7. Pusey brackets these words in his text, presumably because they seem to be an insertion by Nicephorus.

[133]Jn 3:12.

[134]Jn 3:11.

[135]Wis 9:16.

10:11-13 "No one who believes in him will be put to shame."

Let Israel not think that salvation by faith is their own possession. "For everyone who calls on the name of the Lord," he says, "shall be saved," whether they are Jew or Greek, slave or free. God saves everyone without distinction since all are his. Thus we say that "all things are recapitulated in Christ."[136]

11:1 Has God rejected his people? By no means!

Though Israel experienced a darkening, Paul wisely does not allow them to be hardened further by total rejection, but he artfully pursues them, as it were, with kind words. He just accused Israel of unbelief, but he does not strip them of the hope that comes from above, nor does he say that they are completely excluded from relationship with God. He clearly demonstrates this point by presenting himself as an "Israelite" and "a descendant of Abraham."[137] With consummate skill he still calls them God's "people," and to the question about rejection he replies, "By no means!" He says these things as if he were fawning on those who [**238**] chose unbelief and insinuating himself by flattery to redirect them to a godly and obedient disposition. Since it is clear that he himself has been called to apostleship and appointed as a priest of the mysteries of the Savior and as a herald and apostle to the Gentiles[138] even though he is an Israelite, it is obvious that God has not rejected his people.

11:2-5 Do you not know what the Scripture says of Elijah?

He introduces the story of Elijah as an extremely apt image of what happened to Israel. We can easily see by comparison with the events of that time how Israel was in a drunken brawl with itself. When Ahab of Samaria was king, Israel worshiped handmade idols, which is a foreign practice. There were sacrifices and sacred precincts everywhere. Those who were devoted to God lived in utter terror and underwent such unbearable persecution that the prophets hid in caves and in holes in the rocks.[139] At that time even Elijah himself ran up into the remote wilderness and fell before God and said, "They have demolished your altars and killed your prophets; I alone am left, and they are seeking my life." And he immediately heard this reply: "I have kept for myself seven thousand who have not bowed the knee to Baal." Now at that time God was not the one impelling Israel to such terrible sins, but they fell because of their own insanity. In the same way, when God the Father was offering everyone salvation because of Christ, no one was coerced at all but they voluntarily fell into apostasy by rejecting the Redeemer. Therefore, [**239**] God has not rejected his people since he decided beforehand, as I said, that they would share in Christ's salvation if they so chose.

11:6 But if it is by grace, it is no longer on the basis of works . . .

"But if it is by grace," he says, "it is no longer on the basis of works, otherwise grace would no longer be grace." Wherever people think that they please God on the basis of works, there both the name and the reality of grace will be altogether empty and superfluous. "For to the one who works," he says, "wages are not reckoned as a gift but as something due."[140] Therefore, if grace is based on works, it is no longer grace.

---

[136]Eph 1:10.
[137]Rom 11:2.
[138]Cf. 1 Tim 2:7.
[139]Cf. 1 Kings 18:13 (3 Kings 18:13 LXX).
[140]Rom 4:4.

11:7 What then? Israel failed to obtain what it was seeking.

He said that "God has not rejected his people"[141] since it was likely that some would arise who would allege just that and say, How has God not rejected his people, since Israel fell away, even if their fall was not complete but partial? After all, just a remnant has been saved,[142] and that by election. He very wisely responds to this by saying, "What then?" That is to say, What shall I say in response to this? "Israel failed to obtain what it was seeking. The elect obtained it, but the rest were hardened." Israel was seeking the righteousness that comes from the law. So how could they have been justified, he says, since no one has kept the law? Therefore, Israel was seeking the righteousness that comes through a type, but they did not obtain it. But those who were elect and chosen from among the others because of their obedience obtained it. They have been justified through faith. But the rest have been hardened—that is, they are unyielding and unteachable. **[240]**

11:9 And David says, "Let their table become . . ."

"Let their table," he says, "become a snare." . . . For proof of what he said, he cites the writings of not one, but two prophets in combination "that every word may be confirmed by the evidence of two or three witnesses."[143] "Their table," that is, the inhospitality and cruelty that they showed to Christ at the time of his crucifixion, quite rightly became cursed. When he thirsted, they brought him vinegar mixed with gall.[144] Therefore, their minds were darkened and they were bent down so that they could only see earthly things.

[141]Rom 11:2.
[142]Rom 11:5.
[143]Mt 18:16.
[144]Mt 27:34.

11:11 So I ask, have they stumbled so as to fall? By no means!

I admire you for your gentleness, divinely inspired Paul, as you skillfully craft your discussion of God's plan. You stress that the reason the Gentiles were called was not so that Israel might completely fall away from their hope in God and stumble over Christ like some stone, but to make them jealous of those who were unexpectedly received so that they might choose to unlearn their shameful way of thinking and have a better mind than they did before and so receive the Redeemer. This argument may be proved by a brief example. Sometimes small and preadolescent children experience pain that is characteristic of those who are still children. They immediately flee from their father or mother and instantly release a flood of tears from their eyes, and this distresses their parents to no small degree because of the law of natural affection. But the parents skillfully stand aloof from this vain and childish pettiness. They simply grab whatever child is at hand and give him their honor, thus provoking the first child to jealousy and angering him, as it were, **[241]** to get him to return to his love for them. So when Paul refused to despair of Israel even though they offended, I think he was saying that something like this has happened.

11:12 Now if their stumbling means riches for the world.

Now if the world has been enriched by a relationship with God, he says, through Israel stumbling, and the Gentiles were accepted because Israel lacked a sound mind, what would Israel's acceptance be but a veritable redemption from death and life from the dead?[145]

[145]Rom 11:15.

11:13-14 If I somehow make my own flesh . . .

He brings the faithful from the Jews and Gentiles into harmony and peace with each other so that they may not become conceited but give thanks to God for mercifully granting them the forgiveness of sins. He says that he glorifies his own ministry not out of a desire for vainglory, but in order, he says, to "make my own flesh jealous." Here he refers to Israel as his own "flesh," that is, his race according to the flesh. It is as if he were to say: I say that my apostleship is noble and worthy and extremely precious to God and is the most useful thing under the sun. But I do so not to crown my own head with empty honors out of some strange desire for praise, but in order to save my race according to the flesh by pricking them, as it were, with the goad of jealousy and rousing them to the necessary choice of being justified by the grace that comes through Christ. [242]

11:15 For if their rejection is the reconciliation of the world, what will their acceptance be but life from the dead?

Since it is not possible to praise Israel for their faith or behavior, he proceeds to discuss the *oikonomia*, and he says that their unbelief provided the world with a relationship with God. He is trying to say that through the very things by which they have offended, they have perhaps become the benefactors of the world. And though Israel had fallen and was lying on the ground, as it were, he crowns them. He says that their acceptance is "life from the dead," if it is true that their rejection is "the reconciliation of the world."

11:22 If you remain.

The apostle skillfully constructs his statement. On the one hand, he restores Israel, who had missed the mark of what is fitting, and he urges them back to what is profitable and to seek out their root by faith in Christ. On the other hand, he says that the Gentiles have been honored by God, and he urges them to steadfastness in faith and godliness. So if you stay this way, you will remain a noble branch from a holy root. But if you disobey, you will be separated from the root.

11:25-26 Until the full number of the Gentiles has come in. . . . And so all Israel will be saved.

Now let's take a look at this and examine it carefully. He said that "the full number of the Gentiles" will come in, and "all Israel will be saved." But what if someone were to reply, And yet many of the Gentiles have died in unbelief, so how could the "full number of the Gentiles" have come in? [243] So "all Israel" will not be saved, if it is true that the Jews will receive the lawless son after neglecting love for Christ. That is what he himself said: "I have come in my Father's name, and you do not accept me; if another comes in his own name, you will accept him."[146] And the most-wise Paul says, "Because they refused to love the truth and so be saved. For this reason God sends them a powerful delusion, leading them to believe what is false."[147] What then shall we say to this? We say that since God has offered grace through faith ungrudgingly to everyone without exception, hasn't "the full number of the Gentiles" come in, at least when it comes to the mind and intention of the one who called them? Now if some have voluntarily fallen away and failed to obtain the gift, we will not find the word of Scripture to be false on this point, will we? After all, it is within their power to share in the gifts once given, but instead they have voluntarily committed apostasy. Therefore, insofar as it concerns the

[146]Jn 5:43.
[147]2 Thess 2:10-11.

kindness and love of the one who has called them, "the full number of the Gentiles" has come in and "all Israel" has been saved. But since they have become unbending, he says that a hardening has come on part of them.

11:26 As it is written, "Out of Zion will come the Deliverer."

He adds a holy oracle to confirm the hope that even rejected Israel is going to be saved at that time. Indeed, Israel will be saved at that time. They will be called last, after the calling of the Gentiles.

11:28 They are enemies for your sake.

When it comes to the gospel proclamation, [244] they have become "enemies." They have stumbled because of their godless behavior toward Christ. They who were held in high esteem as holy and devoted to God because of the nobility of their fathers could be regarded as "beloved" for their fathers' sake. Yet they have become "enemies" in order to make them jealous of the unbelievers.[148]

11:30-32 Just as you were once disobedient to God.

He shows that the same charges apply to both the Jews and the Gentiles and that both have been healed by the same grace. Israel was called at the right time through Moses and rescued from hard labor. But the worshipers of demons, that is, the Gentiles who go by the name Egyptians, up to this point did not believe in God's mercy toward the Israelites. That is because they gave no credence to the miracles performed by Moses, and they did not want to acknowledge the God of the Hebrews. Right after they sent the Jewish people into the desert to perform sacrifices, they started clinging to their ancient error. But now they have received mercy while Israel stumbled. Israel did not believe in God's mercy toward the Gentiles so that they themselves might receive mercy at the proper time. Therefore, the charge against both of them, as I said, is equal. They both failed in the same way to have mercy and offer assistance. Then Paul says that all have been locked up by God in disobedience "so that he may be merciful to all." Now we should certainly not think that the fact that some disobeyed is a result of God's will so that once they had fallen into that state, they may be shown mercy. Rather, "he imprisoned them in disobedience" to show that they are guilty of the charge of disobedience and that they stand indicted, as it were, for their actions. They reached such a level of wicked behavior that they are practically devoid of mercy and pity. [245]

14:14 I know and am persuaded in the Lord Jesus . . .

"I know and am persuaded in the Lord Jesus," he says, "that nothing is unclean in itself," and the rest. The witness is compelling as he insists that he knows and is persuaded. Then he adds "in the Lord Jesus" to confirm the truth even more and to pursue the unhesitating persuasion of his hearers. He is surely thinking of what Christ says somewhere: "It is not what goes into the mouth that defiles a person,"[149] and that all food goes into the stomach and is expelled into the sewer.[150] And this is food's nature and function. Therefore, as far as its nature is concerned, nothing that serves as nourishment is "unclean" or profane "for it is sanctified by God's word and by prayer."[151] We also recall that when God brought everything into existence, it says that

[148]Cf. Rom 10:19.

[149]Mt 15:11.

[150]Mt 15:17.

[151]1 Tim 4:5.

he saw that it was "very good"[152] and he blessed it. Now since God praises his creation and indeed has even blessed it, who would dare to say that the creation is a patron of what is polluted and profane? Wouldn't that person also be accusing the one who brought it into being? Therefore, no part of creation at all is "unclean" by nature. But if anyone thinks that something is unclean, that person has been polluted by it and has contracted the disease of impurity. All things are pure, but it is the lack of faith on the part of some that renders the unbeliever unclean, not the supposed unclean items themselves. Similarly, those with a mature mind know that God is one by nature and there is none beside him, and no idol really exists in the world and we give no weight to what is sacrificed to idols. After all, how could an idol that cannot know anything realize what is sacrificed to it? But for those who think there are many gods, anything sacrificed to idols will surely be significant. In the same way, for believers, what is made by God is not profane but pure, and nothing at all is unclean by nature. The use of foods has been left completely to our discretion. **[246]** But for those who have not yet reached this understanding, these things are not pure according to the right view (as they see it) but unclean, since their mind cripples them, as it were, on their way to the truth.

14:16 So do not let your good be spoken of as ill.

Do not let the glory of honorable people be torn down in front of the weak, nor let "your good"—that is, your admirable faith—"be spoken of as ill" before anyone. God-pleasing behavior does not come about through meat, but neither is a person godly and worthy of the kingdom of heaven if they eat uncritically whatever is put before them. No, the godly person condescends to the weakness of the weak brothers and refrains. And even though he criticized Peter for living in a Jewish way because of the men from James who came to Antioch,[153] he did not criticize him for condescending to the weakness of the circumcision party and refraining from certain foods. Instead, he criticized him for using his own credibility to drag away many of the Gentiles into thinking that they had to live according to the law. This risked bringing Paul's own proclamation to nothing. Paul was, after all, the teacher of the Gentiles.

14:20-22 Everything is indeed clean, but it is wrong for you to make others fall by what you eat.

It is indeed permissible both to "eat meat" and to "drink wine," but permission in these matters does not completely exempt us from punishment. Now it is beneficial to refrain so that we may not fatten our flesh with luxury and exacerbate its inherent passions. So if we refrain from these things for our own sake, we will do so even more for the sake of our brother so that he may not stumble, according to the statement, "Love your neighbor as yourself."[154] **[247]**

15:7-12 Welcome one another, therefore, just as Christ has welcomed you, for the glory of God.

We who are many are one body and members of one another, as it is written,[155] since Christ knits us together into one by the bonds of his love. "He has made both groups into one and has broken down the dividing wall. He has abolished the law with its commandments and ordinances."[156] Therefore, we should have

[152]Gen 1:31.

[153]Gal 2:12.
[154]Rom 13:9.
[155]Rom 12:5.
[156]Eph 2:14-15.

the same attitude toward each other. "If one member suffers, all suffer together with it; if one member is honored, all rejoice together with it."[157] "Welcome one another, therefore," he says, "just as Christ has welcomed you, for the glory of God." We should welcome one another by committing to having the same mind, bearing one another's burdens,[158] and keeping "the unity of spirit in the bond of peace."[159] That is how God welcomed us in Christ. Indeed, he is telling the truth when he says of God the Father that "he so loved the world that he gave his Son for us,"[160] since he has given him in exchange for the life of us all. We have deliverance from death, and we have been redeemed from death and sin. Furthermore, he clarifies the scope of the *oikonomia* when he says that "Christ has become a servant of the circumcised on behalf of the truth," and so on. God promised to the fathers of the Jews that he would bless their future seed and that they would be "as many as the stars of heaven."[161] That is why the Word, who was God, appeared in the flesh and became human—he who holds all creation together in existence and who, as God, grants well-being to the things that exist. He came into this world in the flesh not to be served, "but," as he himself says, "to serve, and to give his life as a ransom for **[248]** many."[162] Indeed, he explicitly confesses that he came to fulfill the promise to Israel when he says, "I was sent only to the lost sheep of the house of Israel."[163] Therefore, Paul is not lying when he says that Christ "became a servant of the circumcised in order that he might confirm the promises given to the patriarchs" and that he was appointed to this position by God the Father to obtain mercy for the Gentiles so that they too might glorify the Savior and Redeemer as the Creator and craftsman of all things. The ineffable grace of God must not—must not—seem ineffectual due to the great unbelief of the circumcised who godlessly committed an outrage against him and refused his redemption. That is what would happen if only a few Israelite believers were saved, and that just barely. For this reason God's mercy is widened, as it were, to all people, so it is clear that the mystery of wisdom in Christ does not miss its goal of mercy. After all, the whole world under heaven has been saved in place of those who have fallen away, as God has mercy. And this mystery was announced beforehand by the words of the saints who foreknew in the Spirit what would happen—a fact he establishes by the clearest juxtaposition of prophetic testimony.

[157] 1 Cor 12:26.
[158] Gal 6:2.
[159] Eph 4:3.
[160] Jn 3:16.
[161] Heb 11:12.
[162] Mt 20:28.
[163] Mt 15:24.

COMMENTARY ON THE FIRST EPISTLE TO THE CORINTHIANS (FRAGMENTS)

[88]*

1:1-2 Paul, called to be an apostle of Jesus Christ by the will of God, and our brother Sosthenes, to the church of God that is in Corinth, to those who are sanctified in Christ Jesus, called to be saints, together with all those who call on the name of our Lord Jesus Christ in every place, both theirs and ours.

The divinely inspired Paul says that he has been sent by Christ at the good pleasure of God the Father. I think that is what "by the will of God" means. Since the will and activity belong to the Father and come through the Son, we say that the saints have been appointed to apostleship by the same Son.

He makes it quite clear that the force of his message will benefit not only the Corinthians, but also all who have been called by Christ to sanctification through faith with the words, "to those who are sanctified in Christ Jesus" through to "in every place, both theirs and ours." The law did not command people to do this[1] in every place, but to come to the holy temple itself in Jerusalem. The concern here is probably the vacillating nature of their mind. If they were commanded to worship or sacrifice in every place, they might make that command an excuse to turn to disgraceful practices. They might worship carved statues and erect temples and altars for themselves. However, now that we Gentiles have finally been called by faith in Christ into God's family and we have been enriched by steadfastness through the Holy Spirit, we are all commanded to worship not in Jerusalem but in "every place." This is what the statement of the prophets meant, which says, "And each one will worship the Lord from his own place."[2]

Now along with Sosthenes, he writes to the "church of God," which Christ himself presented to himself.[3] And who saw this church? **[90]** All who were sanctified and called to righteousness by Christ and who call on his name "in every place, theirs and ours," that is, whether in the land of the Jews or in the cities and regions of the Gentiles. He proclaims Christ to be God by nature, and with him and through him he gives glory to God the Father. He does that by referring to the sanctified as the church "of God" and then assigning them to Christ, saying, "Anyone who does not have the Spirit of Christ does not belong to him."[4]

*The page numbers in brackets refer to Konrad F. Zawadzki, *Der Kommentar Cyrills von Alexandrien zum 1. Korintherbrief*, Traditio Exegetica Graeca 16 (Leuven: Peeters, 2015). They are all even numbers because Zawadzki puts the Greek text on the even-numbered pages and a German translation on the odd-numbered pages.

[1]In his quotation of 1 Cor 1:2, he leaves out the phrase "who call on the name of our Lord Jesus Christ," but he seems to have this phrase in mind here.

[2]Zeph 2:11.

[3]Cf. Eph 5:27.

[4]Rom 8:9.

1:3 Grace to you and peace from God our Father and the Lord Jesus Christ. I give thanks to my God always for you because of the grace of God that has been given you in Christ Jesus, for in every way you have been enriched in him, in speech and knowledge of every kind—just as the testimony of Christ has been strengthened among you.

He crowns believers with the grace that comes from God the Father and the Lord Jesus Christ. Through him and in him, all things come from God the Father, while he is the co-giver and co-supplier, along with his begetter, of the blessings from above. He is the distributer of gifts from heaven, and he himself is the peace of all things. By his grace, he enlightens principalities, thrones, and powers,[5] and to put it generally, all rational creation.

1:10 That all of you be in agreement and that there be no divisions among you, but that you be united in the same mind and the same purpose. For it has been reported to me by Chloe's people that there are quarrels among you, my brothers. What I mean is that each of you says, "I belong to Paul," or "I belong to Apollos," or "I belong to Cephas," or "I belong to Christ."

It was both necessary and wise to persuade us that the Lord's name must be glorified. <God himself taught us this>[6] by saying through one of the holy prophets, "My servants will be given a new name, which will be blessed on the earth."[7] And we are called "Christians" and have received the riches of the new name. But any who depart from the right ways of the church are justly deprived of it. Those who are devoted to "deceitful spirits"[8] and to the wonders of certain unholy false teachers possess the name of those false teachers, and rightly so, because they do not belong to Christ. They participate in slander against him and they splinter into different views and opinions, even though Christ calls his own to peace.[9] **[92]** Since he himself is one and is not divided, we are all one in Christ and we are united in this regard "in the same mind and the same purpose." He has united[10] us in one heart in a spiritual unity by saying to God the Father about us, I desire that just as you and I are one, so "they too may be one in us."[11]

1:13 Has Christ been divided? Was Paul crucified for you? Or were you baptized in the name of Paul? I thank God that I baptized none of you except Crispus and Gaius, so that no one can say that I baptized in my own name. (I did baptize also the household of Stephanas; beyond that, I do not know whether I baptized anyone else.) For Christ did not send me to baptize, but to proclaim the gospel.

If someone else endured the cross for us, let us count ourselves as his. And if by chance we have been baptized into someone else's name, let that person possess us and let us register him as our Savior and Redeemer. But if "Christ died for our sins"[12] and we have been buried with him alone

---

[5]Cf. Col 1:16.

[6]I follow Zawadzki's conjectural addition of the words καὶ τοῦτο ἐδίδαξεν ὁ θεὸς in order to make sense of the sentence while remaining faithful to Cyril's characteristic expressions. See the discussion of the matter in Zawadzki, 285-89.

[7]Is 65:15-16.

[8]1 Tim 4:1.

[9]1 Cor 7:15.

[10]I follow Zawadzki's conjectural emendation συνθέντος in place of συνδέντος.

[11]Jn 17:21.

[12]1 Cor 15:3.

"by baptism into death,"[13] then let him possess those whom he purchased, since we have been saved by and through him who gave his own life for us.

It is common knowledge that he has been sent to proclaim Jesus to the Gentiles, yet we maintain that it is also the task of an apostle to perform some baptisms, if he so chooses, at times when there is a need. But so that he does not manifestly spend the time required for proclamation on other pursuits, he proclaims the gospel instead, wisely leaving it to all who have been ordained to the episcopacy throughout the regions to do this at their leisure. He devotes himself to the ministry of the word and presents the mystery of Christ with exquisite attention to detail. However, just as the divinely inspired Stephen performed the unavoidable task of mystagogy even though he was appointed to wait on tables,[14] so also the divinely inspired Paul performed the task of baptism at certain times even though he was assigned the duty of proclaiming the mystery of Christ. He had the authority for both, and no one would prevent him if he chose to do this. **[94]**

1:20 Where is the one who is wise? Where is the scribe? Where is the debater of this age? Has not God made foolish the wisdom of this world?

For those who have great minds for earthly wisdom but do not accept faith (that is, faith in Christ), the gospel is foolishness.[15] But for us, this is not the case. Far from it! We are confident that it is the power of God. It is the way of salvation leading to sanctification. It wisely teaches us the knowledge of the truth through abundant proclamation. He here uses the term "wise," at least in my view, to describe those rhetoricians who by their skill with words constantly weave together some plausible argument out of lies and eagerly surround it with the appearance of truth. And I think the term "scribes" refers to schoolmasters or grammarians whose practice was to waste their labors on the writings of the poets and explain them to the youth. And he uses the term "debaters" for those whose practice is to fight over words and conduct truly "painstaking" examination of matters, who in their pursuit of knowledge pretend to seek the truth, as every single one of their propositions seem faultless, but they are not right. No, they are completely negligent since they do not recognize the God of the universe, who effortlessly established all things by his ineffable activity and brought all things from nonexistence into existence with a mere nod. So the wisdom of the world has truly become foolish.

1:21 For since, in the wisdom of God, the world did not know God through wisdom, God decided, through the foolishness of our proclamation, to save those who believe.

He calls human knowledge and eloquence (or rather, flowery diction) the "wisdom of God" in order to teach that God is the Creator of the mind and supplier of intelligence and eloquence, even if some use them for unfitting purposes. But he calls simplicity of speech "the foolishness of our proclamation," since the divinely inspired disciples were ignorant in speech, but rich in knowledge. **[96]**

1:22-25 For Jews demand a sign and Greeks desire wisdom, but we proclaim Christ crucified, a stumbling block to Jews and foolishness to Greeks, but to those who are called, both Jews

[13] Rom 6:4.
[14] Acts 6:2, 5.
[15] 1 Cor 1:18.

and Greeks, Christ the power of God and the wisdom of God. For God's foolishness is wiser than human wisdom, and God's weakness is stronger than human strength.

Paul's statement is right about both. Christ once drove out of the temple precincts those who were selling sheep, cattle, pigeons, and turtledoves, saying, "Stop making my Father's house a marketplace!"[16] They opposed him by saying, "What sign can you show us for doing this?"[17] and, "Who gave you this authority?"[18] Some of the scribes approached him after such a great demonstration of signs and maliciously said, "Teacher, we wish to see a sign from you."[19] So they sought a divine sign while completely disregarding the words of the saints by which they could probably learn that he was the Christ. That is why the Savior told those sent by John, "Go and tell John what you hear and see: the blind receive their sight, the lame walk," and so on.[20] And the Greeks, who seek glory in diction and discourse, consider the manner of the *oikonomia* in the flesh to be foolishness. They say, Why on earth was it necessary for the Word of God, who is God by nature, who is powerful enough to accomplish anything he wants by his will with a mere nod, to become human and endure death? And how could it be, they say, that a virgin gave birth? And how could what has decayed due to death be raised again? Well it is not unreasonable to say this about them: "Those who are unspiritual do not receive the things of the Spirit, for they are foolishness to them."[21] But for us, he is the power and wisdom of God. Through him, God the Father saved the earth under heaven through the power that is in him by nature and through the ineffable wisdom (that is, his own wisdom). The Son is the wisdom and power of God the Father through which he brought all things into being and preserves what he has made. And if any should choose, he says, to compare God's power to human power, they will surely see that those divine works that may perhaps seem to be done in weakness and not by the full power of the Creator nevertheless outstrip and outperform all human strength. In the same way, when it comes to the knowledge of wisdom, that which seems to be foolish [98] is wiser than human wisdom. It is as if someone decided to compare the insignificant and smallest parts of creation with the magnitude and beauty of the elements, I mean the sky and the sun and the rest of the stars and fire and water and the rest. The power and wisdom in the former parts of creation will be found utterly negligible, and because of that, their creator would seem to be foolish.[22] Yet there is no craftsman among us who can produce such admirable[23] works. So it is true that God's weakness is stronger than human strength, and God's foolishness is wiser than human wisdom. Therefore, the *oikonomia* is altogether wise, since Christ rules the whole world under heaven with insight and wisdom.

2:1 When I came to you, brothers, I did not come proclaiming the Testimony of God to you in lofty words and wisdom.

[16]Jn 2:16.
[17]Jn 2:18.
[18]Mt 21:23.
[19]Mt 12:38.
[20]Mt 11:4-5.
[21]1 Cor 2:14.
[22]The last phrase follows Zawadzki's hypothetical reconstruction. The manuscript has a gap of seventeen letters at this point. See Zawadzki, 98.
[23]The word "admirable" is based on Zawadzki's hypothetical reconstruction. The manuscript has a gap of ten letters at this point. See Zawadzki, 98.

He calls Christ the "Testimony of God," since God the Father testified about him saying, "This is my Son, the Beloved, with whom I am well pleased."[24]

2:3-4 And I came to you in weakness and in fear and in much trembling. My speech and my proclamation were not with plausible words of human wisdom, but with a demonstration of the Spirit and of power.

(Cod. Vat. Gr. 762)	(Cod. Pantokrator. 28)
Since I employed such a simple form of instruction, I was very much afraid, he says, that perhaps some would be found to have deeper thoughts than mine, and they would convey not benefit but harm. Those who are infants in their minds, after all, would need soft and gentle instruction that leads to knowledge.[25] "But solid food is for the mature, for those whose faculties have been trained by practice to distinguish good **[100]** from evil."[26] Therefore, he says, my instruction to you took place with great weakness, not with the full power of the mystagogue. Indeed, it was not "with plausible words of human wisdom, but with a demonstration of the Spirit and of power, so that your faith might rest not on human wisdom but on the power of God." That is why the apostles added signs from God to their proclamation, to provide a clear proof of the fact that we ought to believe that God has been made known among them through the Spirit and through the deeds themselves. And they accomplished those miracles easily by using a certain ineffable and indescribable power and activity. The Greek myths, of course, would need the defensive cover of artful language to cloak the ugliness within them. But when it comes to the divine proclamation, unadorned simple language, attested by the power of God, is enough.	**[100]** Therefore, my instruction to you took place in weakness and not in the full power of the mystagogue.

2:6 Yet among the mature we do speak wisdom, though it is not a wisdom of this age or of the rulers of this age, who are doomed to perish.

The language of the holy mystagogues proceeds with humble diction, but it implants in us the unadulterated knowledge of the divine mysteries and reveals that Christ is Wisdom. He is attested not by the beautiful rhetoric of earthly wisdom, but by his own nature. None of the rulers of this age recognized him. The rulers of this age are the wicked and hostile powers who speak through the wise of the world. **[102]**

2:7-8 But we speak God's wisdom, secret and hidden, which God decreed before the ages for our glory. None of the rulers of this age understood this; for if they had, they would not have crucified the Lord of Glory.

[24]Mt 3:17.
[25]Cf. 1 Cor 3:1.
[26]Heb 5:14.

(Cod. Vat. Gr. 762)	(Cod. Pantokrator. 28)
This statement is very true. Christ has triumphed over the wicked and hostile powers through his cross. He nailed the "record that stood against us"[27] to the tree and drove Satan out of his position of tyranny over us. He nullified the sin of the world, and by opening the gates of Hades for the spirits below, he took away the power of death. So how could his suffering on the cross not be infuriating to the unclean demons? They would not have crucified him if they had clearly known that he was the Redeemer and the Lord of Glory. The divinely inspired John made it clear that the crucifixion of Christ by the madness of the Jews was an act of the devil's brutality when he said of Judas, "After he received the piece of bread, Satan entered into him."[28] Satan did not know that Jesus was God. After all, if he did know it and believe it, why did he tempt him in the desert saying, "If you are the Son of God, command these stones to become loaves of bread"?[29] The Savior himself was obviously **[104]** eager to hide from the rulers of this age so that he might suffer and with his own blood win the earth under heaven for himself and his Father without them realizing it.	**[102]** If they had known the blessings that would come to human beings through the crucifixion of Christ, and that Jesus Christ was the Redeemer and the Lord of Glory, and that the crucified one was God and the true Son of God the Father by nature, and that the one begotten of the holy virgin was God by nature in that the Word has become flesh,[30] then the Jews, who did not recognize Christ, would not have crucified him. **[104]** For the Lord himself was eager to hide so that he might suffer and by his own death redeem the earth under heaven without them realizing it.

2:10-11 These things God has revealed to us through the Spirit; for the Spirit searches everything, even the depths of God. For who knows a person's thoughts except the spirit of that person, which is in him? So also no one comprehends the thoughts of God except the Spirit of God.

"Depths of God" refers to the secret and hidden knowledge in the Holy Scriptures. The Spirit has this knowledge and reveals it to the souls of the saints, rendering their mind divine, in a sense.

2:14 The natural man does not grasp the matters of God's Spirit, for they are foolishness to him, and he is unable to understand them because they are spiritually discerned.

The "natural man"[31] is someone who lives according to the flesh[32] and whose mind is not yet enlightened by the Holy Spirit. He only has innate human knowledge, which the Creator implants in the souls of all.

2:15-16 The spiritual man discerns all things, and he himself is subject to no one else's scrutiny. "For who has known the mind of the Lord so as to instruct him?" But we have the mind of Christ.

[27]Col 2:14.
[28]Jn 13:27.
[29]Mt 4:3.
[30]Jn 1:14.
[31]ψυχικός. Cyril is distinguishing between matters pertaining to the soul (ψυχή), which everyone has by virtue of being created, and matters of the Spirit (πνεῦμα), which come only from the Holy Spirit.
[32]Cf. Rom 8:4.

(Cod. Vat. Gr. 762)	(Cod. Pantokrator. 28)
The spiritual man discerns all things and winnows them, as it were, with exactitude. But he himself is subject to no one else's scrutiny. On the other hand, Paul makes it clear that those whom he calls "natural" absolutely require spiritual teachers for their benefit and education **[106]** by adding, "For who has known the mind of the Lord so as to instruct him?" It is as though he should say: No one could instruct the natural man without having the mind of Christ. By "instruct" he means "prepare for knowledge." Then he indicates who has the mind of the Lord by saying, "But we have the mind of Christ," that is, the Spirit speaking in the saints and revealing mysteries to them and rendering their mind divine, in a sense.	**[106]** No one can instruct the natural man without having the mind of Christ. By "instruct" he means "prepare for knowledge." Those who have the mind of Christ are those who have the Spirit, who speaks in the saints and reveals mysteries to them. This is the same Spirit who searches the depths of God. "Depths of God" refers to the secret and hidden knowledge in the Holy Scriptures. The Spirit has this knowledge and reveals it to the souls of the saints, rendering their mind divine, in a sense. And even though they were able to understand and explain the most excellent and lofty matters, whenever they wrote they adapted the level of their instruction to the condition of those whom they were leading into the mysteries.

3:1 And so, brothers, I could not speak to you as spiritual people, but rather as people of the flesh, as infants in Christ.

It is not because I lacked for words that were strong enough to bring you complete knowledge that I was prevented from talking to you about more perfect matters, but because you are infants in your disposition and your mind is unsteady. Your mind has not advanced to more perfect knowledge, and it is not yet ready to proceed to the mysteries. **[108]**

3:6 I planted, Apollos watered, but God gave the growth.

Paul planted, and Apollos watered, but God was the one who called forth the growth. What is the planting but the beginning of faith and the recognition and confession that God is the Lord of the universe? And what is the watering but a sowing, as it were, and pouring on of instruction in doctrine that nourishes and strengthens the mind of the believer so that it bears fruit? And what is the growth that Christ gives but toughening by the Spirit and growing up to be a "mature man,"[33] given in accordance with the zeal and desire of each person.

3:7-8 So neither the one who plants nor the one who waters is anything, but only God who gives the growth. The one who plants and the one who waters have a common purpose, and each will receive wages according to the labor of each.

Since Christ endured the death of the flesh and purchased us with his precious blood, we belong completely to him who purchased us, not to any others, even though we do have deacons and reconcilers and mediators and mystagogues by his grace. Therefore, we are not named after the others, but after Christ alone. He is our Lord.

[33]Eph 4:13.

3:10-11 According to the grace of God given to me, like a skilled master builder I laid a foundation, and someone else is building on it. Each builder must choose with care how to build on it. For no one can lay any foundation other than the one that has been laid; that foundation is Jesus Christ.

(Cod. Vat. Gr. 762)

Since he referred to believers as the house of God,[34] he naturally refers to Christ as the foundation. And Paul boasts that he came before the others and was a kind of firstfruits of those who preached to them the mystery of Christ, who is the unshakeable foundation. Christ supports those who are built on him. He intimates that they are temples **[110]** and that they are joined with one another through faith and by the grace of the Holy Spirit, who brings them together in one heart. God the Father spoke of this foundation through the prophet: "See, I am laying as a foundation in Zion a costly stone, a precious cornerstone as her foundation. Whoever trusts in him will not be put to shame."[35] So Paul is quite right to say that he has laid the foundation and that the others can work and build on it, but they cannot now lay another foundation besides the one that has already been laid. "There is no other name under heaven given among men by which we must be saved."[36] "For there is one God, the Father, from whom are all things and for whom we exist, and one Lord, Jesus Christ, through whom are all things and through whom we exist."[37] "He is the head of the body, the church."[38] Therefore, whoever denies the foundation and rejects the rock does not build on rock but on sand.[39] Because of that, he will be very easily shaken. Anything that Christ does not support will surely be moved since it does not have a stable foundation. **[112]**

(Cod. Pantokrator. 28)

[108] Since he called believers the house of God,[40] he naturally refers to Christ as the foundation. Now the Corinthians had many teachers, but Paul boasts that he came before the others and was the first of those who proclaimed the mystery of Christ, who is the foundation. So there is one foundation, and that is Christ.

[110] Paul says that he laid a foundation and that the others can work on it, but they cannot lay another foundation besides the one that has already been laid. "There is no other name under heaven given among men by which we must be saved."[41] That is because, though he was God by nature, he became human and was begotten through the holy *theotokos*[42] Mary according to the flesh. Yet even in his humanity, he remained God. Therefore, whoever denies the foundation and the rock builds completely on sand and is easily shaken.[43] Anything that Christ does not support will surely fall and have no firm foundation.

4:18-19a But some of you, thinking that I am not coming to you, have become arrogant. But I will come to you soon, if the Lord wills.

Since there were some in Corinth who thought that they were self-sufficient and did not need teachers and that they surpassed Paul in the wisdom of worldly rhetorical skill, they became puffed up and proud because of it. They looked down on others, though their own lives were not blameless. Since some have become arrogant in my absence and think that I left because I was

[34]In 1 Cor 3:9, Paul refers to believers as the "building" (οἰκοδομή) of God. Cyril, however, claims Paul refers to them as the "house" (οἶκος) of God. This may mean either that Cyril's text of 1 Cor 3:9 has a different reading or that Cyril simply saw "building" and "house" as synonyms.

[35]Is 28:16.

[36]Acts 4:12.

[37]1 Cor 8:6.

[38]Col 1:18.

[39]Cf. Mt 7:24-27.

[40]See note 34.

[41]See note 36.

[42]The appearance here of the term θεοτόκος could suggest that the commentary was written after the outbreak of the Nestorian controversy in 428, although the term had been used already by previous patristic writers.

[43]See note 39.

afraid to come and speak with them (which is not the case), I will come when God wills and commands it.

He announced that he would come, but not unequivocally. Rather, as was fitting, he rightly added the necessary qualification, "if the Lord wills." Indeed, this is the only way we should think or speak.

4:19b-20 And I will find out not the talk of these arrogant people but their power. For the kingdom of God depends not on talk but on power.

What use is glorious rhetorical style if it contains nothing good, as is the case with the style of the Greeks? But the style of the divinely inspired Scripture is simple and ordinary, yet it brings rich profit and leads gloriously to the true knowledge of him who is God by nature. It prepares us for every admirable good work. And when that happens, we receive the boundless riches of the grace of the Spirit's gifts, which we yearn for. "For the kingdom of God depends not on talk but on power." Now you should understand "power," when applied to the holy apostles themselves, to refer to the might and activity of the Spirit by which they perform miracles. But in our case, you should take the term to refer to the power of a holy and pure life. **[114]**

4:21–5:1 What would you prefer? Am I to come to you with a stick, or with love in a spirit of gentleness? It is actually reported that there is sexual immorality among you, and of a kind that is not found even among pagans; for a man is living with his father's wife.

Do you want me to apply a wise rebuke to those who have sinned, he is saying, as with some kind of stick? Or shall I come to you in a spirit of gentleness and love and pass over the matter in silence? But a rebuke would be better for them, a rebuke that strikes at the terrible and reckless nature of even the attempt at such a transgression. The divinely inspired Scriptures spoke of this in the case of the Israelites through the voice of Joel: "A father and his son go in to the same girl, so that they profane the name of their God."[44] Such sexual immorality, he says, is not even heard of among the pagans. He had probably heard somewhere that Theseus was angry with his own son and cursed him and actually killed him because he was accused by his stepmother.[45] And others who are guilty of such things may be found in the sweet-sounding verses of the poets.[46]

5:5 You are to hand this man over to Satan for the destruction of the flesh, so that his spirit may be saved in the day of the Lord.

By the fact that he gave the sexual offender over "for the destruction of the flesh" in order that his spirit may be saved, Paul makes clear what the statement "the kingdom of heaven depends not on talk but on power" means. This is a clear demonstration of marvelous authority given to him from above. For our Lord Jesus Christ has honored his saints.

6:1 When any of you has a grievance against another, do you dare to take it to court before the unrighteous, instead of taking it before the saints?

[44]Amos 2:7.

[45]Cyril is referring to Euripides's tragedy *Hippolytus*. See Zawadzki, 346.

[46]Zawadzki points out that similar examples may be found in Homer (*Iliad* 6.155-205) and Pindar (*Nemean Odes* 5.26). See Zawadzki, 347.

He calls those who have been sanctified by the Spirit "saints." Those who have not yet believed he calls "unrighteous" since they are more than ready to indulge in every kind of wickedness. After all, it is not strange that those who do not yet know him who is true God by nature are not qualified. **[116]**

6:2a Do you not know that the saints will judge the world?

They will preside as judges and judge the world, though not in an absolute sense. "For there is one lawgiver and judge."[47] Nevertheless, by their holiness of life and obedience in all things, they will for all practical purposes point out the sin of the world, since the world did not become imitators of them.[48] We are all of the same nature since we have the earth as our mother and we are in these perishable bodies. But since some of us have become God-loving and good, what excuse will finally avail at God's tribunal for those who have chosen an infamous and cursed life? They could have been exalted just like the others, but they voluntarily went after all sorts of perversity.

6:2b-3 And if the world is to be judged by you, are you incompetent to try trivial cases? Do you not know that we are to judge angels—to say nothing of ordinary matters?

We should read this verse as a question with a question mark, since the next verse must also be read as a question with a question mark.[49] After all, who would dare to claim that you are incompetent for such paltry cases when you judge the world by the glory of your life? Next he extends the logic of his statement and emphasizes its reliability by comparison with something greater. Here he is speaking not of the holy angels but rather of the apostate angels, who did not maintain their rank. Even though they are from above and do not bear earthly bodies, they will be condemned by the saints and accused for all their shameful behavior in the same way as the world will be: by the virtue of the saints. So if the saints are better than the angels, how could they be incompetent in trivial cases regarding worldly matters? **[118]**

6:4 If you have ordinary cases, then, appoint as judges those who have no standing in the church.[50]

(Cod. Vat. Gr. 762)

For those who are very competent in the church, it is trivial and unimportant to judge earthly matters. We learn this from the Lord. When someone came to him and said, "Teacher, tell my brother to divide the family inheritance with me," he replied, "Friend, who set me to be a judge or arbiter over you?"[51] Rather, it would be appropriate for the wisest members of the church to judge spiritual matters, to examine the utterance of faith with skillful discrimination. This was numbered among the good gifts given by the Spirit from above. For to some are given the utterance of wisdom and the utterance of knowledge, while to others also the discernment of spirits.[52]

(Cod. Pantokrator. 28)

[118] For the very competent select members of the church, it is trivial and unimportant to judge earthly matters. But it is more important to speak at length about spiritual matters and to discern carefully who is speaking by the Holy Spirit and says "Jesus is Lord," and who is speaking by Beelzeboul and for this reason says, "Let Jesus be cursed."[53]

[47] Jas 2:14.
[48] Cf. 1 Cor 11:1.
[49] In other words, 1 Cor 6:2b should be read as a question because 1 Cor 6:3 must also be a question.
[50] Cyril understands this verse to be a statement, not a question as it is commonly rendered in English translations.
[51] Lk 12:13-14.
[52] 1 Cor 12:8, 10.
[53] 1 Cor 12:3.

6:15-17 Do you not know that your bodies are members of Christ? Should I therefore take the members of Christ and make them members of a prostitute? Never! Do you not know that whoever is united to a prostitute becomes one body with her? For it is said, "The two shall be one flesh." But anyone united to the Lord becomes one spirit with him.

(Cod. Vat. Gr. 762)

How could our members be members of Christ? We have him in ourselves both physically and spiritually. He dwells in our hearts through the Spirit, and we participate **[120]** in his holy flesh. So we are doubly sanctified. And he dwells in us as the living life-giver in order that through himself he may destroy death, which rules our members.

Now if he is "the head of his body, the church,"[54] then we are the individual members. So when we fall into alien pleasures, then—oh then we will offend him whose members we have become since we will give what is his to prostitutes!

(Cod. Pantokrator. 28)

Our bodies are members of Christ in that we have him in ourselves both physically and spiritually. He dwells in our hearts through the Holy Spirit, **[120]** and we participate in his holy flesh. Thus, he dwells in us as life and life-giver. This frees us from decay and from the snares of death and makes us superior to carnal passions. We take the unleavened instruction of the divine sayings into ourselves, which nourishes our intellect, and we are yoked with Christ (obviously in a spiritual way) so that we overcome the passions of the flesh. Now since Christ is the head of the church,[55] we are surely the individual members. So if we go to a prostitute, we offend Christ, whose members we have become. His members are then stained by sin and are made members of a prostitute. Just as one who unites himself to a woman will be one body with her, so also one who unites himself spiritually to God will be one spirit with him. That is because we have become "participants of the divine nature,"[56] and we have been united and sanctified by the Spirit in Christ.

[122]

6:18 Every sin that a person commits is outside the body; but the fornicator sins against the body itself.

(Cod. Vat. Gr. 762)

(Cod. Pantokrator. 28)

[122] Someone may say, Tell me, how does the murderer commit murder? Is it not through blood? And if someone should decide to criticize others, does this not take place through the tongue? So what offense could there be that is not committed through the body? Is the Spirit Bearer, then, somehow shown to be a liar in the end? By no means! After all, he speaks in Christ, and Christ is the Truth. Therefore, he will tell the truth. Let us examine the matter carefully. If someone should choose to behave badly, such a person will surely behave that way toward others, not toward themselves. After all, murderers are not going to kill themselves but others. Slanderers are not going to insult themselves but others. The greedy are not going to wrong themselves but others. And you will find a similar course of action in every outrageous deed. In that sense, then, "every sin is outside the body,

[54] Col 1:18.
[55] See note 54.
[56] 2 Pet 1:4.

(Cod. Vat. Gr. 762)

[124] As long as the members of our body remain members of Christ through chastity, they will surely participate in his life and glory. "He will transform the body of our humiliation that it may be conformed to the body of his glory."[57] But if they should become members of a prostitute, how could they receive the transformation and spiritual glory that comes from being conformed to him? **[126]**

(Cod. Pantokrator. 28)

but the fornicator sins against the body itself." Such a person will be caught spoiling their own body, **[124]** and I will tell you how. As long as the members of our body remain members of Christ through chastity, they will surely participate in his life and glory. But if they should become members of a prostitute, how could they receive the transformation and spiritual glory that comes from being conformed to him? When our bodies are raised from the ground at the time of the resurrection, "the righteous will shine like the sun,"[58] while the ungodly and profane who have lived their lives intemperately will be raised, but they will not live the good life. Instead, they will remain without a share of glory. They will not rise "in the judgment or in the counsel of the righteous,"[59] but they will live in outer darkness as their punishment and sentence.[60] How could someone who is being punished live in glory? Then he adds something else that is not without the ability to persuade us to hate the cursed lusts of the body. [. . .][61]

{Even though the murderer, the insolent person, and the slanderer commit sin with their body, nevertheless they do it to others. That is the sense in which he says, "Every sin is outside the body, but the fornicator **[126]** spoils the body itself." Our bodies remain members of Christ through chastity, and they receive life and glory from him. But if they are defiled, they will be deprived of this glory.}[62]

6:19-20 Or do you not know that your body is a temple of the Holy Spirit within you, which you have from God, and that you are not your own? For you were bought with a price; therefore glorify God in your body and in your spirit, which is from God.

(Cod. Vat. Gr. 762)

In you dwells the "Spirit of adoption" (that is, the Holy Spirit) "by whom we cry, 'Abba! Father!'"[63] Furthermore, we were bought with a price when Christ the Savior of us all laid down his own life for us.[64] We are therefore temples of the living God since Christ dwells in us through the Holy Spirit, and he also has God the Father in his own nature, from whom he shines forth essentially. He himself said, "Those who love me will keep my word, and my Father will love them, and we will come to them and make our home with them."[65] Therefore let us keep the stench of

(Cod. Vat. Gr. 762)

In us dwells the "Spirit of adoption" (that is, the Holy Spirit) "by whom we cry, 'Abba! Father!'"[66] Furthermore, we were bought with a price when Christ the Savior of us all laid down his own life for us.[67] Now Christ dwells in us through the Holy Spirit, and he also has God the Father in his own nature, from whom he shines forth essentially. Therefore, it is fitting for us to bring our petitions to the divine temple and to lift up our praises and to offer continuous sacrifices of a pure body and soul. And so let us keep the stench of lust far from our minds. Indeed, let the sweet fragrance of self-control arise like incense.

[57]Phil 3:21.
[58]Mt 13:43.
[59]Ps 1:5.
[60]Cf. Mt 8:12; 22:13; 25:30.
[61]The copyist seems to have left out the rest of the thought. See Zawadzki, 371.
[62]Zawadzki (371) puts this section in braces because he thinks its style suggests that it is a summary of Cyril's position by the catenist rather than a text from Cyril himself.
[63]Rom 8:15.
[64]Cf. 1 Jn 3:16.
[65]Jn 14:23.
[66]Rom 8:15.
[67]See note 64.

(Cod. Vat. Gr. 762)

lust far from our minds as from the temple of God. Indeed, let the sweet fragrance of self-control arise like incense, and let us offer "our bodies as a living sacrifice, **[128]** holy and acceptable to God, which is our spiritual worship." For we were bought "not with perishable things like silver or gold, but with his precious blood," as it is written.[68] Let us therefore serve the one who bought us and present ourselves to him as obedient servants and our members to God "as instruments of righteousness."[69] For it is written, "The body is meant not for fornication but for the Lord, and the Lord for the body."[70] When we keep the members of our body free from the defilement of carnal desire, then he will be the Lord of our body. After all, he who is holy by nature as God dwells in those who are holy.

7:8-11 To the unmarried and the widows I say that it is well for them to remain unmarried as I am. But if they are not practicing self-control, they should marry. For it is better to marry than to be aflame with passion. To the married I give this command—not I but the Lord—that the wife should not separate from her husband (but if she does separate, let her remain unmarried or else be reconciled to her husband), and that the husband should not divorce his wife.

(Cod. Vat. Gr. 762)

The Israelites were caught having a frivolous mind that is easily led astray into all sorts of pleasure. That is why they were rightly kept from giving their own opinion on the law. It says that one must not add to these things **[130]** or take away from them.[71] The authors of the Gospels, on the other hand, have a mind fixed on the good and have Christ himself speaking in them. So they rightly dared to offer words of guidance from their great authority even where the Holy Scriptures do not say explicitly what should be done. The divinely inspired Paul acts this way when he says, "To the unmarried and the widows I say that it is well for them to remain unmarried as I am," and the rest. Where it is not a divine law for us, he uses the words "I say," but where Christ is the one who gives the command, he says, "I give this command," but he immediately adds, "not I but the Lord." So what necessary instructions did Christ overlook when he gave his law? What better instruction did the mystagogues come up with? How could it not be ignorant and completely insane to think that the instructions given by Christ are not perfect? What then shall we say? The divine proclamation of the gospel did not deny marriage since God, I think, took human nature into account when he gave his command. After all, when the Pharisees

(Cod. Pantokrator. 28)

[130] I marvel at the mystagogue. I am astonished at the beauty of the wisdom he possesses, at the superiority of his insight, and the exactitude of his mystagogy. Where it is not a divine law for us, he appropriately uses the words, "I say," but where Christ is the one who gives the command, he says, "I give this command," but he immediately adds, "not I but the Lord." He advises us as a brother and a fellow servant. Now when Paul adds the qualifier that these words come from him, he does not do so because the evangelical laws are incomplete. Rather, even though the present age is drawing to a close and there is no longer a need to have children,[72] the evangelical word passes over the exhortation to self-control as something difficult to bear so that its yoke and burden may not seem heavy.[73] It did not explicitly impose this command.

[68]1 Pet 1:18-19.
[69]Rom 6:13.
[70]1 Cor 6:13.
[71]Cf. Deut 4:2; 12:32.
[72]Cf. 1 Cor 7:29.
[73]Cf. Mt 11:30.

(Cod. Vat. Gr. 762)

tested him by asking, "Is it lawful for a man to divorce his wife" for reasons besides fornication,[74] the Lord replied, "Anyone who divorces his wife, except on the ground of fornication, **[132]** causes her to commit adultery."[75] At this, the disciples say to him, "'If such is the case of a man with his wife, it is better not to marry.' But he said to them, 'There are eunuchs who have been so from birth, and there are eunuchs who have been made eunuchs by others, and there are eunuchs who have made themselves eunuchs for the sake of the kingdom of heaven. Let anyone accept this who can.'"[76] He set this out for those who want to do well, but he did not subject them to a law since he did not believe that everyone could master the impulses of the flesh. The shadow of the law contains something like this as well when it institutes the ways of performing sacrifice to the glory of God. Some are for sins and unknown errors,[77] and some are for purification and elimination of defilement.[78] Some are offered on the Sabbath, some on the first of the month, and some at the festivals.[79] In addition to these, the law allowed people to make a freewill offering, that is, to bring it before God. These freewill offerings were beyond what was required by the law. They were like the fruit of a good and godly love of honor. Now it was **[134]** not permitted to be remiss in offering the sacrifices prescribed by the law. But the people God considered worthy of praise were the ones who, in addition to the prescribed sacrifices, also offered something of their own on their own initiative. We maintain that this arrangement holds in the present case as well. Christ did not forbid people to engage in lawful unions, if they chose to do so. But nothing should prevent us from achieving something even better if we strive to lay hold of the ultimate glory. So Paul is completely right to say, "To the unmarried and the widows, it is well for them to remain unmarried as I am. To the married I give this command—not I but the Lord," and the rest. He brings up himself as an example of the chosen life that is free from distraction and clearly prefers the unmarried life to the married one. Let those who do take off the yoke of the law maintain their self-control, he says. For in this way they will inherit the kingdom of heaven. And the one who distributes the crowns will make this pledge to them: "Thus says the Lord to the eunuchs: 'Those who keep my Sabbaths and choose what I will and hold fast to my covenant—I will give them in my house and within my walls a place and a name, better than that of sons and daughters. I will give them an eternal name, and it will never die out.'"[80]

(Cod. Pantokrator. 28)

But when it pronounced a blessing on those who have made themselves eunuchs for the kingdom of heaven, it gave us to understand **[132]** that even though it did not annul the law of childbearing, it approves of those who have made themselves eunuchs for the kingdom. So it did not impose this as a law but merely gave permission to those who wanted to do it, since it did not believe that everyone could master the impulses of the flesh. That is why it adds, "Let anyone accept this who can."[81] Knowing this, Paul gives these instructions to those who wish to reach for a more perfect way of life, since it is not prohibited by Christ but left to the decision of those who want it. And he presents himself as an image of this preferred life, honoring singleness more than marriage and placing self-control higher than marriage. He advises the widows to remain pure. And he himself is holy and pure, superior to carnal pleasures, thus showing the reward for self-control to be more credible.

But if any are too weak for self-control, he commands them to marry in the Lord, saying that it is better to marry than to be aflame.

After all, if they might surrender themselves to the flame of pleasures **[134]** and fall into godlessness because they are unable to do right, it is better that the law should help them and that they should have an irreproachable remedy for their weakness rather than that they should feign self-control even though they are not yet able to practice it. For "God is not mocked."[82] Therefore, be strong and walk uprightly in self-control, or do not be ashamed to admit your weakness by getting married. For I think pardonable sickness is better than feigned courage that results in being aflame.

[74]Mt 19:3.
[75]Mt 5:32; cf. 19:9.
[76]Mt 19:10-12.
[77]Lev 5:17-19.
[78]Cf. Lev 5:12-15.
[79]Cf. Num 28:9-31.
[80]Is 56:4-5.
[81]Mt 19:12.
[82]Gal 6:7.

(Cod. Vat. Gr. 762)	(Cod. Pantokrator. 28)
The **[136]** reward of self-control is precious. But for those who are already bound by marriage, he does not permit them to leave their wife once they are married so that the saving proclamation may not raise an uproar in the world. Christ the Savior of us all does not approve of that, even though the law permitted the ancients to do this as an accommodation due to the "hardness of their hearts," as the Savior himself says.[83] From the following fact as well, anyone who is willing can easily see that those in Christ are steadier and stouter than the ancients: the law prohibited the Israelites from uniting themselves with foreigners and binding themselves together in marriage,[84] but Paul says to us, "If any brother has a wife who is an unbeliever,"[85] and so on.	**[136]** For those who are married, he does not permit them to leave or divorce their wife once they are married so that the proclamation may not càuse an uproar among the people. Through Moses God permitted the Jews to have certificates of divorce in the beginning[86] because they were weak, but he does not permit this for us since we are strong in godly faith.

7:12-15 To the rest I say—I and not the Lord—that if any believer has a wife who is an unbeliever, and she consents to live with him, he should not divorce her. And if any woman has a husband who is an unbeliever, and he consents to live with her, she should not divorce him. For the unbelieving husband is made holy through his wife, and the unbelieving wife is made holy through her husband. Otherwise, your children would be unclean, but as it is, they are holy. But if the unbelieving partner separates, let it be so; in such a case the brother or sister is not bound.

(Cod. Vat. Gr. 762)	(Cod. Pantokrator. 28)
Their mind is shaky and unsound, but we **[138]** are not like that. We have been anointed for adoption by the Holy Spirit, and Christ dwells in us. So since we are solid in our commitment to every kind of good work, we do not at all fear to associate with an unbeliever. Rather, we have courage that we will net them for godliness and that we ourselves will not become prey to their ignorance. We bless those who do not yet believe; we are not polluted by them. "For an unbelieving husband," he says, "is made holy through his wife."	Because of the strength of the believers, he does not permit them to dissolve their **[138]** marriage and live with others. Nor does he forbid them from staying with unbelievers, as the ancient law did because of the feeble mind of the Jews. So also now he permits believing husbands to remain with unbelieving wives since they have the confidence that they will convert their unbelieving wives and that they will not be turned to evil. They will bless their wives; they will not be polluted by them.
In this way our children are holy as well since the sanctification that believers have surely overcomes the uncleanness of those who do not yet believe. "But if the unbelieving partner separates," he says, "let it be so; in such a case the brother or sister is not bound."	In this way your children are holy as well, since the sanctification of believers overcomes the uncleanness of those who do not yet believe.
Let the polluted partner leave the holy one, if the polluted partner wants to do so, incurring the penalty for this as the payment for that decision. But the one who follows the divine commands is completely blameless since that partner will be blessed as obedient by Christ the Savior of us all.	Let the polluted partner leave and separate from the holy one, receiving the penalty for this as a payment for that decision. But the one who follows the divine commands is completely blameless since that partner will be blessed as obedient by God.

7:18-24 Was anyone at the time of his call already circumcised? Let him not seek to remove the marks of circumcision. Was anyone at the time of his call uncircumcised? Let him not seek circumcision. Circumcision is nothing, and uncircumcision is nothing; but obeying the

[83]Mt 19:8, cf. Deut 24:1.

[84]Cf. Deut 7:3; Ezra 10:3; Neh 13:23-29.

[85]1 Cor 7:12.

[86]Cf. Deut 24:1.

commandments of God is everything. Let each of you remain in the condition in which you were called. Were you a slave when you were called? Do not be concerned about it. Even if you can gain your freedom, make use of your present condition now more than ever. For whoever was called in the Lord as a slave is a freed person belonging to the Lord, just as whoever was free when called is a slave of Christ. You were bought with a price; do not become slaves of human masters. In whatever condition you were called, brothers, there remain with God.

(Cod. Vat. Gr. 762)

[140] Some of those who were circumcised were probably saying among themselves, How can we be accepted and honor our life in Christ when we are already circumcised? Perhaps we should remove the marks of circumcision, that is, apply force to the nature of our flesh and return to being uncircumcised. Those who came from the Greek error, on the other hand, perhaps learned from those who still value the shadow of the law that circumcision is a precious thing that is observed by all the saints. Though they once accepted the faith, they tried to complete it with the flesh, just like some in Galatia whom Paul rebukes by saying, "Having started with the Spirit, are you now ending with the flesh?"[87] Therefore, it was necessary to open the way for them with a clear and utterly unambiguous proclamation of the truth that circumcision is nothing apart from the other commands of God. Likewise, uncircumcision is nothing if it is not adorned with the life of the gospel. It is therefore fitting that those who are called remain in the calling in which they find themselves. He has to intervene **[142]** because he must once again scare away another blasphemy, as it were, to keep it away from the divine proclamation. That is because there is a spirit of slavery in those under the law, but he says that the gospel message inserts a Spirit of adoption in those who want to believe, and that Spirit calls them no longer to slavery but to a rank of freedom.

(Cod. Pantokrator. 28)

[Scholion 1][88]

[140] Now the apostle is speaking as a spiritual man. He does not allow types now that we have the revelation of the truth, that is, Christ. He helps both the Greeks and the Jews. He does not compel the former to be circumcised, nor does he compel those who are circumcised to apply force to the nature of their flesh to return it to uncircumcision. That is because circumcision in type has come to an end, while circumcision in spirit is brought about spiritually by Christ. After all, what benefit is circumcision to someone who leads an ungodly life? Let's say there is an uncircumcised man who is conspicuous among those who pride themselves on goodness. And let's say there is another man, a Hebrew of Hebrews who is circumcised in the flesh but unholy in his ways. He is beset by great weakness and lowers himself to every kind of alien and shameful act. Which of the two is worthy to be admired? Well I think it should be clear that we ought to honor not the circumcision that has been disfigured but the uncircumcision that contains virtue. The mystagogue, then, is telling the truth when he says, "Circumcision is nothing, and uncircumcision is nothing." Therefore, those who are called should **[142]** remain in the calling into which they have been called, that is, in which they find themselves, whether they are uncircumcised or circumcised. Now when some hear that faith sets them free and grants them the rank of adopted sons, they run away from the yoke of slavery. But Paul urges them not to do this but rather to remain in their physical slavery since they have been called by faith, he says, into a free sonship and have become "participants of the divine nature."[89] After all, their labor in slavery will not go unrewarded, since the Creator created nature free and knew it to be so. However, greed slipped in and spoiled the freedom. Nevertheless, we ought to love freedom because it provides help and reward, at least where God preserves it for everyone. On the other hand, we as human beings cannot escape slavery, since everything that is created is a slave. Therefore, even if you could gain your freedom, he says, "make use of your present condition now more than ever." Indeed, the yoke is not without profit for those who have a good heart, and physical slavery does no harm to virtue.

---

[87]Gal 3:3.

[88]Cyril's comments on 1 Cor 7:21-22 are presented in two different scholia in the Athos catena. These correspond to the paragraphs here labeled "Scholion 1" and "Scholion 2." (Scholion 2 ends with the words "the one who is called to freedom is surely a slave.") Scholion 1 comments more broadly on 1 Cor 7:18-22, while Scholion 2 focuses narrowly on 1 Cor 7:21-22. There is a great deal of verbal repetition between the two scholia, which suggests that they are each based on the same underlying text. See the discussion of the matter in Zawadzki, 389-92.

[89]2 Pet 1:4.

(Cod. Vat. Gr. 762)

For this reason, some who were called by faith to spiritual freedom tried to escape from their physical slavery. Paul writes to them in another place and says, "Only do not use your freedom as an opportunity for the flesh."[90] He exhorts **[144]** them also with these words: "Were you a slave when you were called? Do not be concerned about it. Even if you can gain your freedom, make use of your present condition now more than ever." This means: Even if you have the yoke of physical slavery imposed on you, you have been called by faith to freedom and sonship. And since you have become participants in the divine nature,[91] transcend pettiness! You will find that your toil in slavery will not go unrewarded. Those who endure slavery by the oppression of another will certainly be free of that evil when the Lord transforms all things in the coming age to the way they were in the beginning. The Creator has made nature free, and that is how it will be, as I said, in the coming age. "And it shall be, as with the people, so with the priest; as with the slave, so with his master; as with the maid, so with her mistress," according to the prophecy of Isaiah.[92] Therefore even if you can "gain your freedom," he says, "make use of your present condition now more than ever." For those who have a good heart and lead an upright life, the yoke of slavery is not without profit, as I said. In any case, he says, it would not be possible for us as human beings to escape the name *slavery*. After all, everything that is created is a slave. That means that "the slave is a freed person belonging to Christ," and that the one who is called to freedom is surely a slave, just as the psalm says: **[146]** "For all things are your slaves."[93] Indeed the mystagogue shows us in another way as well that those who are saved by Christ are debtors to him. That is what he means when he says, "You were bought with a price; do not become slaves of human masters." As we all know, we were bought with a price when Christ the Savior of us all offered his own blood for us. We were rescued from the violence of the devil and from the savagery of the demons, and we were called to freedom through Christ. Since we were purchased and bought, we owe our life to him. So "do not become slaves," he says, "of human masters." Now we are not saying that he is urging them to run away from their physical slavery. Rather, he is quite rightly teaching them this: do not become slaves to those who try to carry off believers to the observance of the law and who pour into the souls of the simple

(Cod. Pantokrator. 28)

[Scholion 2]

Since some who are worthy of the grace of the Holy Spirit have shaken off the yoke of slavery, he writes somewhere else, "Only do not use your freedom as an opportunity for the flesh."[94] But here he bewitches them, as it were, **[144]** with a highly sophisticated discourse: "Were you a slave when you were called," and the rest. This means: Even if you have the yoke of physical slavery imposed on you, you have been called by faith to freedom and sonship. And since you have become participants in the divine nature,[95] transcend pettiness! You will find that your toil in slavery will not go unrewarded. The Creator knew a nature that was free because he created it that way. But greed rushed in at a certain time and spoiled the beauty of the freedom. Those who have endured slavery must surely be free of that evil when Christ transforms all things to the way they were in the beginning. What is in him is a new creation.[96] There is neither slave nor free, but he is "all in all."[97] And Isaiah lifted up his voice ahead of time to describe the conditions and the equality before God that there will be in the life to come that we wait for. He said, "And it shall be, as with the people, so with the priest; as with the slave, so with his master; as with the maid, so with her mistress."[98] Therefore, even if you could gain your freedom, he says, "make use of your present condition now more than ever." For the yoke is not unprofitable, as I said, for those who have a good heart and lead upright lives under it. The oppressive imposition of physical slavery on some people now will not harm them as long as **[146]** the same freedom is preserved for everyone before God, who judges justly and weighs our deeds in holiness. In any case, he says, it would not be possible for us as human beings to escape the name *slavery*. After all, everything that is created is a slave, and everything that has been called into being is subject to the divine scepter. That means that "the slave is a freed person belonging to Christ," and that the one who is called to freedom is surely a slave.

We were bought with the precious blood of Christ and rescued from the oppression of the devil and the rulers of the world when we washed away the filth of their wickedness and were called to freedom through

[90] Gal 5:13.
[91] 2 Pet 1:4.
[92] Is 24:2.
[93] Ps 119:91 (Ps 118:91 LXX).
[94] See note 90.
[95] See note 91.
[96] Cf. 2 Cor 5:17.
[97] Col 3:11.
[98] Is 24:2.

(Cod. Vat. Gr. 762)	(Cod. Pantokrator. 28)
the poison of the ancient deception and convince them to observe days and months[99] and who practice what is termed "self-imposed piety"[100] and persuade others to do so as well. Since you were bought with a price, he says, and "you were ransomed not with perishable things like silver or gold, but with the precious blood of Christ, like that of a lamb without defect or blemish,"[101] let us be subject to his laws instead. **[148]**	Christ. So since we owe our life to him who bought us, "Do not become slaves," he says, "of human masters." He is not saying, Do not serve as physical slaves, but rather, Do not be slaves to the observation of laws that command circumcision and refraining from certain foods. Instead, let us be subject to him who purchased us not with perishable things but with his precious blood,[102] and let us obey his laws. **[148]**

8:1 Now concerning food sacrificed to idols: we know that "all of us possess knowledge." Knowledge puffs up, but love builds up.

The believers in Corinth were convinced that there is only one who is God by nature and that the idols are not gods. They ridiculed those who sacrificed to them and said that what is offered as a sacrifice is nothing at all. They ate these sacrifices without discrimination, confident that no pollution could come from this. In so doing, they caused the weak to stumble, who assumed it would not offend God if they honored the feasts of idols. For this reason Paul put a stop to these feasts, since he wanted the believers to be single-minded in their worship of the all-holy God.[103]

8:4-6 Hence, as to the eating of food offered to idols, we know that "no idol in the world really exists," and that "there is no God but one." Indeed, even though there may be so-called gods in heaven or on earth—as in fact there are many gods and many lords—yet for us there is one God, the Father, from whom are all things and for whom we exist, and one Lord, Jesus Christ, through whom are all things and through whom we exist.

For those who are completely unfamiliar with idols and for those who know exactly what they are (wood and mere stone), "no idol in the world really exists."[104] They think this because they do not consider idols worth mentioning. They believe in "one God, the Father, from whom are all things," and in "one Lord Jesus Christ, through whom are all things." God the Father has the glory of lordship and the one who was born of him has the supremacy of the one who bore him, since he is considered to be (and actually is) God in his own nature. By participation in him through the Spirit, many are called gods and lords, but few realize this.

By being deemed worthy of participation in the Holy Spirit, many are called gods and lords. But few have this mystical knowledge. The unbelievers think that there are many gods, and even some of those who believe in Christ have not completely abandoned the custom of idol worship.[105] **[150]**

[99]Cf. Gal 4:10.

[100]Col 2:23.

[101]1 Pet 1:18-19.

[102]See note 101.

[103]Paul does not mention putting a stop to the feasts of idols in 1 Cor 8. This comment seems to be directed at Cyril's contemporaries who were trying to adhere both to Christianity and pagan religion. See Zawadzki, 399.

[104]Cyril is referring here to two groups of Christians. The first group presumably consists of people born to Christian families who have no contact with the worship of idols. The second group consists of those Christians who lived in areas where idols were worshiped. Cyril's comments on this passage indicate that pagan practices still continued to pose a threat to Christianity even after the antipagan reforms of Theodosius (379–395) (Zawadzki, 398-99).

[105]Cyril's argument here is that all who worship idols fail to realize that they themselves can be "gods" by participation in Christ or the Holy Spirit (Zawadzki, 400).

8:7 It is not everyone, however, who has this knowledge. Since some have become so accustomed to idols until now, they still think of the food they eat as food offered to an idol; and their conscience, being weak, is defiled.

Some who believe in Christ have not completely abandoned the worship of idols. "Their conscience, being weak, is defiled." Perhaps because of the weakness of their soul, they imagine that they benefit themselves when they participate in the holy offerings and sample them and treat the sacrifices as food. We must guide the weak with spiritual teachings so that they do not eat indiscriminately and recline at table with unbelievers.

8:9 But take care that this liberty of yours does not somehow become a stumbling block to the weak.

When they ate food sacrificed to idols without discrimination and reclined at table with unbelievers in their sacrifices, they turned the demonstration of their strength into an occasion for others to stumble. One ought not exercise one's freedom in the faith at every occasion or at the wrong time or indiscriminately. Rather, everything we do should be done with decency.

8:11-12 So by your knowledge the weak brother for whom Christ died is destroyed. But when you thus sin against your brothers and wound their conscience when it is weak, you sin against Christ.

If we cause our brothers to stumble, we will sin against Christ himself, who has died for the salvation of us all. What wrong could be compared with that? "For by your knowledge, the one who is weak is destroyed." What is good has become a sin for you, and the strength of your faith has become a stumbling block for your brothers, and your knowledge has become a pothole.

It is a terrible thing when you all but attack your brothers' weaknesses instead of being eager to strengthen the weakness of their conscience. We should not "put stumbling blocks or hindrances in front of our brother,"[106] but bear in mind what is written: "Take care that you do not despise one of these little ones; for, I tell you, in heaven their angels continually see the face of my Father."[107] Wouldn't it be completely terrible for us to be denounced by their holy angels for all but attacking the weaknesses of our brothers rather than being eager to strengthen the weakness of their conscience? [152]

10:1-5 I do not want you to be unaware, brothers, that our fathers were all under the cloud, and all passed through the sea, and all were baptized into Moses in the cloud and in the sea, and all ate the same spiritual food, and all drank the same spiritual drink. For they drank from the same spiritual rock that followed them, and the rock was Christ. Nevertheless, God was not pleased with most of them, and they were struck down in the wilderness.

[106]Rom 14:13.
[107]Mt 18:10.

(Cod. Vat. Gr. 762)

We maintain that these things are prefigurations of what God would accomplish. Before faith in Christ, we too were subject to the oppression of demons and we were slaves to the spiritual Pharaoh, that is, Satan, the origin of all evil. We toiled for him in vain since we engaged only in the works of the flesh, which was our clay brick-making, as it were. And we too were rescued by "the mediator between God and humankind, the man Christ Jesus, who gave himself as a ransom for all."[108] He brought us too through the storms of this present life, as through a sea, and perfected us through holy baptism. He himself is the spiritual cloud from above that gives a supply of living water to those who love it. And this living water is the Spirit. Christ said, "As the Scripture has said, 'Out of the believer's heart shall flow rivers of living water.'"[109] **[154]** To clarify what he said, the divinely inspired Evangelist immediately added to these words the following statement: "Now he said this about the Spirit, which believers in him were to receive."[110] We too ate the bread that truly gives life, and we drank the spiritual drink just as they drank water from the rock. "And the rock was Christ," who for us too sent his own blood, mixed with water, gushing from his side when Pilate's soldiers pierced him with the spear. He is called the rock because he is invincible as God, even though he voluntarily suffered the assault of death. And what happened to the ancients after that? How did they offend God? They were profaned at Shittim, they worshiped idols, and they were consecrated to the Baal of Peor.[111] Since they were entangled with idol worshipers and associated with them and took part in the table of idols, they fell into apostasy and danced in a chorus with women, "and the people entangled itself with a harlot," as the prophet says.[112] That is what it means that they "rose up to revel."[113] Therefore, it is dangerous to associate with the wicked and with unbelievers. As Solomon said somewhere, **[156]** "Whoever walks with the wise becomes wise, but whoever walks with fools will be known."[114]

(Cod. Pantokrator. 28)

Paul exhorts those with truly perfect knowledge not to eat food sacrificed to idols. Then he appeals to the experiences of the ancients to try to persuade them that this act is not beneficial but dangerous, and that the penalty is not trivial that comes on those whose conduct is unrighteous. After all, this eating leads them to break God's law, since the human mind is easily shaken and quickly drawn to what is not right. Paul employs an image of this phenomenon that is not without beauty, indeed it is extremely fitting: the experiences of Israel's descendants in the desert. He demonstrates with great force that the desire to associate with unbelievers is not harmless even for those who are firm in the faith. What he says is this: those who were freed from slavery were perfected through the cloud in the sea. The cloud hung over them, and Moses was their mediator. **[154]** They ate the bread from heaven. They drank the life-giving drink. Christ himself provided them with drink, since he was the rock. Indeed, he is invincible as God, even though he voluntarily suffered the assault of death. We maintain that these things are prefigurations of what God would accomplish. And what happened to the ancients after that? How did they offend God? They were profaned, they worshiped idols, and they were consecrated to the Baal of Peor. Notice how they who were baptized in the cloud and the sea and who ate the bread from heaven and drank the spiritual drink nevertheless entangled themselves with idolatry. Since they associated with idolaters and took part in the table of idolatry, they quickly became distracted and fell into apostasy and worshiped the Baal of Peor. Therefore, it is dangerous to live with the wicked and with unbelievers. Christ freed us when we were under the power of the spiritual Pharaoh. He brought us through the storms of this present life, as through a sea, and he perfected us through holy baptism. He himself is the spiritual cloud from above **[156]** that supplies living water, which is the Spirit. We ate the life-giving bread from heaven. We drank the spiritual drink, just as they drank the water from the rock. "And the rock was Christ," who for us too sent his own blood, mixed with water, gushing from his side when Pilate's soldiers pierced him with the spear.

10:7-8 Do not become idolaters as some of them did; as it is written, "The people sat down to eat and drink, and they rose up to play." We must not indulge in sexual immorality as some of them did, and twenty-three thousand fell in a single day.

[108]1 Tim 2:5-6.
[109]Jn 7:38.
[110]Jn 7:39.
[111]Cf. Num 25:1-3.
[112]Hos 4:14.
[113]Ex 32:6; cf. 1 Cor 10:7.
[114]Prov 13:20.

He brings up the entire narrative in the book of Numbers to teach that those who were baptized in the cloud and the sea, who were deemed worthy of the spiritual food, nevertheless fell when they ate with idolaters. And "they rose up to play" stands for "they committed sexual immorality with the Moabite women."
(Cod. Pantokrator. 28)

10:28-29 But if someone says to you, "This has been offered in sacrifice," then do not eat it, out of consideration for the one who informed you, and for the sake of conscience. For the earth is the Lord's and everything in it. I mean the other's conscience, not your own.

"For the sake of conscience you must abstain from those things you ought to abstain from. I do not mean your own conscience, since it has knowledge, but the other's conscience. This is so that he will not be falsely emboldened to imitate out of ignorance what he does not understand, thus becoming a despiser rather than a high-minded person."[115] **[158]**
(Cod. Pantokrator. 28)

11:3 But I want you to understand that Christ is the head of every man, and the husband is the head of his wife, and God is the head of Christ.

(Cod. Vat. Gr. 762)	(Cod. Pantokrator. 28)
[160] By "head" he means here the archetypal beauty. Each of the aforementioned people, enriched by that image, may rightly be understood to share in that essential nobility, or to put it another way, they share in the same nature. The first man, that is, Adam, was created in the image and likeness of God. The Creator of the universe says somewhere, "In the image of God he made the man."[116] Therefore, Christ is the head of the man. As God, he is the archetype, but by the	Since some of the Corinthians were recent converts who were just settling into the faith, they did not know how to pray and they did not observe the proper custom as they entered the house of God. When they drew near to pray to God and brought their petitions on their own behalf, their appearance was most inappropriate. Men approached without taking their customary coverings off their heads, and women came before God with their hair uncovered and unveiled,[117] all but crying out against nature. To the man is given the boldness to speak, while the woman covers her hair for decency out of a sense of modesty. It was fitting to use logical necessity to shame them into thinking rightly and to make the law of nature a kind of referee of what is fitting for each gender. So Paul tries to use the natural law to persuade them to think the way they should.[118] So he goes back to the creation of the human being in the beginning.[119] **[160]** By "head" he means the archetypal beauty in whose likeness one is created. Adam was created in the image and likeness of God. Therefore, Christ is the head of the man. As God, he is the archetype, but also by the law of our nature since he became a human being, even though the Word is God. In fact, he calls himself the Son of Man in many places, even though he has an ineffable birth from God. Finally, the woman is created in the image of

[115]This is a quote from Clement of Alexandria's *Stromateis* 4.15.98.2. The catenist either erroneously ascribed this scholion to Cyril or copied a section from Cyril in which Cyril was quoting Clement. I agree with Zawadzki's analysis (415-16) that the latter is more probable because the catenist never cites Clement elsewhere.

[116]Gen 9:6.

[117]1 Cor 11:4-5.

[118]Cf. 1 Cor 11:14-15.

[119]Cf. 1 Cor 11:7-9.

(Cod. Vat. Gr. 762)

law of our nature, he is also the same as us since he became a human being, even though the Word is God and has an ineffable birth from God the Father. The woman was created in the image and likeness of the man, that is, Adam. She is not at all alien to him, but she is of the same nature and species as he is. Our forefather Adam explicitly acknowledged this when he said, "This is now bone of my bones and flesh of my flesh," and so on.[120] But if they claim that the Word of God the Father is originate and should be numbered among the creatures since he is the "head of every man," would we not have to think, by the same logic, that the Father himself is created and **[162]** made? After all, he is the head of the Son, and the Son has our essential nature, or more precisely, the essential nature of creatures. And as they themselves incessantly claim, the head is united by the laws of nature to the rest of the body so that they are identical. Therefore, kinship with every man will extend via the Son to God the Father himself. But we will not follow the idiotic teachings of these people. How could we? No, we believe that the Word who sprang from the Father is unoriginate from an unoriginate Father. And we maintain that he is called the "head of every man" as an archetype, as I said. But since he became a human being in the last times of the age, it is also as a member of the human race (at least according to his human nature) that he is the head "of the church, which is his body."[121] For he holds first place in all things, as Paul says.[122]

(Cod. Pantokrator. 28)

Adam. She is of the same nature and species as he is, not at all alien to him. So the man is the head of the woman, Christ is the head of the man, and God is the head of Christ. But some[123] say that the Son is originate like the rest of creation of which Paul says Christ is the head, since Paul says, "Christ is the head of every man." These people ought to consider above all else that the force of this blasphemy does not reach only to the teaching concerning the Son, but it will rush ahead on an unstoppable course, as it were, to reach the Father himself. I will tell you how. If they claim that the Word of God the Father is begotten[124] and should be numbered among the creatures since he is the "head of every man," would **[162]** we not have to think, by the same logic, that the Father himself is created and made? After all, he is the head of the Son, and the Son has our essential nature, or more precisely, the essential nature of creatures. And as they themselves incessantly claim, the head is united by the laws of nature with the rest of the body so that they are identical. Therefore, kinship with every man will extend via the Son to God the Father himself. So how does he still transcend the nature of originate beings? Whom shall we look to as the Creator of all things? They are forced to say that even the Father is begotten if he is called the head of Christ, and Christ has, according to them, the nature of us creatures, and kinship with every man extends via the Son in some way even to God the Father himself. So we must ultimately look for some other creator besides him. Therefore, lest we veer off into this bizarre nonsense, we must hold that the Son is unoriginate from an unoriginate Father, and that he is called the "head of every man" as an archetype in that he is by nature God. But since he became a human being as well, he is also considered the head "of the church, which is his body."[125] For he holds first place in all things,[126] and in this sense he is understood to be the head of everything else.

[164]

11:4-10 Any man who prays or prophesies with something on his head disgraces his head, but any woman who prays or prophesies with her head unveiled disgraces her head—it is one and the same thing as having her head shaved. For if a woman will not veil herself, then she should cut off her hair; but if it is disgraceful for a woman to have her hair cut off or to be shaved, she should wear a veil. For a man ought not to have his head veiled, since he is the image and glory of God; but woman is the glory of man. Indeed, man was not made from

[120]Gen 2:23.
[121]Eph 1:22-23.
[122]Col 1:18.
[123]The Arians say this. The main proponent of Arianism that Cyril probably has in view is Eunomius of Cyzicus.
[124]Codex Vat. Gr. 762 has γενητόν (originate) rather than γεννητὸν (begotten). "Originate" fits better with Cyril's point here.
[125]See note 121.
[126]See note 122.

woman, but woman from man. Neither was man created for the sake of woman, but woman for the sake of man. For this reason a woman ought to have a symbol of authority on her head, because of the angels.

(Cod. Vat. Gr. 762)

Do you see how he makes the law of nature the judge that determines what is fitting for each gender? Bold speech is most appropriate for men, while the modesty of veiling is most appropriate for a woman. And unseemliness on the part of the image would quite reasonably constitute an insult to the archetype. So since a man is the image and glory of God (for according to the Scriptures he is created as such), then let him preserve for God a fitting boldness of speech by keeping his head unveiled, since the law of nature does not force him to be veiled. After all, the divine nature is free and beyond all criticism. It is rich with its own glory, and it is wonderful. And since woman is in the likeness of man **[166]** and she is the image of the image and the glory of the glory, and since nature decrees that she let her hair grow long, why would the gender that comes later engage in a battle over grace with the gender that came first? She too is in the image and likeness of God, but mediately through the man, so that there is a slight difference between her nature and his. I will level no charge against a woman who modestly covers her body, as far as possible, and who crowns her head with hair. But bold speech is surely not without penalty for a woman. Therefore, "she should wear a veil," he says, "because of the angels." Clearly this refers to the angels whom God appointed over the churches.

[168] They are exceedingly upset whenever anyone neglects proper decorum since they too know the Creator's will for us.

(Cod. Pantokrator. 28)

By the term "prophesy" he means singing the Psalms and praising God. He makes the law of nature the judge of what is fitting for each gender. Bold speech is most appropriate for men, while the modestly of veiling is most appropriate for women. And unseemliness on the part of the image would quite reasonably constitute an insult to the archetype. So since man is the image and glory of God, let him preserve for God a fitting boldness of speech by keeping his head unveiled. After all, the divine nature is free, and the law of nature does not force him to be veiled. And since woman is created in the likeness of man and she is, as it were, the image of the image and the glory of the glory, and since nature decrees that she let her hair grow long, why would the gender that comes later engage in a battle over grace with the gender that came first? **[166]** She too is in the image and likeness of God, but mediately through the man, so that there is a slight difference between her nature and his. I will level no charge against a woman who modestly covers her body, as far as possible, and who crowns her head with hair. But bold speech is surely not without penalty for a woman. It would be more fitting for them gladly to veil themselves.

"She should wear a veil because of the angels" whom God appointed over the churches. Not that they suffer anything when they see women. Human beings are actually the ones who would suffer harm, since they have this coarse earthly body and are dragged down by innate pleasure to what is shameful. They would be the ones aroused by the beauty of these women to commit inappropriate acts. But how could anyone either think or say this about the holy angels? They are holy, after all, and far above all filth because they use bodies that are incorporeal, subtle, spiritual, and beyond human comprehension. **[168]** No, the phrase "because of the angels" means that the angels are upset whenever proper decorum is neglected. Being veiled is appropriate for a woman, and nature is a witness of this fact. "For her hair," he says, "is given to her for a covering."[127] Therefore, appropriate behavior should be observed for this reason as well: because of those who know the Creator's will for us.

11:11-12 Nevertheless, in the Lord woman is not independent of man or man independent of woman. For just as woman came from man, so man comes through woman; but all things come from God.

[127] 1 Cor 11:15.

(Cod. Vat. Gr. 762)

The divinely inspired Paul employs yet another skillful device. He just said that the man was created in the image and likeness of God. And after that, he made it clear that the female gender was subordinated to his honor and glory by adding the following:

"For the woman," he says, "is the glory of man. For man was not created for the sake of woman, but woman for the sake of man."[128] But then he quite rightly puts a veil over anything further that would likely cause grief to the female gender, and he adds, "Nevertheless, woman is not independent of man nor man independent of woman." The woman certainly came **[170]** from the man. This is true. But she is not without contribution in the origination of man. The plan of nature has established a need for each other that brings them both into a unity and binds them in love. Paul also confirms that the Creator of all things is God when he adds, "But all things come from God." For he has brought all things into being through Christ.

(Cod. Pantokrator. 28)

In the foregoing material, he said that the female gender is lacking in many respects compared to the male. So to prevent the female from being upset by this, he shows care for her by saying, "Nevertheless, woman is not independent of man or man independent of woman." The woman certainly came from the man. **[170]** This is true. But the woman also plays a role in the origination of man. After all, the plan of nature knew that their union would not[129] be ineffectual, and it gave each of them a need for the other, thereby uniting them in love. But the Creator of all things is God.

12:3-6 Therefore, I want you to understand that no one speaking by the Spirit of God ever says, "Let Jesus be cursed!" and no one can say, "Jesus is Lord" except by the Holy Spirit. Now there are varieties of gifts, but the same Spirit; and there are varieties of services, but the same Lord; and there are varieties of activities, but it is the same God who activates all of them in everyone.

(Cod. Vat. Gr. 762)

Our Lord Jesus Christ promised that after he departed, he would send to us the Paraclete, and he added this: "He will glorify me."[130] We are right to think that Christ's Spirit glorifies him by making everyone he enters wise and by making Christ to dwell in the saints through himself, since Christ is in us through the Holy Spirit. He glorifies him in another way as well. He performs works that bring glory to Christ through the hands of the saints. So if Christ's Spirit glorifies the Son, how could anyone speaking by the Spirit speak ill of Christ? **[172]** You will say, rather, "Jesus is Lord." Therefore, those who classify him as a creature, even though all things were brought into being through him, must be completely devoid of participation in the Holy Spirit. But those who reverently confess him as God and Lord thereby prove that they have been led by the Spirit to experience the vision of God in him. "For the Spirit searches everything, even the depths of God."[131] The Spirit, who knows what is hidden in God, conveys it to the souls of the saints and inserts into them knowledge that is sure and irreproachable.

(Cod. Pantokrator. 28)

When the Lord promised to send the Paraclete to the holy apostles, he added, "He will glorify me."[132] We should understand this to mean that when he makes those he enters wise and when he makes Christ dwell in them through himself, then he glorifies Christ. He also glorifies him when he performs works that bring glory to the Son through the saints. So if the Spirit glorifies the Son, how could anyone speaking by the Spirit speak ill of Christ? He will say, rather, "Jesus is Lord." Therefore, those who classify him as a creature, **[172]** even though all things were brought into being through him, are surely devoid of participation in the Holy Spirit. After all, they clearly say, "Let Jesus be cursed!" But those who confess that Jesus is God and Lord thereby reverently demonstrate that they have been led by the Spirit to experience the vision of God in him.

---

[128]1 Cor 11:7, 9.

[129]I follow Zawadzki's conjectural addition of οὐκ (not) as the only way to make sense of this sentence. See his discussion in Zawadzki, 428.

[130]Jn 16:14.

[131]1 Cor 2:10.

[132]See note 130.

(Cod. Vat. Gr. 762)	(Cod. Pantokrator. 28)
The divinely inspired Paul himself is a witness to this when he adds, "Now there are varieties of gifts, but the same Spirit; and there are varieties of services, but the same Lord; and there are varieties of activities, but it is the same God who activates all of them in everyone." Just as those who rule over earthly affairs, resplendent on the thrones of their kingdoms, crown their noble servants with various honors, so also the holy and consubstantial Trinity distributes his abundant blessings from above on those who love him with a pure heart and a full understanding. This takes place from the Father through the one Spirit just as through Christ, since all things are from the Father through the Son in the Spirit.	The Holy Trinity richly grants his manifold gifts from the Father through the one Spirit, just as through Christ, since all things are from the Father through the Son in the Spirit.

[174]

12:7-11 To each is given the manifestation of the Spirit for the common good. To one is given through the Spirit the word of wisdom, and to another the word of knowledge according to the same Spirit, to another faith by the same Spirit, to another gifts of healing by the same Spirit, to another the working of miracles, to another prophecy, to another the discernment of spirits, to another various kinds of tongues, to another the interpretation of tongues. All these are activated by one and the same Spirit, who allots to each one individually just as the Spirit chooses.

(Cod. Vat. Gr. 762)	(Cod. Pantokrator. 28)
He knows, yes he knows the right time for everything he does! "In him are hidden all the treasures of wisdom and knowledge," as it is written.[133] And he clarifies what the gifts are and what their distribution is and indeed what the workings of miracles are as well when he says, "To one is given through the Spirit the word of wisdom."	He knows the right time for everything he does. "In him are all the treasures of wisdom."[137]
The phrase *word of wisdom* means, in my opinion, that when someone "opens his mouth,"[134] he is articulate and fluent.[135] "And to another the word of knowledge." There are some among us who do not have the aptitude for speaking and who do not possess the confidence they need to be able to express themselves with ease, but they do have a profound capacity for understanding, and they approach the holy words with great insight.[136] Both the former and the latter word are given through the one Spirit to those who are worthy to receive them from the Father through the Son, who is said to distribute the ministries. **[176]**	The phrase *word of wisdom* means, in my opinion, that when someone "opens his mouth,"[138] he is articulate and fluent and proceeds with an exquisitely eloquent tongue. "And to another the word of knowledge." There are some among us who do not have the aptitude for speaking and who do not possess the confidence they need to be able to express themselves with ease, but they do have a profound capacity for understanding, and they approach the holy words with great insight and nuance. They can also lead others into the mystery and easily lay out the objects of contemplation. But **[176]** both the word of wisdom and the word of knowledge

[133]Col 2:3.
[134]Eph 6:19.
[135]Similarly, in his comments on 1 Cor 1:20, Cyril understands Paul's term "wisdom" to refer to rhetoricians.
[136]Zawadzki suggests that Cyril may have the Egyptian monks in mind here (Zawadzki, 438).
[137]See note 133.
[138]See note 134.

(Cod. Vat. Gr. 762)

He commanded some of the holy apostles to preach the word of faith to those of Israel's bloodline. Others he assigned to Gentile regions. And he did this through the Holy Spirit. Indeed, we find written in the Acts of the Holy Apostles, "While they were worshiping the Lord and fasting, the Holy Spirit said, 'Set apart for me Barnabas and Saul for the work to which I have called them.'"[139] The divinely inspired Paul was appointed as apostle to the Gentiles, and that is the ministry he received. He himself proves it when he writes, "Inasmuch then as I am an apostle to the Gentiles, I glorify my ministry."[140] So the Son apportions the ministries, but the Holy Spirit carries out the task with power, since he is the Spirit of the Son. But it is also the case that God himself accomplishes for us the workings of miracles, that is, the divine signs done by the saints, **[178]** since all things, as I said, are from the Father through the Son in the Holy Spirit. In everything that is accomplished, the holy and consubstantial Trinity is praised. Notice how Paul begins from the Spirit, since he is in us and he brings about the distribution of the divine gifts. Then he ascends to the Son, who is Son by nature. And finally he reaches the Father and ascribes to him the activity that is carried out by the Spirit through the mediation of the Son.[141] "To another faith by the same Spirit." Faith here means, in my opinion, steadfastness in all good things and in whatever God wills. That is the sense in which we say that the priest Moses was faithful "in all his house."[142] Faith should not be construed in thought or word to mean the mere belief that the God of the universe is truly one by nature. Rather, it means having a steadfast spirit and being "ready to walk with the Lord God," as the prophet says.[143] At any rate, the divinely inspired disciples once approached Christ and said explicitly, "Increase our faith!"[144] And they were given more than

(Cod. Pantokrator. 28)

are given through the one Spirit to those who are worthy to receive them from the Father through the Son. It is a word of knowledge when someone knows the meaning of the divine sayings and is capable of unpacking that meaning but he cannot teach it eloquently. Both the former and the latter word are given to the worthy through the one Spirit, from the Father, through the Son, who is said to distribute the ministries. He commanded some of the apostles to preach the word of faith to Israel according to the flesh, while he commanded others to preach it to the Gentiles. And this too he did through the Holy Spirit, who says, "Set apart for me Barnabas and Saul."[145]

But it is also the case that God himself does the workings of miracles, the divine signs done by the saints, since all things are from **[178]** the Father through the Son in the Holy Spirit. In everything that is accomplished, the holy and consubstantial Trinity is praised.

He uses "faith" here to mean not bare knowledge, which even the unclean spirits have since they believe that God is one.[146] No, "faith" here should be understood to mean not only believing in God, but also doing everything that pleases him, having genuine love for him, having a steadfast spirit, and being "ready to walk with the Lord God."[147] After all, if faith is understood to mean merely believing that God is one and this is classified as one of the divine gifts, why can't we who believe also command the mountains to be moved?[148] The term *gifts of healing* refers to the healing of the sick that Christ performs through the Spirit.

139 Acts 13:2.
140 Rom 11:13.
141 Zawadzki suggests that Cyril is referring to Paul's mention of the Sprit, the Lord, and God (in that order) in 1 Cor 12:4-6 (Zawadzki, 440).
142 Heb 3:2.
143 Mic 6:8.
144 Lk 17:5.
145 See note 139.
146 Cf. Jas 2:19.
147 See note 143.
148 Cf. Mt 17:20.

(Cod. Vat. Gr. 762)	(Cod. Pantokrator. 28)
that: "gifts of healing by the one Spirit." Now please pay careful attention to the following: Christ is the giver of the Spirit **[180]** who Paul says distributes the gifts of healing. That is because Christ gave the holy apostles "authority over unclean spirits, to cast them out."[149] In particular he told them to "cure the sick, raise the dead, cleanse the lepers, cast out demons. You received without payment; give without payment."[150] Surely the working of miracles also came from him, but by the one Spirit. Moses threw his staff on the ground and it became a snake.[151] He turned the waters into blood.[152] He drew out water from a rock.[153] The blessed prophets performed an exceeding number of acts beyond reason and wonder. We maintain that these are the working of miracles through the same Spirit. Someone else can prophesy, but not without the Spirit. Someone can have the discernment of spirits, but only by the same Spirit. I have previously discussed what kind of spirits these are. Now he also maintains that the knowledge of various kinds of tongues is given to others, and to still others is given the knowledge of how to interpret them. We say that this gift is private and is given to certain people at the proper time when the circumstances call for it. Some spoke in tongues even though they previously did not know them, while others knew how to interpret them, **[182]** even though they were previously unacquainted with the vocabulary. However, the divinely inspired Paul maintains that speaking in tongues was given to people in those days not as a gift but as a sign to unbelievers.[154] And in particular, he cites the prophetic saying that goes like this: "In other tongues and by the lips of foreigners I will speak to this people, yet even then they will not believe."[155] The Spirit brings about the distribution of gifts differently in each person. He does this, Paul says, so that just as this coarse earthly body is composed of parts, so also Christ or his body, which is the church, may be put together from a great multitude of saints into the most perfect spiritual unity. Along the same lines the divinely inspired David says that she is robed in a "golden garment" of many shades,[156] signifying by this, it seems to me, the multiplicity and precious value of the gifts. **[184]**	The term *working of miracles* refers to miracle-working and prophecy through the **[180]** Spirit. "Discernment of spirits" is the ability to identify which teachings are heretical and erroneous and which are orthodox. Speaking in tongues is a private gift that is given to certain people at the proper time when the circumstances call for it. Others did not speak in other tongues but interpreted what was spoken in them. The Spirit brings about the distribution of gifts differently in each person.

12:12-13 For just as the body is one and has many members, and all the members of the body, though many, are one body, so it is with Christ. For in the one Spirit we were all baptized into one body—Jews or Greeks, slaves or free—and we were all made to drink of one Spirit.

[149]Mt 10:1.
[150]Mt 10:8.
[151]Cf. Ex 7:9-10.
[152]Cf. Ex 7:20.
[153]Cf. Ex 17:6.
[154]Cf. 1 Cor 14:22.
[155]1 Cor 14:21.
[156]Ps 45:12 (Ps 44:10 LXX).

We have been united with one another and have become part of the same body in Christ.[157] He has gathered us together and practically tied us to each other through the one Spirit who is in all. And we have been given the Spirit as a life-giving drink. Indeed, when Christ was speaking to the woman at Jacob's well, he said, "Everyone who drinks of this water will be thirsty again, but those who drink of the water that I will give—a spring of water will arise in them gushing up to eternal life."[158] And he said somewhere to the Jews, "As the Scripture has said, 'Out of the believer's heart shall flow rivers of living water.' He said this," it says, "about the Spirit, which believers in him were to receive."[159] And do not be astonished by this! If he who is full of water is "the river of God," as the psalmist says, "flowing with abundance,"[160] and God the Father is said to give him as a drink to those who love him, how could we not understand his Spirit to be a drink and life-giving water? Therefore, since we have been called to unity through the Spirit and we have been made one body with Christ, let us keep the unbreakable bond of love.

14:1-3 Pursue love and strive for the spiritual gifts, and especially that you may prophesy. For those who speak in a tongue do not speak to other people but to God; for nobody understands them, since they are speaking mysteries to the Spirit. On the other hand, those who prophesy speak to other people for their upbuilding and encouragement and consolation.

(Cod. Coisl. 25)

He gave them tongues as a sign that the mystagogues of the world would preach the gospel proclamation (that is, the saving proclamation) in every tongue and every nation. Though the men were Galileans and were raised **[186]** in Judea, Hebrews descended from Hebrews, they spoke in the tongues of Medes, Parthians, Elamites, and residents of Mesopotamia, Cappadocians, and Egyptians.[161] They accomplished this by the activity and grace of the Spirit. As it is written, "Divided tongues, as of fire, appeared among them," and so on.[162] Now what they did was a way of furthering God's plan of salvation, but not everyone understood this. Once they began to speak in other tongues, they made the grace of the Spirit into a kind of show and took the sign as an opportunity for boasting. They neglected their duty to speak the message of the holy prophets to the crowds and counsel them with the evangelical dogmas, as these were long proclaimed from above. They were proud only of their ability to speak in tongues and thought that they should strive for this alone. That was what they wanted the most.

(Cod. Vat. Gr. 762)

He disabuses them of the idea that speaking in tongues is more glorious than interpreting **[188]** the words of the prophets. Once we have in ourselves faith, hope, and especially love for God and the brothers, which is the fulfillment of the entire law, then let the rest be added as

(Cod. Pantokrator. 28)

When those who received the gift of tongues became more proud than they ought, they took the sign as an opportunity for boasting and they neglected the proclamation of the gospel. They were proud, as I said, only of their ability to speak in tongues and thought that they should strive for this alone. Paul teaches that the duty of speaking the message of the holy prophets to the crowds and counseling them with the evangelical dogmas is better than speaking in tongues.

[188] Once we have in ourselves faith, hope, and love for God and the brothers and we prize those virtues above all, which is what the entire law commands, then I will be amazed by the gifts of the Spirit. I am

[157]Cf. Eph 3:6.
[158]Jn 4:13-14.
[159]Jn 7:38-39.
[160]Ps 65:10 (Ps 64:10 LXX).
[161]Cf Acts 2:9.
[162]Acts 2:3.

(Cod. Vat. Gr. 762)

well. Then—then!—will be just the right time for us to be filled with God's graces and enriched by the gifts of the Spirit! I am referring to the ability to prophesy, that is, to interpret the words of the prophets. After all, once the Only Begotten became man, once he suffered and rose and accomplished the *oikonomia* for us, what prophecy could still be needed? What deeds could still be foretold? Therefore, the term *prophesying* in this passage could have no other meaning than the ability to interpret prophecy. When we elucidate a passage for our hearers as best we can, confirming our interpretation by comparing it with the truth, then we will be correct and error-free interpreters of the most beautiful things. Now the one who speaks in tongues, he says, does not speak to other people but to God. Why is that? "For nobody understands them," he says. So, for example, if one of the disciples happens to receive the ability to speak in the language of the Medes and another receives the ability to speak in the language of the Elamites, **[190]** and the men I am talking about want to converse in the Jewish synagogues or with the Greek flocks, who would understand them? What would be the benefit of such a conversation? No one would understand them except for God alone, who knows everything, "since they are speaking mysteries to the Spirit," he says. Notice how the one who speaks to God speaks to the Spirit. Therefore, the Spirit is God. Now "those who speak in a tongue speak to God," he says, "and not to other people." But "those who prophesy speak to other people for their upbuilding and encouragement and consolation." He understands the term *prophesying* here to mean interpreting the words of the prophets, by which the message of encouragement is confirmed and the mind of the catechumens is led to the truth of Christ. So he adds further clarification that interpreting the words of the prophets is incomparably better than speaking in a tongue. "Those who speak in a tongue," he says, "build up themselves."[163] That is because no one else understands them. But those who employ the words and predictions of the holy prophets as evidence "build up the church."[164] Therefore, prophesying is greater. It has the utmost renown and brings glorious hope since it is obviously better to build up the church than to speak only to oneself in a tongue. **[192]**

(Cod. Pantokrator. 28)

referring to the ability to prophesy, that is, the ability to interpret the words of the prophets. After all, once the Only Begotten became man, once he suffered and rose again and fulfilled the *oikonomia* for us, what prophecy could still be needed? What deeds could still be foretold? Therefore, the term *prophesying* in this passage could have no other meaning than the ability to interpret prophecy. When we elucidate prophecies as best we can for our hearers, then we will be correct and error-free interpreters of the most beautiful things.

For example, if one of the disciples happens to receive the ability to speak in the language of the Medes, and another receives the ability to speak in the language of the Elamites, and then they speak with the Greeks or the Jews, **[190]** who would understand them? What would be the benefit of such a conversation? No one understands them except God alone, who knows everything, "since they are speaking mysteries to the Spirit." Now if the one who speaks to God speaks to the Spirit, then the Spirit is God.

Now "those who speak in a tongue build up themselves,"[165] since they are the ones who understand what they are saying. But those who explain the words of the prophets and employ their predictions as evidence "build up the church."[166] Therefore, prophesying is greater since it is better to build up the church than to speak only to oneself in a tongue. **[192]**

14:5 Now I would like all of you to speak in tongues, but even more to prophesy. One who prophesies is greater than one who speaks in tongues, unless someone interprets, so that the church may be built up.

[163] 1 Cor 14:4.
[164] 1 Cor 14:4.
[165] See note 163.
[166] See note 164.

(Cod. Vat. Gr. 762)	(Cod. Pantokrator. 28)
Since it was unusual and truly a gift from God that men who were Hebrew could speak in the language of other people, and so that no one may think that the apostle was foolishly discounting what happened and saying that the gift given through the activity of the Spirit was nothing, he approves of it and says, "Now I would like all of you to speak in tongues." But he abruptly and decisively cuts short any eagerness for this gift and transfers it to a better one by immediately adding, "but even more to prophesy." He is thereby saying in the clearest way possible that the one who prophesies is greater than the one who speaks in a tongue. Then he shows that it is not altogether useless for those who have it and for their hearers when he adds, "unless someone interprets," that is, unless there is always someone there to interpret for the catechumens. **[194]**	Since it was unusual and truly a gift from God that men who were Hebrew could speak in the language of other people, and so that no one may think that Paul was rejecting the gift of tongues and saying that the gift given through the activity of the Spirit was in vain (since it was given as a sign to unbelievers), he approves of it and adds, "Now I would like all of you to speak in tongues." However, he says that prophesying is better than speaking in a tongue, except that even speaking in tongues can bring some benefit to the hearers if there is always someone there to interpret for the catechumens in a language that the catechumens know how to speak and understand. **[194]**

14:9-11 So with yourselves; if in a tongue you utter speech that is not intelligible, how will anyone know what is being said? For you will be speaking into the air. There are doubtless many different kinds of languages in the world, and nothing is without language. If then I do not know the meaning of a language, I will be a foreigner to the speaker and the speaker a foreigner to me.

(Cod. Vat. Gr. 762)	(Cod. Pantokrator. 28)
	Some who regularly went to church possessed the ability to speak in tongues by the activity of the Spirit. Now in church, one should offer prayers and, more importantly, make petitions and sing psalms in the language of those present, but they did not do so. They took pride only in the gift of tongues and did not offer prayers or psalms. Paul teaches that if the hearers do not know the language in which the possessor of the gift is speaking, there is no benefit from this activity. After all, there are multitudes of nations and many human languages, and there is no example of a rational or human creature that is without language.
He says that there is absolutely no example of a rational or human creature that is without language. But if someone does not happen to know the meaning of another's words and they do not know each other's language, they will be foreigners to one another, even though they speak their own languages correctly. Therefore, those who want to teach others **[196]** must produce speech that is comprehensible to their hearers.	If someone does not happen to know the meaning of another's words and they do not know each other's language when one speaks, they will be foreigners to one another, even though they speak their own languages correctly. Therefore, those who want to teach others must produce speech that is comprehensible **[196]** to their hearers. If the utterance is meaningless and the language is unknown, then they have labored in vain and assaulted the hearing of the learner with a pointless cacophony.
	He says that those who want to teach must speak words that are comprehensible to the hearers or else they labor in vain. That is because the one who speaks only in tongues does not edify the church.

14:13-15 Therefore, one who speaks in a tongue should pray for the power to interpret. For if I pray in a tongue, my spirit prays but my mind is unproductive. What should I do then? I will pray with the spirit, but I will pray with the mind also; I will sing psalms with the spirit, but I will sing psalms with the mind also.

(Cod. Vat. Gr. 762)

In this passage he uses the term "spirit" to refer to the grace given by the Spirit, that is, the ability to speak in tongues. If, he says, I pray prayers in church with the spirit, that is, employing the tongue given by the Spirit, my mind will remain unfruitful. I should pray earnestly and ask God for those things that pertain to salvation. I should not pride myself in speaking in a tongue **[198]** or concentrate only on speaking in a tongue, since my mind is unfruitful and it derives no benefit from such ambition.

When I sing psalms in a tongue, if I want to be approved and make use of a tongue given by the Spirit and earnestly try not to leave my mind unfruitful but raise up my mind within myself, as it were, then I must sing the psalm no less with my mind as well—that is, I must understand the meaning of the psalm in detail and not allow the words of the prophecy to go unexamined. Therefore, it is better to desire to prophesy or interpret the Holy Scriptures in church than simply to make use of tongues. **[200]**

(Cod. Pantokrator. 28)

"Therefore, one who speaks in a tongue should pray for the power to interpret," since speaking in tongues by itself would not have the power to build up the church. Here he uses the term *spirit* to refer to the grace given by the Spirit, that is, the ability to speak in tongues. **[198]**

The meaning of this passage is not entirely clear. Yet I will attempt to explain it as best I can. If I want to pray in a tongue, that is, if I want to be approved when I speak in a tongue and to try earnestly not to leave my mind unfruitful, if I want to be someone who does not only speak in a tongue but also rouses my mind within myself when I sing a psalm in a tongue, then I must sing the psalm no less with my mind by understanding the meaning of the psalm and the prophecy, and I must not allow their words to go unexamined. That is because if I should speak empty words, then "I am a noisy gong."[167] Therefore, it is better to prophesy or to interpret the divine Scriptures in church than simply to make use of tongues. What then will be better? "I will pray with the spirit, but I will pray with the mind also." He uses the term "spirit" here to refer to the gifts given by the Spirit. It is his goal to use as many considerations as he needs in order to show that speaking in a tongue is useless unless it is accompanied by the ability to explain the words of the prophet to others. Therefore, he adds additional considerations by which one may see clearly what he is saying. **[200]**

14:16-17 Otherwise, if you say a blessing with the spirit, how can anyone in the position of a private person say the "Amen" to your thanksgiving, since that person does not know what you are saying? For you may give thanks well enough, but the other person is not built up.

[167] 1 Cor 13:1.

(Cod. Vat. Gr. 762)	(Cod. Pantokrator. 28)
When you yourself speak in a tongue, he says, but someone in the rank of the laity does not know your language, how can that person supply the "Amen" in their own thanksgiving or prayers so that what seems to be lacking in completeness on the part of the priests may be supplied by the laity and God may receive "the small along with the great,"[168] as it were, in the unity of the Spirit?	When you yourself speak in a tongue, he says, but someone in the rank of the laity is ignorant of your language, how can that person supply the "Amen" to their own thanksgiving or prayers? Everyone knows that there is a custom in the church that the prayers of the presiders and the prayers of those under them come to an end at the same time. The people supply the "Amen" for those who pray to God on their behalf, adding the conclusion to the priest's words. That way whatever seems to be lacking in completeness on the part of the priests may be supplied by the laity and God may receive "the small along with the great,"[169] as it were, in the unity of the Spirit. For the laity under the priests' supervision believe that their own prayers will be received when they unite them to the prayers of the priests. This was the reason God commanded even humble offerings to be brought to the altar of burnt offerings, so that what is modest may be combined with what is complete and may become acceptable to God, since we are all one in the Lord. So, he says, when you speak in a tongue (since that is what "say a blessing with the spirit" means), how can those who do not know what you are saying "say the 'Amen' in **[202]** their own thanksgiving?" You yourself may act rightly, at least when it comes to your intentions, but "the other person is not built up." We must do everything for the sake of building up and benefiting the brothers. {You who speak in a tongue, that is, say a blessing with the spirit, act rightly in your intentions, but the other person is not built up. Everything must be done for the benefit and edification of the brothers.}[170]

15:1-2 Now I would remind you, brothers and sisters, of the good news that I proclaimed to you, which you in turn received, in which also you stand, through which also you are being saved.

(Cod. Vat. Gr. 762)	(Cod. Pantokrator. 28)
He very appropriately and wisely uses the term *good news* to refer to the proclamation of the resurrection from the dead and the proclamation of Christ himself more generally. It is, after all, an announcement of every good thing for those who have accepted the faith. He says that in it they stand and are being saved. "Standing" means that believers have a steadfast hope and right doctrine. "Being saved" means that they are found to be stronger than sin itself and they have escaped the snares of death. **[204]**	He fittingly uses the term *good news* to refer to the proclamation of the resurrection from the dead and the proclamation of Christ himself, since it supplies every good thing to believers. He says that they stand in it, signifying their steadfast hope, and that they are being saved, indicating their superiority to the very snares of death. **[204]**

15:3-9 For I handed on to you as of first importance what I in turn had received: that Christ died for our sins in accordance with the Scriptures, and that he was buried, and that he was

[168]Ps 115:13 (Ps 113:21 LXX).

[169]See note 168.

[170]Zawadzki notes that the words in braces are a repetition of the foregoing content and should not be considered genuinely Cyrilline (Zawadzki, 467n353).

raised on the third day in accordance with the Scriptures, and that he appeared to Cephas, then to the Twelve. Then he appeared to more than five hundred brothers at one time, most of whom are still alive, though some have died. Then he appeared to James, then to all the apostles. Last of all, as to one untimely born, he appeared also to me. For I am the least of the apostles, unfit to be called an apostle, because I persecuted the church of God.

(Cod. Vat. Gr. 762)

He says that he did not hand on to you something that just came into his mind or that he accepted without careful examination, but the good news that he received. He received it from the one who placed in his mind the knowledge of him who became a human being for us. Paul himself elsewhere says of the good news, "For I did not receive it from a human source, nor was I taught it, but I received it through a revelation of Jesus Christ."[171] Now if the one who hands this on is taught by God, how could what he proclaimed be untrue, namely, that "Christ died for our sins in accordance with the Scriptures" (that is, both the Old and New Testaments)? After all, there were a great many witnesses of Christ's death and resurrection. There is therefore no doubt that Christ Jesus died for us according to the flesh to take away the sin of the world[172] and that he was raised again and trampled death so that **[206]** we too may profit from this event. It is also imperative in the present passage for him to say not only that Christ died but also that he was buried. Emmanuel was placed in the tomb to give us confidence that he truly died. But he rose again, as I just said. By dying in the flesh, he proves that he was made flesh, even though the Word is God. And by trampling death, he manifestly demonstrates that he is God by nature. However, the Word of God the Father does not give life to someone else's temple or to a body that strictly belongs to someone else. Rather, he gives life to his own body through which he is said to die for us so that the benefit of the resurrection may truly be ours as well.[173] You see, the entire human nature was trampling death in him. That is why we are said to be buried and raised with him[174] and seated with him "in the heavenly places."[175] Then he says that he was raised in accordance with the Scriptures and that he appeared to the holy apostles, first to a select few and then to a great many. Then "as to one untimely born" among the apostles, "he appeared also to me." He is very humble and insists that he persecuted the church, but he received mercy from Christ

(Cod. Pantokrator. 28)

He says that he did not hand on something that just came into his mind or that he took to heart without careful examination, but the good news that he received from Christ himself, who placed in his mind the knowledge of him who became a human being for us.

{He says that he did not hand on something that just came into his mind, but the good news that he received from the one who placed in his mind the knowledge of him who became a human being for us.}[176]

After all, the death of Christ was prophesied by the Law and the Prophets as well as the evangelical and apostolic oracles. There is therefore no doubt that Christ died for us according to the flesh to take away the sin of the world[177] and he was raised again and trampled **[206]** death so that we too may profit from this event.

By dying in the flesh he proves that he was made flesh, even though he is God and therefore impassible. And by rising again, he proves that he is God by nature. Just as suffering is a human characteristic, so also conquering death is a divine one. Thus we are said to be buried and raised with him[178] and even to be seated with him in heaven.[179] He is not talking about Christ's two natures,[180] but he is saying that in Christ all of humanity, or rather the entire human race, obtains immortality and the other blessings.

Then he was raised and appeared to the holy apostles, first to a select few.

[171]Gal 1:12.
[172]Cf. 1 Pet 4:1; Jn 1:29.
[173]This comment seems to be directed against the view of Nestorius.
[174]Cf. Col 2:12.
[175]Eph 2:6.
[176]Since this section is almost a verbatim repetition of the previous sentence, Zawadzki notes that it should not be considered genuine (Zawadzki, 470n356).
[177]See note 172.
[178]See note 174.
[179]See note 175.
[180]φύσεις. Cyril often says that Christ has one nature, but here he speaks of two.

(Cod. Vat. Gr. 762)	(Cod. Pantokrator. 28)
and was called to his apostolic office. He made known the great mystery of the resurrection. **[208]** This mystery was not unknown to the ancient saints, since it was announced beforehand, nor was it unknown to those chosen to be apostles, who were "eyewitnesses and servants of the word."[181]	He is very humble, and he persecuted the church, yet he insists that he received mercy from Christ and was called to his apostolic office. **[208]**

15:12 Now if Christ is proclaimed as raised from the dead, how can some of you say there is no resurrection of the dead?

(Cod. Vat. Gr. 762)	(Cod. Pantokrator. 28)
He is astounded at those who are persuaded (I know not how) to oppose the holy and divine Scriptures and have the audacity to take a different position. After all, if Christ died not to remain dead, but to overpower death and decay and to become for human nature a road, as it were, and a door leading to the power to overcome decay and return to life, and if the one who died for us has risen again so that we may have life with him, how can they now bind with the cords of death those for whom Emmanuel, who is God by nature, is said to have died and returned to life? How can they remove the human race from the benefits of the resurrection and misrepresent the culmination of the *oikonomia* in the flesh? If Christ has become "the firstfruits of those who have died"[182] and "the firstborn from the dead,"[183] then all the rest will surely follow their firstfruits. **[210]** They will accompany the firstborn, and rightly so, since he is the firstborn. The divinely inspired Paul himself will be our witness: "For if we have been united with him in a death like his, we will certainly be united with him in a resurrection like his."[184]	He is astounded at the audacity of those who dare to contradict the entirety of the Holy Scriptures. After all, if Christ died not to remain dead, but to overpower death and decay and to become a way for human beings to return to life and overcome decay, and if Christ who died for us (even though he is God by nature) rose again so that we may be made alive with him, how can some deprive the human race of the benefits of the resurrection and misrepresent the culmination of the *oikonomia* in the flesh? Those who claim that Christ has not been raised deny the consummation of the *oikonomia* in the flesh. If Christ has become "the firstfruits of those who have died,"[188] and "the firstborn from the dead,"[189] all the rest will surely follow the **[210]** firstfruits and the firstborn. They are the ones of whom he is the firstborn.
Now when some people acknowledge that Christ has been raised but deny the mystery of the resurrection of the dead, they are utterly ignorant of the reason for the incarnation[185] of the Only Begotten. God the Word did not become a human being for his own benefit, but "instead of the joy that was set before him, he endured the cross, disregarding its shame."[186] The most-wise Paul himself teaches us the reason when he says, "Since, therefore, the children share flesh and blood, he himself likewise shared the same things, so that through death he might destroy the one who has the power of death, that is, the devil, and free those who all their lives were held in slavery by the fear of death."[187]	Now when some people acknowledge that Christ was raised but reject the mystery of the resurrection of the dead, they are ignorant of the reason for the incarnation[190] of the Only Begotten. The Word of God did not become a human being for his own benefit, but to free us from death.
Now if death has not been rendered powerless, then his plan is pointless and the mystery of	Now if death has not been rendered powerless, then his plan is pointless and useless to us, since we have utterly failed to obtain the hope of life.

[181]Lk 1:2.
[182]1 Cor 15:20.
[183]Col 1:18.
[184]Rom 6:5.
[185]ἐνανθρωπήσεως. Literally "inhumanization."
[186]Heb 12:2.
[187]Heb 2:14-15.
[188]See note 182.
[189]See note 183.
[190]See note 185.

(Cod. Vat. Gr. 762)

the *oikonomia* in the flesh is useless to us. We have utterly failed to obtain the hope of life. How then have we been called to adoption and how are we the children of God, as **[212]** the wise John says?[191] If it is true that "we wait for adoption, the redemption of our bodies,"[192] what kind of redemption will it be if Christ has not made us stronger than death? How will he "transform the body of our humiliation that it may be conformed to the body of his glory"?[193] When will this happen if death has not been neutralized? What kind of transformation will they have who will stay the same, or rather change for the worse? Notice how skillfully he brings us around to the necessary conclusion that we must say that our earthly bodies will be returned to life at the right time. If, he says, throughout the entire divinely inspired Scriptures Christ has been proclaimed as risen from the dead, "how can some of you say there is no resurrection from the dead?" He died, as we said before, not for himself but for us so that—since he is life by nature as God—he might destroy death by the death of his own flesh and human nature might follow him. He returned to life and became a kind of firstfruits of a humanity that crosses over to life, is re-created in incorruption, and conquers death. Whatever is in Christ is a new creation.[194] **[214]** Since this has begun, how will we remain in the ground? How can some of you have the audacity to claim that the dead will not return to life? These people seem to be the Sadducees, since they are the ones who said that "there is no resurrection, or angel, or spirit."[195] Hymenaeus and Alexander also falsified the mystery of the resurrection "by claiming that the resurrection has already taken place."[196] But they suffered shipwreck in the faith,[197] along with everyone who wants to follow their foolishness.[198]

(Cod. Pantokrator. 28)

When he says "some" he is hinting at the Sadducees, who deny that there is a resurrection or angel or spirit.[199] Hymenaeus and Alexander also falsified the mystery of the resurrection. But they suffered shipwreck in the faith.[200]

15:13-15 If there is no resurrection of the dead, then Christ has not been raised; and if Christ has not been raised, then our proclamation has been in vain and your faith has been in vain. We are even found to be misrepresenting God, because we testified of God that he raised Christ—whom he did not raise if it is true that the dead are not raised.

[191]Cf. 1 Jn 3:2.
[192]Rom 8:23.
[193]Phil 3:21.
[194]Cf. 2 Cor 5:17.
[195]Acts 23:8.
[196]2 Tim 2:18; cf. 1 Tim 1:19-20.
[197]Cf. 1 Tim 1:19.
[198]It is not entirely clear who was denying the resurrection in Cyril's day. Zawadzki suggests that Cyril probably has the Origenists in mind, since Methodius of Olympus had earlier attested that they deny the resurrection. See Zawadzki 477n377.
[199]See note 195.
[200]See note 197.

(Cod. Vat. Gr. 762)	(Cod. Pantokrator. 28)
The second follows from the first, as it were, and the first goes with the second. When this happens, that is, when we believe this, the proclamation of the holy apostles will be in vain, and the faith is in vain. So is the word of faith[201] that through the saints guides initiates all over the world. How then **[216]** can we still believe if he did not return to life, as some claim? "We are even found," he says, "to be misrepresenting God," because we said that "he raised Christ—whom he did not raise if it is true that the dead are not raised." In that case, how could such a great multitude of saints escape the charge of falsification? They should not even be saints. How could they be? They would suffer from the sin of lying against God. But that is not how things are. The mystagogues are not lying when they say that Christ has been raised.	Now if the dead are not raised, neither has Christ been raised. The second follows from the first, and the first goes with the second. When this is believed, the proclamation of the apostles will be in vain and impotent. The faith too will be in vain. It will turn out to be a lie, and the apostles could be accused of telling pointless fables. If we say that this claim is true, it will carry us to other absurdities too. **[216]** A great multitude of saints will be subject to the charge of falsification as well, since they testified in contradiction to God, who did not raise Christ. They should not even be called saints. They suffer from the sin of lying against God, and they should be punished. The faith is futile.

15:17 If Christ has not been raised, your faith is futile and you are still in your sins.

(Cod. Vat. Gr. 762)	(Cod. Pantokrator. 28)
He is quite right and utterly truthful to add this to his other statements. Faith justifies,[202] but if someone subscribes to the futile notion that Christ was not raised, what difference does it ultimately make? We are still subject to the ancient charges, and our sin is not washed away. In vain did the divinely inspired psalmist say, "Lord, you were favorable to your land. You forgave the iniquity of your people; you covered all their sin."[203] And again, "Blessed are those whose transgressions are forgiven, whose sins are covered. Blessed is the man to whom **[218]** the Lord imputes no iniquity."[204] And the blessed Paul says in the epistle to the Romans that the blessedness referred to in this passage extends both to the circumcised and to the Gentiles.[205] For we have been justified in Christ, "who was handed over for our trespasses and was raised for our justification."[206]	If Christ has not been raised, what is left to justify us? We are still subject to the ancient charges since we have not washed away the filth of our sin. **[218]**

15:18 Then those also who have fallen asleep in Christ have perished.

(Cod. Vat. Gr. 762)	(Cod. Pantokrator. 28)
They have been deceived, it seems, and have given their lives for him without reward if Christ has not been raised.	The holy martyrs have been deceived, it seems, and they have given their lives for him without reward. They can in no way boast of the glory of their genuine relation to him, even though the blessed Stephen became the firstfruits of the holy martyrs when he offered his own

[201]Cf. Rom 10:8.
[202]Cf. Rom 5:1.
[203]Ps 85:1-2 (Ps 85:2-3 LXX).
[204]Ps 32:1-2.
[205]Cf. Rom 4:9.
[206]Rom 4:25.

(Cod. Vat. Gr. 762)	(Cod. Pantokrator. 28)
If the hope of the saints is not full of immortality,[207] if they do not expect to reign with him, then perhaps they have perished. But away with such terrible ignorance! "For the dead will be resurrected and those in the tombs will be raised," as the prophet says.[208] **[220]**	death as a sweet-smelling offering to God. But if Christ has not been raised, if the hope of the saints is not full of immortality,[209] if they do not expect to reign with him, then perhaps they have perished and receive a penalty for their efforts in that they have endured death itself to no benefit. But away with such terrible ignorance! "For the dead will be resurrected"[210] and the distributor of crowns will weigh out to each one what is most appropriate, and he will surely impose punishment on the ungodly. **[220]** As God, he is the judge of all. {And perhaps they have perished if the hope of the saints is not full of immortality, if they do not expect to reign with him.}[211]

15:20-23 But in fact Christ has been raised from the dead. He has become the firstfruits of those who have fallen asleep. For since death came through a human being, the resurrection of the dead has also come through a human being; for as all die in Adam, so all will be made alive in Christ. But each in his own order: Christ the firstfruits, then at his coming those who belong to Christ.

(Cod. Vat. Gr. 762)	(Cod. Pantokrator. 28)
He takes it as a given that we must believe that Christ returned to life and became the firstfruits of those who have fallen asleep, the first one on earth to trample death, just as our forefather Adam was of course the first one to enter into death and to become the firstfruits of those who have fallen into decay. And he adds that the resurrection of the dead will follow the resurrection of our Savior when he says, "For since death came through a human being, the resurrection of the dead has also come through a human being." Observe how once again he shows that the mystery of the *oikonomia* in the flesh is replete with God-befitting craftsmanship. It was necessary—necessary, he says—that a human being conquer death on our behalf. This is the reason why God the Word, who came from God, did not take on[212] the nature of angels, as Paul says, but the seed of Abraham: to **[222]** be made like his brothers in all things.[213] It was necessary, as I said, that what was sick be healed and what had fallen be raised up. It was necessary that what had come under the power of death through transgression and sin should overcome death through obedience and righteousness. This is why the only begotten Word of God, who knew no sin, became a human being: so that	Since it is a given that Christ returned to life and became the firstfruits of those who have fallen asleep, the first one on earth to trample death, the resurrection of the dead will surely follow the resurrection of the Savior. **[222]**
just as all were condemned in Adam when human nature experienced death, so also we will be justified in Christ and put off sin along with the death that springs from it.	Just as all were condemned in Adam when human nature experienced the fall through his disobedience, so also we will be justified in Christ and put off sin along with the death that springs from it.

[207]Cf. Wis 3:4.
[208]Is 26:19.
[209]See note 207.
[210]See note 208.
[211]The words in braces are a repetition of foregoing material. Zawadzki considers them inauthentic (Zawadzki, 485n386).
[212]The verb here echoes Phil 2:7, "taking on the form of a slave."
[213]Heb 2:16-17.

(Cod. Vat. Gr. 762)

The divinely inspired Paul himself will be our witness when he says, "Just as by the one man's disobedience the many were made sinners."[214] Therefore, "as all die in Adam," since our nature was condemned in him by his transgression, as I said, "so all will be made alive in Christ," since our nature is correspondingly blessed in him in the same way by his justification. The second condition, then, redeems us from the first. "For he was handed over for our transgressions and was raised for our justification."[215] Therefore, when he was raised, we were raised with him as well. The Word of God is life by nature, and he grants this good attribute of his nature (I mean life) not only to his own flesh, but **[224]** he conveys it to the entirety of human nature. Christ has undoubtedly been raised as the firstfruits "so that he might come to have first place in everything," as it is written.[216] Then the resurrection of the others will follow at the proper time. However, as you might expect, this will not take place chaotically but decorously and in order, "with a command." You see, it is only after the firstfruits (that is, Christ) that it says that those who belong to him will be raised. This clearly refers to those who lived at the time of his advent, or more precisely those who were born after the incarnation and fell asleep in faith. There were, of course, holy people in Israel at that time, when the life of the law was held in high regard and still held sway. But those in Christ were better, since they were justified by faith and became participants of the divine nature[217] and were enriched by the spirit of adoption.[218] They have been called into brotherhood by the grace of him who is the true Son by nature. Those under the law had the spirit of slavery, but we cry out, "Abba! Father!"[219] Therefore, those in Christ are better, as I said, than the ancients. And so **[226]** he says that they will be raised first since they followed in the footsteps of him who is the first of all. Because they are bound more closely to him, they also receive greater honor than the others. Our Lord Jesus Christ himself hints at something like this in the Gospel parables as well. He said that when evening came, the master who hired laborers for his vineyard said to his manager, "Call the laborers and give them their pay, beginning with the last and then going to the first."[220]

(Cod. Pantokrator. 28)

The second condition, then, redeems us from the first, and the righteousness and obedience that we find in Christ effect an overthrow of what happened to our nature because of sin. Therefore, when Christ was raised, we were raised with him as well. Since the Word of God is life by nature, he granted this good attribute of his nature (I mean life) not only to his own flesh, **[224]** but he conveyed it to the entirety of human nature.

[226]

15:24 Then comes the end, when he hands over the kingdom to God the Father, after he has destroyed every dominion and every authority and power.

[214]Rom 5:19.
[215]Rom 4:25.
[216]Col 1:18.
[217]2 Pet 4:1.
[218]Rom 8:15.
[219]Rom 8:15.
[220]Mt 20:8.

He says that the kingdom will be handed over to God the Father by the Son when every dominion of the unclean spirits has been destroyed and when death itself is utterly neutralized.

15:28 When all things are subjected to him, then the Son himself will also be subjected to the one who put all things in subjection under him, so that God may be all in all.

Some try to disparage the Son, to the extent that they can, by saying that he hands the kingdom over to the Father and is subjected to him since the Father is greater. We must reply that the Son submitted to a voluntary emptying when he became like us. He came from the heights, as it were, and humbled himself. When he was in the same form as and equal to the Father, he was hidden in God, but he will be revealed in glory at the end of the present age. He now sits at the right hand of the Father. But if he is dragged down from the honor that he now has, is he therefore subjected to a second emptying? And if he hands over the kingdom, how will he come "with the holy angels in the glory of his Father?"[221] **[228]** If he reigns with the Father now but loses the kingdom then, it would not be desirable for the Son "to put all his enemies under his feet."[222] Though the Son is subjected to the Father, he is not for that reason less than the Father. The concept of subjection is not a definition of nature or substance, but it indicates a manner of action. Even when it occurs among us, it does not indicate that people are of different substances from each other. How could it? The son is subject to the father, the slave to the master, the student to the teacher, the subordinates under a yoke to the leader. But in none of these cases is the principle of consubstantiality compromised. They are still the same species as each other. And even though they have this manner of action, the subjects and the leaders are similar to each other, and they do not dishonor the lesser condition since it is beneficial. Furthermore, how can these people let our weak condition hold sway for God? If the Son's subjection is an attribute or a capacity of his nature, as they claim, then freedom from subjection is an attribute of his other nature.[223] And I suppose the latter nature is in a better condition than the former, if indeed subjection is worse. In the *oikonomia*, he is subjected for us, after all. This is how: When humanity sinned, it became subject to decay and the devil and the demons, and it was separated from him who is God by nature. The Only Begotten became human for us and neutralized the power of death. He also took away the root of death, which is sin. He cast out the ruler of this world.[224] After he has accomplished all these things and the entire *oikonomia* has been fulfilled, he will hand over (that is, present) the kingdom to the Father—the kingdom that was once stolen and taken over by others—and restore the Father's rule over everything on earth. Once death has been destroyed along with the tyrant Satan, the Son will once again have superiority in the coming age over all authority. **[230]**

15:35-38 But someone will ask, "How are the dead raised? With what kind of body do they come?" Fool! What you sow does not come to life unless it dies. And as for what you sow, you do not sow the body that is to be, but a bare seed, perhaps of wheat or some other grain. But God gives it a body as he has chosen, and to each kind of seed its own body.

[221]Mt 16:27.

[222]1 Cor 15:25.

[223]Note that Cyril explicitly refers to Christ as having two *natures*.

[224]Cf. Jn 12:31.

(Cod. Vat. Gr. 762)

The prophet Isaiah announces ahead of time the mystery of the resurrection of the dead, saying that it will take place at the proper time when God gives the nod and by his ineffable power restores to life those who have been overcome by death. Isaiah says, "The dead will be raised and those in the tombs will be awakened and those in the earth will rejoice. For your dew is their medicine."[225] I think dew refers figuratively to the life-giving energy of God by which he ascribes being to those who do not exist and he grants well-being to those who have already been called into existence. All things hold together in him just as surely as they were brought into being through him. The divinely inspired David also sings somewhere to God the Savior of all regarding those on earth: "When you open your hand, all creatures will be filled with good things. When you hide your face, they will be dismayed; when you take away their breath, they will die and return to their dust. When you send forth your spirit, they will be created and you will renew the face **[232]** of the ground."[226] Human nature has experienced a turning away from God's face in Adam because of his transgression. Therefore, it has all but been thrown into confusion and disorder. It has reverted to its own dust and has been dragged down into death and decay. But since the Only Begotten Word of God has become like us and we have been enriched by participation in the Holy Spirit,[227] we are transformed to our original condition and we have been re-created, as it were. For we have been called to newness of life,[228] and so we escape the power of death. The most-wise Paul will be our witness of this when he says, "If the Spirit of him who raised Jesus from the dead dwells in you, he who raised Christ Jesus from the dead will give life to your mortal bodies also through his Spirit that dwells in you."[229] Now since Christ has returned to life, trampling the power of death, and has become the firstfruits of those who have fallen asleep—which means that they will surely follow in his footsteps—would you not have to be completely out of your mind to have any more doubt about the mystery of the resurrection? **[234]**

(Cod. Pantokrator. 28)

If any should decide out of too much curiosity to apply the eye of their mind to the works of the divine nature and to try to examine the manner in which each thing **[234]** was brought into being and the origin of its existence, they would never stop asking the insane question, "How?" How was the sky made? Out of what kind of matter and where did it come from? What kind of foundation does it have? How, where, and when was the earth fixed firm? How was the course of the sun brought into being? How about the moon and the stars and the rest of creation? How did the Creator of the universe take dust from the earth and fashion the man? How was earth transformed into bones and sinews and flesh? If we are not in a position to give an explanation for everything that is created and for that reason we deny that they have come into being at all, where would that line of reasoning (or rather, that attempt at mischief) ultimately lead us?

[225]Is 26:19.
[226]Ps 104:28-30 (Ps 103:28-30 LXX).
[227]Cf. Heb 6:4.
[228]Cf. Rom 6:4.
[229]Rom 8:11.

(Cod. Vat. Gr. 762)

But perhaps you will say the following: Yes, you are correct. I will now drop my insistence on asking how the dead are raised. But I must still know with what kind of bodies they come. Will this earthly body that is subject to decay come to life? Or will it be a different body, though one that comes from it? I, at least, would give this direct answer: the orthodox faith teaches that we will be resurrected with the same flesh. After all, that is how Christ returned to life as "the firstborn **[236]** from the dead, the firstfruits of those who have fallen asleep."[230] But since this teaching intensely displeases some people, come let us bring up the position they think is correct and then say what is actually right. (Then he presents the myths of those who say that souls preexist their bodies. He then continues:) In that case how can God be glorified for fashioning humanity? He says somewhere to the blessed Job, "Did you take clay from the ground, form a living creature, and set it with the power of speech on the earth?"[231] I think that fashioning a rational being from the earth would surpass all wonder. Furthermore, how did the Creator bless the newly created man who was formed from the earth, saying, "Increase and multiply and fill the earth"?[232] (And he brings up many other arguments against them and then adds:) the divinely inspired Paul uses the most excellent example when he says that the body falls into the ground like a seed. A seed does not rise bare, as it was sown, but with the clothing and adornment that its nature ordinarily provides for it. I mean a stalk and leaves. "For God gives," he says, "to each kind of seed its own body." He is saying that not all who sleep will return to life in glory, though they will all have imperishability. After all, it would not be fitting for God to crown the violent and the evildoers with glory. **[238]** Thus he profitably reminds us of the different seeds to which God distributes however he wills, giving one form to one and another to another. For he says, "As for what you sow, you do not sow the body that is to be."

(Cod. Pantokrator. 28)

In the wake of Christ's resurrection, it is foolish, ignorant, and pretentious to cast doubt on the resurrection and ask "how?" regarding the works of God. It is just as silly to ask with what kind of bodies the dead are raised. Clearly, the bodies are the same. Indeed, the Lord raised his own flesh just as it was before. **[236]**

The most-wise Paul skillfully says that the body falls into the ground like a seed. But it will not rise this way. Rather, it will rise with clothing and adornment that its nature ordinarily provides for it. In this way he teaches that in the resurrection, the body is clothed with the glory of God and it is enriched with imperishability.

15:40 There are both heavenly bodies and earthly bodies, but the glory of the heavenly is one thing, and that of the earthly is another.

Each body, insofar as it is a body, has and is named by the same definition. But they are distinguished from one another by some other principle. The bodies of all people will be raised to life in incorruption, but there will be a difference regarding their glory and adornment. God will bring this about when he distributes to each one what that person deserves.

15:41-42a There is one glory of the sun, and another glory of the moon, and another glory of the stars; indeed, star differs from star in glory. So it is with the resurrection of the dead.

[230]Col 1:18; 1 Cor 15:20.
[231]Job 38:14 (LXX).
[232]Gen 1:28.

Paul just introduced two examples for us: that of the seed and that showing the difference in glory of the heavenly bodies. We must understand that he makes the first into an image of the resurrection of the dead. He says the following:

15:42b-43 What is sown is perishable, what is raised is imperishable. It is sown in dishonor, it is raised in glory. It is sown in weakness, it is raised in power.

(Cod. Vat. Gr. 762)

Just as the grain of wheat elicits wonder since it is thrown bare and dead into the dirt but grows up clothed with a body and outfitted with beauty, so also the human body is sown perishable, **[240]** weak, and dishonored but it is brought back to life in honor and imperishability and it is clothed with power. The sobriety of the divinely inspired author is worthy of our admiration. He is firm in the faith and believes without a doubt that he will rise again. So he likens the perishing of the body with sowing, drawing a very skillful and exceedingly apt comparison between the nature of the matter and the illustration. Like a seed, the body will come to life not bare, he says, but clothed with imperishability, glory, and strength as well. Indeed, grace from above and the incomparable power of the Creator of the universe will transform it to the opposite of its present condition by enriching it with a spiritual mind. Within the body that is fallen and sown into the earth, as it were, in perishability and weakness, there is a natural mind lacking in beauty. We say that this is the same thing as a fleshly and earthly mind. When it was brought into being in the beginning, however, it was not like this by nature. Rather, this condition slipped in because of the transgression and the judgment of death. Nature, however, calls us back to what we were in the beginning. **[242]** The removal of this interposed condition must be accomplished by the power and working of God. Then the participation in the original good that we had in the beginning will be restored. We have been renewed in Christ according to the Scriptures. As the holy prophet said, "Take heart, Zion! Do not let your hands grow weak. The Lord, your God, is in your midst. He is mighty to save you, and he will renew you in his love."[233] When God the Father loved us, then—then!—he also renewed us in Christ. Indeed, it is true that in him everything is a "new creation. Everything old has passed away and has become new."[234] What does he mean by "old"? That which is past. And what is "new"? That which has been introduced. Perishability and weakness are old, as are shame and the accusations against the natural mind. But through Christ, glory and imperishability and power and a spiritual mind are new. They will be our "spiritual body." **[244]**

(Cod. Pantokrator. 28)

Like a seed, the body will come to life not bare, but clothed with imperishability, glory, and strength. Indeed it will be enriched by having a spiritual mind.

Within the body that is sown into the earth in perishability and weakness, there is a lack of beauty. **[242]**

By the power of God, the participation in the original good that we had in the beginning is brought about once again: imperishability, glory, and power. After all, that which is renewed does not somehow return to the beginning of its existence, but it returns to the condition it had in the beginning. **[244]**

---

[233] Zeph 3:16-17.
[234] 2 Cor 5:17.

15:44-45 It is sown a soul body, it is raised a spiritual body. There is a soul body, there is also a spiritual body. Thus it is written, "The first man, Adam, became a living soul"; the last Adam became a life-giving spirit.[235]

(Cod. Vat. Gr. 762)

I, however, would say that a spiritual body is not a body that is in the form of a shadow or an incorporeal spirit, but rather a body that is completely freed from a carnal earthly mind.

If some should choose to refer to our earthly body as a soul body, it would be unreasonable to think they are giving it the form of a soul. Rather, they are using the term to refer to the "soul" kind of mind, or more specifically, the mind of the flesh, just as of course **[246]** we also consider our human wisdom to be related to the soul and earthly.[236] Thus, even though the body may be called "soul," I do not think anyone who gives it the form of the soul would escape the charge of error, since depending on how people live even while they are still in these earthly bodies, some are called "soul" people and some are called "spiritual." It is written, "Those who are soul people do not receive the gifts of God's Spirit, for they are foolishness to them. Those who are spiritual people discern all things, and they themselves are subject to no one else's scrutiny."[237] And since it was fitting for him to confirm this statement with facts, he adds, "The first man, Adam, became a living soul; the last Adam became a life-giving spirit." Now he called Adam a soul person (since that is what I think it means that he was created a living soul) because Adam was not completely free of carnal desires. Now if you examine the nature of the matter, the yearnings that are directed and turned to the passions of the flesh, even when they have the approval of the law, are nevertheless actually failings of carnal weakness. Let me give you an example. "Let marriage be held in honor, and **[248]** let the marriage bed be kept undefiled."[238] The motion of the sexual appetite was implanted in the nature of the body by the Creator of the universe to give the living being a desire for procreation. It was said to the man,

(Cod. Pantokrator. 28)

What would a "spiritual body" be, O mystagogue? Will it no longer be flesh? Will it no longer consist of bones and tendons, as it does now, by which the nature of our body is completed? Is he saying that it will be subtle and airy and less than shadows? Not at all! If any think this is the case, then what will return to life is surely not what fell into the ground, but something else that does not resemble it at all. I, however, would say that a spiritual body is not a body that is in the form of a shadow or an incorporeal spirit, but rather a body that is completely freed from a carnal earthly mind. If there is, he says, a soul body, there is also a spiritual one. If some should choose to refer to our earthly body as a soul body, it would be unreasonable to think they are giving it the form of a soul. Rather, they are using the term to refer to the "soul" kind of mind, or more specifically, the mind of the flesh. **[246]** Thus, even though the body may be called "soul," I do not think anyone who gives it the form of the soul would escape the charge of error. It would be reasonable to understand carnal thinking as related to the soul and spiritual thinking as spiritual. **[248]**

---

[235]Cyril has the same Greek text as modern New Testaments. Modern English translations, however, translate σῶμα ψυχικόν (soul body) as "physical body" or "natural body" to make it read more smoothly in English. I have opted for a more awkward literal translation so that the reader can more easily follow Cyril's argument. Cyril links the soul with the flesh on the basis of Paul's citation of Gen 2:7, which states that Adam became a living "soul." The word *soul*, therefore, is associated with the first Adam, while the word *spirit* is associated with Christ, the second Adam.

[236]Jas 3:15. Cyril is here rejecting the Origenist view that the term σῶμα ψυχικόν (soul body) refers to an incorporeal resurrection body. See Zawadzki, 509.

[237]1 Cor 2:14-15. Again, I have rendered ψυχικὸς ἄνθρωπος as "soul people" so the reader can more easily follow Cyril's argument.

[238]Heb 13:4.

(Cod. Vat. Gr. 762)

"Be fruitful and multiply, and fill the earth."[239] And the Creator, it says, in the beginning "made them male and female."[240] Therefore, the desire that is aimed only at procreation is blameless. Yet as far as the nature of the act is concerned, the passion is carnal or related to the soul. It is the same with the other innocent passions. Therefore, the first man, Adam, became a living soul, while the second man from heaven, that is, Christ, became not so much a soul, but a life-giving spirit. God the Word, who came from God the Father by nature, united what was human to himself and lived not a human life like ours, but a divine, God-befitting, and completely blameless life. He "committed no sin"[241] since his mind was untouched by inordinate pleasures and was not overcome by the desire for food. Even though we see him partaking in food and drink (since we believe he was truly human like we are), **[250]** he partook of them in freedom. Though he was in the flesh for us in the *oikonomia,* he was still superior to the flesh. As God, he was a life-giving spirit. Our forefather Adam did not handle his desire for food in a completely blameless fashion. He was created as a "living soul" and as such was weaker than the desire for food. He ate from the tree of life even though God's law forbade him from doing it. Now the term *soul*[242] does not refer to distinctions in our nature, but rather to the quality of the morals and behavior in our life. One person is held down by a mind that is more earthly and carnal, while another is glorious in the freedom of the spirit. He makes this clear from his comparison of the first and second Adam. Both of them came to have earthly bodies, but the quality of their minds and the fact that they chose different ways of life showed that one was "soul" and the other was incomparably better, that is, "spiritual."

(Cod. Pantokrator. 28)

A "spiritual" body is not one that is shadowy and airy. No, it too is composed of bones and sinews. But it is completely free of a carnal earthly mind. Furthermore, we say that this "soul" body does not have the form of a soul. Rather, it has a "soul" kind of mind, that is, a carnal mind. In the same way, we understand our human wisdom to be a "soul" kind of wisdom.[243]

15:46 But it is not the spiritual that is first, but that which is related to the soul, and then the spiritual.

Next he takes up the topic of the time in which they came to be. He says, "But it is not the spiritual that is first, but that which is related to the soul, and then the spiritual." Since he said that the "soul" kind of body is sown into the earth and the "spiritual" body comes back to life, he shows clearly that it is not contrary to human nature to transform from a "soul" kind of mind to a "spiritual" one. How could what is related to "soul" be older than the "spiritual"? What could be the proof of this?[244] [252]

15:47-49 The first man was from the earth, a man of dust; the second man is the Lord from heaven. As was the man of dust, so are those who are of the dust; and as is the man of heaven,

[239]Gen 1:28.
[240]Mt 19:4.
[241]1 Pet 2:22.
[242]ψυχικός. The Greek word is an adjective, but there is no adjectival form of "soul" in English.
[243]Cf. Jas 3:15.
[244]Since the text we have does not answer these questions, it seems likely that the catenist omitted part of Cyril's interpretation of this verse (Zawadzki, 515).

so are those who are of heaven. Just as we have borne the image of the man of dust, we will also bear the image of the man of heaven.

He says that the first man (that is, Adam) was created a living soul (that is, earthly and carnal), while the second man is from heaven. That is because even though the Word of God became flesh according to the Scriptures,[245] he was nevertheless "from above" and "from heaven" and "above all,"[246] as John says. So they were both in earthly bodies, as I said, but they were not the same when it came to their thinking and way of life. The first man had a carnal mind, while the second was a life-giving spirit from heaven. "We have borne the image of the man of dust" (that is, the likeness of Adam), and so we are subject to passions and we sin in our weakness and we bear the yoke of perishability. In the same way, "we will also bear the image of the man of heaven" (that is, Christ), and so we have become superior to carnal desires and the will to sin and we have now conquered death itself, that terrible ancient foreboding tyrant that ruled so fiercely over us.

15:50 What I am saying, brothers, is this: flesh and blood cannot inherit the kingdom of God, nor does the perishable inherit the imperishable.

With these words he introduces the mystery of the resurrection. As long as the human body is flesh and blood (that is, mortal and perishable), it could not inherit the kingdom of God (that is, continuous existence). Therefore, it is absolutely necessary that perishability be swallowed up and the withering body be taken away. It must be transformed to imperishability and gleam with a kind of divine and ineffable glory. Then it will inherit the kingdom of God. **[254]**

15:51-52 Behold, I will tell you a mystery! We will not all fall asleep, but we will all be changed, in a moment, in the twinkling of an eye, at the last trumpet. For the trumpet will sound, and the dead will be raised imperishable, and we will be changed.

Great and truly heavenly is the mystery! It was surely revealed to him through Christ, who is speaking in him[247] "in whom are hidden all the treasures of wisdom and knowledge."[248] He himself is the distributor of the coming good gifts that we wait for. He himself will transform creation and renew the whole of it and free it from slavery and bring it "into the glory of the children of God."[249] And if that is true, then how could it not be altogether necessary that the one for whom creation exists be renewed along with creation? I mean humanity. Humanity must be new, not tyrannized by the original perishability, not forced into sin by carnal lusts, but rather raised in imperishability and strength and clothed in honor and a kind of divine glory. The divinely inspired Isaiah has said, "Your righteousness will go before you, and the glory of God will be your garment."[250] Indeed, our Lord Jesus Christ himself explicitly stated that the dead would be raised at the close of this age: "Those who are wise will shine like the brightness of the

[245]Jn 1:14.
[246]Jn 3:31.
[247]Cf. 2 Cor 13:3.
[248]Col 2:3.
[249]Rom 8:21.
[250]Is 58:8.

sky."[251] However, the grace of such honor and glory will not be given to everyone indiscriminately. That grace is fitting for those who have been chosen before others, who are conformed "to the image of his Son."[252] To be sure, the bodies of all will be raised, clothed with the grace of imperishability, but not all will be changed.[253] Rather, the wicked will remain in their dishonorable form simply because they must be punished, while only the righteous will be changed so that they have the good attribute of imperishability and are enriched by the adornment of divine glory. And so he, by his own power and God-befitting activity, "will transform the body of our humiliation that it may be conformed to the body of his glory."[254] What is the body of our humiliation? It is this body from the earth that is held by death because of that ancient curse that Christ dissolved "by becoming a curse for us."[255] The transformation will not change us into some other nature.[256] We will remain what we are, that is, human beings, but incomparably better. We will be imperishable and indestructible and glorified as well. Now what the last trumpet that wakes the dead refers to, the divinely inspired Paul himself explains to us **[256]** when he says, "For the Lord himself, with a cry of command, with the archangel's call and with the sound of God's trumpet, will descend from heaven, and the dead in Christ will rise first."[257] He likens the voice of the archangel and that divine and terrifying command to a trumpet. And even though the archangel is the one who cries out and gives the signal of resurrection to those lying in the earth, it will nevertheless be the voice of Christ. He is in fact the one who wakes the dead by his own power. It is surely not the voice of the archangel that does it. After all, all rational creatures are subject to the Lord's commands.

15:53 For this perishable body must put on imperishability, and this mortal body must put on immortality.

As far as its own nature is concerned, the human body is subject to death and decay. But it is covered with immortality when God completes it as he knows how.[258] We say that this is how the first human was created in the beginning. But when the curse came, when he ignored the command that had been given to him, he was stripped of imperishability and the robe of divine glory. That is the sense in which "they knew that they were naked."[259] At the time of the resurrection, however, there will be a restoration of the good attributes they had in the beginning. The flesh will rise clothed with immortality and enriched by the robe of divine glory.[260]

15:54b-57 Death has been swallowed up in victory. Where, O death, is your sting? Where, O Hades, is your victory? The sting of death is sin, and the power of sin is the law. But thanks be to God, who gives us the victory through our Lord Jesus Christ.

---

[251]Dan 12:3; cf. Mt 13:43.

[252]Rom 8:29.

[253]Cyril seems to be following a textual variant of 1 Cor 15:51 that reads, "we will not all be changed." See Zawadzki, 520.

[254]Phil 3:21.

[255]Gal 3:13.

[256]This comment is directed against the Origenists (Zawadzki, 522).

[257]1 Thess 4:16.

[258]Cf. Gen 2:7.

[259]Gen 3:7.

[260]This scholion is preserved in Codex Vatopedi 236, and it is not explicitly attached to a verse. Zawadzki (523) attaches it to 1 Cor 15:53 on the basis of verbal similarities.

(Cod. Vat. Gr. 762)	(Cod. Pantokrator. 28)
What kind of resurrection will it actually be if we say that what will rise is not the same thing as what was held prisoner by death? Or how will we practically prance on top of decay and say, **[258]** "Death has been swallowed up in victory," and so on? Now we must realize that the blessed Paul employed the arrangement of words in the present passage in accordance with the Hebrew version.[261] The Septuagint version does not read this way. There it is written in the prophets, "Where is your penalty, O death? Where is your sting, O Hades?"[262] However, he adds, "The sting of death is sin, and the power of sin is the law."	If what fell into the earth is not raised, but remains in the ground, how has death been conquered? How will we practically prance on top of decay and say, "Death has been swallowed up in **[258]** victory," that is, complete victory? The apostle then cited the verse in accordance with the Hebrew version,[266] not the Septuagint, which reads, "Where is your penalty, O death? Where is your sting, O Hades?"[267]
After all, the one who has the power of death (that is, Satan) strikes like a scorpion. And he strikes in no other way than through sin. But the Savior has given us the power to "tread on snakes and scorpions, and over all the power of the enemy."[263] The sting of death was destroyed when sin was removed so that it no longer has the law as its power, since the law condemns sinners. That is why the divinely inspired Paul says that the law is the power of sin. This too has been dissolved in Christ, since sin will not rule over us because we are not under law but under grace.[264] "Apart from the law, sin lies dead."[265] Who then supplies us with all these things? Who is the prince of righteousness? Who is the giver of freedom? Who is the fount and cause of every good thing? We can learn this from the blessed Paul, who says, "Thanks be to God, who gives us the victory through our Lord Jesus Christ."	Satan, who has the sting of death, strikes like a scorpion in no other way than through sin. Christ, however, destroyed the sting of death when sin was removed so that it no longer has the law as its power. The law is the power of sin because it condemns sinners. This too has been dissolved in Christ. Therefore, death has been destroyed as well.

[261] Paul's words do not match either the Hebrew or the Septuagint, so we may infer either that Cyril is not basing his comment on analysis of the Hebrew (Zawadzki, 526) or that Cyril has access to a textual tradition that is no longer available to us.

[262] Hos 13:14 (LXX).

[263] Lk 10:19.

[264] Cf. Rom 6:14.

[265] Rom 7:8.

[266] See note 261.

[267] See note 262.

COMMENTARY ON THE SECOND EPISTLE TO THE CORINTHIANS (FRAGMENTS)

[320]* Book 1, Logos 1

1:1 Paul, an apostle of Jesus Christ by the will of God, and Timothy our brother.

The most-wise apostle Paul says that he was chosen and placed into ministry for Christ "by the will of God." He thereby rejects the glory of the false prophets and apostles. He speaks in the Spirit and has Jesus himself dwelling in his soul. That is why he says in one place, "And I think that I too have the Spirit of God,"[1] and in another, "Since you desire proof that Christ is speaking in me."[2] He says that he is Christ's servant, even though God alone rules and has authority over all things. After all, the statement "All things are your servants"[3] is addressed to God. So is he not clearly ascribing to Christ the natural and truly God-befitting glory of lordship? **[321]**

He proclaims Jesus to be God truly and by nature by the fact that he calls himself an apostle of Jesus. No one would be an apostle of human beings; one would only be an apostle of one who is God by nature. Furthermore, he shows that he was not called to his apostolic office against the will of the Father, nor does he speak from his own heart like the false prophets, but he is a minister of the oracles of God. And he makes Timothy the coauthor of the letter because Timothy is tested and follows in his footsteps. The fact that they agree makes him all the more persuasive. As the law says, "Every matter will be established by the mouth of two or three witnesses."[4]

To the church of God that is in Corinth.

They write, "to the church of God that is in Corinth," even though the church is said to belong to Christ since he presented her to himself as a holy virgin.[5] Therefore, if the church belongs to God, and Christ presented her to himself, then he who is from holy Mary, *theotokos*,[6] is himself God by nature.

1:2 Grace to you and peace from God our Father and the Lord Jesus Christ.

If he did not believe that the Son was God by nature, would he not have to say, "Grace to you and peace from God the Father" alone? But in fact he includes Christ and makes him a co-bestower of the graces that the divine nature imparts. So he is clearly not unaware that he is God by nature. **[322]** Therefore, we must include the Son along with the Father in the definition of identity and consubstantiality so that we recognize that one God supplies spiritual blessings. When he mentions Christ

*The numbers in bold brackets refer to the page numbers in P. E. Pusey, *Sancti Patris Nostri Cyrilli Archiepiscopi Alexandrini in D. Joannis Evangelium Accedunt Fragmenta Varia Necnon Tractatus ad Tiberium Diaconum Duo*, vol. 3 (Oxford, 1872; repr., Brussels: Culture et Civilisation, 1965). Though this is volume 3 of a subsection of Pusey's series, it is actually volume 5 of the entire series. Therefore, it is hereafter cited as "Pusey 5."

[1] 1 Cor 7:40.

[2] 2 Cor 13:3.

[3] Ps 119:91 (Ps 118:91 LXX).

[4] 1 Cor 13:1; Deut 19:15.

[5] Eph 5:27.

[6] "God-bearer," often rendered in English as "Mother of God." This term was the main point at issue in the Nestorian controversy.

Jesus, he is referring to the Word of God, who appeared in the flesh. And if Christ is the supplier of the things that God the Father himself supplies, does that not make him God by nature according to the union with his own flesh that takes place in the *oikonomia*? The most-wise Paul too says the following about the Israelites: "To them belong the patriarchs, and from them, according to the flesh, comes the Christ, who is over all, God blessed forever. Amen."[7]

Book 1, Logos 2

1:18-20 As surely as God is faithful, our word to you has not been "Yes and No."

No one says, "'Jesus is Lord,' except by the Holy Spirit."[8] And "the Spirit is the truth," as it is written.[9] Filled, then, with the truth, or rather with the Holy Spirit, the heralds of the gospel oracles could not lie. Whatever they said about Christ was altogether definitive and correct. This is confirmed when Christ himself says, "For it is not you who speak, but the Spirit of your Father speaking through you."[10] So when some try to slander him by claiming that he contradicts himself when he sometimes proclaims Jesus to be God by nature and sometimes proclaims him to be man, he denies that there is any contradiction. It is as if he is compelled to attack their misrepresentation. He assures us that his word is not equivocal and obscure but straightforward and true [323] by saying, "Our word to you has not been 'Yes and No.'" This means that his word is not self-contradictory. It does not suffer from inconsistency by praising something in one moment and blaming it the next. Rather, he is telling the truth in his proclamation. So "God is faithful"—that is, he is true and does not lie.

The Greek elite[11] will have various opinions about their supposed gods, saying both "Yes" and "No." That is because they do not have the truth, but rather falsehood. Therefore, they vacillate between different opinions. But he who is truly the natural Son of the Almighty God—how could he be "Yes and No"? . . . And the Son who is from him by nature, "whom we proclaimed among you, Silvanus and Timothy and I," cannot be "Yes and No." Every statement about him that comes through the voice of the theologians[12] is true. "In him," he says, "every one of God's promises is a 'Yes,'" that is, in him we have every lavish gift and promise from God the Father. And this happens in the "Yes," that is, in the truth. These promises have reached their maximum point through Christ. "For death has been swallowed up in victory,"[13] the power of decay has been shaken, and weakness will cease along with dishonor, just as the most-wise Paul said in his former epistle. We have been made heirs and participants in the very kingdom of the saints. He who sits on the divine judgment seat, in whom is the "Yes," will say to us, "Come, you that are blessed by my Father, inherit the kingdom prepared for you from the foundation of the world."[14] We are servants as far as our nature is concerned, but we have been called out of slavery into the dignity of freedom through him. We have been called from decay to incorruption. We have been freed from slavery to the devil. Therefore, every promise [324] of God contains only a "Yes" through Christ. A "No" (which is a denial) is utterly impossible, since he himself is the truth. This also proves in a singular fashion that he is by nature God. After all, if he cannot falsify the promises but

[7]Rom 9:5.
[8]1 Cor 12:3.
[9]1 Jn 5:6.
[10]Jn 10:20.

[11]λογάδες. Literally "picked men." This is an ironic term of contempt.
[12]"Theologians" refers to the biblical writers.
[13]1 Cor 15:54.
[14]Mt 25:34.

will rather fulfill them for the saints, even though God the Father is the one who give the good gifts, how could he not be the true and natural Son—God from God, in whom is "every generous act of giving and every perfect gift"[15] without falsification?

Because Christ's word cannot lie, Paul adds, "For this reason it is through him that we say the 'Amen,' to the glory of God." He himself is the mediator. We have access to the Father through him alone. In him is every spiritual gift. That is why we end every prayer through him, that is, with the "Amen." On top of that, the Son himself teaches us this when he says to the holy apostles, "On that day you will ask nothing of me. Very truly, I tell you, if you ask anything of the Father in my name, he will give it to you. Until now you have not asked for anything in my name. Ask and you will receive, so that your joy may be complete."[16] That is why it is "through him that we say the 'Amen,' to the glory of God the Father." It is our custom to close every prayer in the name of Christ. We can easily see that it is fitting for him to share in the doxology from the prophecy of the blessed Jacob: "Judah, your brothers shall praise you,"[17] since Christ sprang from the tribe of Judah according to the flesh. And then there is the prophet Isaiah, who says, "I saw the Lord of hosts sitting on a throne, high and **[325]** lofty," and the seraphim standing around him calling him "holy" and referring to him as the "Lord of hosts" and saying that heaven and earth are full of his glory. The wise John proves that Isaiah saw the Son himself when he says, "Isaiah said this because he saw his glory and spoke about him."[18] Since the Father is glorified through him, and since he has been placed as a "sacrifice of atonement"[19] and has become a "minister in the sanctuary"[20] according to his human nature, he offers the prayer of each of the saints as a spiritual sacrifice. For our "Amen" is through him. And we should not consider him excluded from the due worship and glorification that we and the multitude of holy spirits above owe him along with the Father. The divinely inspired Paul said somewhere, "And again, when he brings the firstborn into the world, he says, 'Let all God's angels worship him.'"[21] And who is there who cannot see that he is Only Begotten according to that nature by which he is recognized to be God? After all, he is the only one who came from the only Father. But since he came down into our condition, he came to have many brothers,[22] and at that point he was established as having first place.[23] In addition to the fact that he is Only Begotten as God, he is also called firstborn according to his human nature.

1:21 But it is God who establishes us with you in Christ . . .

God the Father "establishes us in Christ." He sets in place an orthodox and unshakeable faith in the souls of all by convincing them that Christ is true God by nature, even though he is found to be in our form, since he who is above all creation was begotten of a woman according to the flesh. So when Peter confessed his faith in clear words, "You are the Christ, the Son of the living God,"[24] our Lord Jesus Christ himself answered, "Blessed are you, Simon **[326]** son of Jonah! For flesh and blood has not revealed this to you, but my Father in heaven." Since the mystery was immense, it makes sense that he would need mystagogy from above given by the Father.

[15]Jas 1:17.
[16]Jn 16:23-24.
[17]Gen 49:8.
[18]Jn 12:41.
[19]Rom 3:25.
[20]Heb 8:2.
[21]Heb 1:6.
[22]Cf. Rom 8:29.
[23]Cf. Col 1:18.
[24]Mt 16:16.

Therefore, it is God himself who "establishes us in Christ and has anointed us, by putting his seal on us and giving us his Spirit in our hearts as a first installment." And on the basis of these words, it should be evident to us that the Son was not "Yes and No." Rather, God is true, and "in him is a Yes" for all good things. Now when it says God has put his seal on us and anointed us and that he gives us "his Spirit as a first installment," once again Christ is the one who accomplishes these things in us. And he does so not as an underling or as one anointing and sealing us with someone else's Spirit, but it is his own Spirit and the Spirit of the Father. The Holy Spirit is inseparably in both because of the identity of essence. But he came to creation from the Father through the Son. Jesus breathed on the holy apostles and said, "Receive the Holy Spirit,"[25] and we too have been sealed in the divine and spiritual image through him and in him. The divine apostle himself wrote to the Galatians and said, "My little children, for whom I am again in the pain of childbirth until Christ is formed in you."[26] Now if we receive in ourselves the riches of the divine image by being formed to be like Christ, then he himself is the image and precise likeness of God the Father. He is not like us. We have been called to this similarity by participation in holiness, but he has it essentially and by nature. After all, there could be no dissimilarity between him who is God by nature and the one born of his essence, who is also truly God by nature. The most-wise John says that the Son has been sealed by God the Father: "He who received his testimony has set his seal because God is true."[27] **[327]** However, he has not been sealed in the same way that we have, but the Father inscribes himself, as it were, entirely in the nature of the Son and impresses himself, so to speak, on him essentially. That is why he said, "Whoever has seen me has seen the Father."[28]

2:14 But thanks be to God, who in Christ always leads us in triumphal procession, and through us spreads in every place the fragrance that comes from knowing him.

The apostles give thanks as they labor and undergo trials, and they boast in their trials for the sake of Christ. Just as Christ was led in triumph for us when he endured death on the tree and was made perfect through sufferings,[29] so also they say that they are led in triumph for him. That means they are made known to people everywhere, they are famous because of their trials, and they overcome the world because they are willing and even eager to suffer all things for the name of Christ.[30] They are—they are!—sharers in his sufferings. And, as it says, they are partakers in "the glory to be revealed."[31] Furthermore, they say that the one who leads them in triumph is God—not that he throws them into suffering or heaps tribulation upon them, but that according to his will, as they proclaim Jesus to people everywhere under heaven, they encounter trials for his sake. That is because without trials, they could not be famous. The fruit of all this is that they suffer "in Christ," that is, on account of Christ. This is glorious and fills them with good hope.

What then is the "fragrance" of the knowledge of God the Father, which is made known to the world "in every place" through the holy apostles, **[328]** as they themselves say? The divinely inspired Paul himself teaches us the answer when he says, "For we do not proclaim ourselves; we proclaim Jesus Christ as Lord and

[25]Jn 20:22.
[26]Gal 4:19.
[27]Jn 3:33.
[28]Jn 14:9.
[29]Cf. Heb 2:10.
[30]Cf. Acts 5:41.
[31]1 Pet 5:1.

ourselves as your slaves for Jesus' sake."[32] And again, "For I decided to know nothing among you except Jesus Christ, and him crucified."[33] Now how can one who was begotten of a woman and who endured the cross and underwent death (though he did come to life again) be the "fragrance" of the knowledge of God the Father if, as some think, Christ was a mere man like us or the mere bearer of God?[34] No, he is God by nature, even though the Word of God did take on human nature in the *oikonomia*. He cannot exude the scent of God the Father's nature by being like us and nothing more, nor could he who endured death become the fragrance of him who does not know death. How then is Christ the "fragrance" of the knowledge of the Father? Is it not clear that he is this in that he is understood to be (and actually is) God, even though he appeared in the flesh for our sake? Otherwise, how could those who proclaim Christ show the world him who is truly God by nature? How could they see Jesus in the first place? How could the holy mystagogues say that God the Father reconciles the world to himself in Christ[35] if he has not brought the Word who sprang from the Father into unity with the human nature, since this is what the carefully devised *oikonomia* requires? After all, the divinely inspired disciples, speaking in the Spirit, declare not that the Word of God dwelt in a man, but that he became flesh—that is, he was united to flesh that has a rational soul. That is how he who was crucified could also be the Lord of glory.[36] **[329]** We, therefore, know him in the flesh. But even when he is not in the flesh but is by himself, so to speak, before he becomes flesh, the Word of God is the "fragrance" of the knowledge of God the Father since by his own nature he gives us the scent of the one he comes from. Now if what I say is true, how could he be originate or numbered among those who have their origin from nothing? The fragrance of the uncreated one could not itself come into being, nor could it exist originately. We cannot see the originate nature in one who is unoriginate, nor can we see the unoriginate nature in one who is originate. Yet the Son has revealed the Father in himself. Therefore, he is God by nature because of the identity of essence. We too, then, should say to the Son, "Your name is perfume poured out."[37] For through him and in him we know God the Father, from whom he was begotten.

2:15-17 For we are the aroma of Christ to God among those who are being saved and among those who are perishing.

They send forth our Lord Jesus Christ as an aroma to God the Father in three ways. First, they have him dwelling in them and inhabiting them through the Holy Spirit. Second, they proclaim him to people everywhere and spread the word about him as they offer their zeal in this endeavor to God as a fragrant sacrifice. And third, they are conformed to him and are perfected through the same suffering. Next they say that they are the aroma of Christ "among those who are being saved and among those who are perishing; to the one a fragrance from **[330]** death to death, to the other a fragrance from life to life." We will now examine this statement. If we interpret it appropriately, it would be reasonable for us to understand those who are being saved and those who are perishing to refer to those who believe and those who reject the faith, who do not acknowledge him who is truly God by nature but worship the creature

[32]2 Cor 4:5.
[33]1 Cor 2:2.
[34]θεοφόρος. This is a term that Cyril condemns in the fifth anathema of his *Third Letter to Nestorius*. See Edward R. Hardy, trans., *Christology of the Later Fathers*, Library of Christian Classics (Louisville, KY: Westminster John Knox, 1954), 353.
[35]2 Cor 5:19.
[36]1 Cor 2:8.

[37]Song 1:3.

rather than the Creator.[38] These people do not accept the message of the divine proclamation. Instead, they ridicule it and think that the mystery of Christ is foolishness.[39] So they receive the "fragrance of the knowledge" of the Father "from death to death." This expression means they are dead because of their ignorance and hard hearts, and they are caught almost falling into the second death. However, those who have been brought by their instruction in the law to an incipient knowledge of God are in that sense alive. And if they were to believe, they would receive the aroma of the knowledge of the Father "from life to life." After all, Christ says somewhere to God the heavenly Father, "And this is eternal life, that they may know you, the only true God, and Jesus Christ whom you have sent."[40] Next he says, "Who is sufficient for these things?" And rightly so. It is truly difficult to find someone who can speak of the mystery of Christ correctly and without error the way the divinely inspired disciples could. They set straight the perversity of the heterodox, who habitually and intently focus on "peddling God's word," as it were, and who always love to mix their explanation of the faith with error and falsehood. It is impossible to find any truth among them that is unmixed, so to speak, and unadulterated. The divine mystagogues, however, when they are speaking by the Spirit do and say everything "as persons of sincerity in God's presence." **[331]**

3:2 You yourselves are our letter, written on our hearts.

We have no need of verbal testimony. By your deeds, you have been shown to be respectable and faithful disciples of Christ, and so you crown the head of your teachers and show us to be respectable as well. Therefore, "You yourselves are our letter, written on our hearts"—that is, You are always and perpetually in our memory since we are always proud of you.

3:3 Not on tablets of stone but on the fleshly tablets of the heart.

He confirms his statement with prophetic testimony: "Not on tablets of stone but on fleshly tablets of the heart." He is pointing out that God said somewhere through the voice of the prophet, "Behold, the days are coming, says the Lord, when I will make a new covenant with the house of Israel and the house of Judah. It will not be like the covenant I made with their fathers when I took them by the hand to bring them out of the land of Egypt because they did not remain in my covenant, though I overlooked it, says the Lord. I will put my law in their minds, and I will write it on their hearts. This is the covenant that I will make with the house of Israel after those days, says the Lord."[41] Indeed, in ancient times the divinely inspired Moses received the law as a pedagogue on tablets of stone, as it is written.[42] And we say that this has become a type of the hard heart of the Jews. It shows that the law has not penetrated into their minds, but just like on stone it barely scratches the surface and is utterly dispensable and quite easy to spit out. **[332]** Indeed, God says somewhere, "These people draw near to me with their mouths and honor me with their lips, while their hearts are far from me; in vain do they worship me, teaching human precepts as doctrines."[43] Our Lord Jesus Christ, on the other hand, inscribes his holy and divine law in us "on fleshly tablets of the heart," meaning

[38]Rom 1:25.
[39]1 Cor 1:18.
[40]Jn 17:3.
[41]Jer 31:31-33 (Jer 38:31-33 LXX).
[42]Ex 31:18.
[43]Is 29:13; Mt 15:9.

sentient tablets. That is why he said through the voice of the prophet Ezekiel, "And I will remove the heart of stone from their flesh and give them a heart of flesh, so that they may walk in my commands."[44] So anyone who does not lean on the shadows given through Moses or hold to the law written in ink as on tablets of stone, but rather has the law written in the mind by the Spirit—that person is the "letter of Christ, known by all." **[333]**

3:4 Such is the confidence that we have through Christ toward God . . .

Paul knows that the honor of his apostleship is not due to human power, but rather to the power of the Almighty God, who extends it to those who are worthy to receive it through Christ the mediator. That is why it says that the saints have all good things in Christ,[45] and also that "every perfect gift is from above, from the Father of lights."[46] Now Christ is the one through whom all things are and in whom all things are.[47] He is the mediator between us and God in accordance with the *oikonomia*, but he is also the one who carries out all things that originate from God the Father in that he is the Father's own wisdom and power. What is this confidence through Christ toward God? Listen to what he says next: "Not that we are competent of ourselves to claim anything as coming from us."[48] ("For all wisdom is from the Lord," as it is written.)[49] "But our competence is from God, who has made us competent to be ministers of a new covenant, not of letter but of spirit; for the letter kills, but the Spirit gives life."[50] And what is the "letter"? It is the **[334]** type contained in the law. It refers to those things that are still accomplished in shadows. "Spirit," on the other hand, is the power of worship that is in Christ. It makes people spiritual when they approach it through faith. And just as the type is less than the truth, to the same extent those who serve the type are inferior to those who minister to the truth. After all, Christ sprinkles us with his own blood, and not merely for the "purification of the flesh,"[51] which of course even the rituals of the law accomplish. No, more than that, he purifies "our conscience from dead works"[52] and drives us away from transgression. On top of that, he freely grants us the hope of life as well. Indeed it is true that "whoever believes in the Son has eternal life."[53] That is because he has promised them resurrection of their bodies and a return to an incorruptible and unending life.

3:10 Indeed, what once had glory has lost its glory because of the greater glory.

Once again he takes up the incomparably surpassing honor of divine apostleship. He compares the ministries, skillfully presenting what is proper to each one. Then he makes clear that the ministry in Christ through the Spirit is the more illustrious of the two. The thrust of his meaning runs along these lines, but he does not express it with the greatest clarity. It does not seem to be very easy to see even for those who are eager to see it. After all, what **[335]** does "what once had glory has lost its glory . . ." actually mean? He is trying to say something like this: Moses "had glory," he says, as a minister of the law that was set aside, but since the glory of the new proclamation in Christ surpasses the first glory, he declared that the former glory seems to have no glory at all. You know that when it is still night and night's

[44]Ezek 11:19-20.
[45]Cf. Philem 6.
[46]Jas 1:17.
[47]Cf. 1 Cor 8:6.
[48]1 Cor 3:5.
[49]Sir 1:1.
[50]2 Cor 3:5-6.
[51]Heb 9:13.
[52]Heb 9:14.
[53]Jn 3:36.

shadow darkens everything, the orb of the moon blazes, as it were, and the chorus of the stars has its own glory. But when the sun rises and unfurls the glory of its brilliance, the light of the moon is overcome by the superior light and seems to have no brightness at all. I think you should understand the meaning of this passage in the same way. You see, he is saying that "what once had glory" (that is, the ministry of the law), even though it received glory from God, seems to lose its original glory "because of the greater glory" (that is, the glory given to the minister of the divine gospel proclamation). What is less always gives way to what is in first place.

3:11 For if what was set aside came through glory, much more has the permanent come in glory!

What has been "set aside"? The shadow and the law, or rather, the type. What is "the permanent"? The Word of God. Therefore, the shadow was "in glory" but the teachings of Christ are in more illustrious glory. They are permanent since they will surpass any glory under heaven.

3:12 Since, then, we have such a hope, we act with great boldness.

What hope is that? To be made competent by God and prepared by grace to be "ministers of a new covenant, not of the letter."[54] And it is fitting for such people to speak "with great boldness," ashamed neither of the impotence of the types, [336] nor of the simplicity of the hearers. Indeed the Holy Spirit has taken up residence in the souls of the believers and allows them easily to understand even deep sayings.

3:13 Not like Moses, who put a veil over his face.

Here again in this passage the disciples of Christ are more illustrious in glory because they have the clear and irresistible word of proclamation that contains nothing obscure, as Moses' proclamation does. When the Israelites failed the test by making the calf even after such great miracles, Moses put on a mask and he used a veil when he spoke the divine law to them. He was teaching them through enigmas that they were not strong enough to see the true face of the law (that is, Christ). Rather, they were attending to what amounts to its second face, the shadow that has no glory. This shadow and type is no longer in effect. It ceased when the new covenant was introduced along with Christ, who is "the end of the law" that was set aside. And so Christ, the veiled glory of Moses, was "the end of the law" that was set aside.[55] Those who remove the shadow and strip off the visible second face, as it were, that is contained in the letter, will see Emmanuel represented in many ways at each point, both as he endures slaughter for the sake of the world and as he saves the earth under heaven so that he may be glorified among us and worshiped by the holy angels. The light of the Savior's glory is truly inaccessible to the minds of the Jews. Since all spiritual contemplation focuses on the mystery of Christ, and the unhappy Jews do not accept faith in him, the veil has remained over them, but it is eliminated in Christ. [337]

3:16 But when one turns to the Lord, the veil is removed.

The Lord himself is the light and he reveals the "deep and hidden things."[56] He shows the true shining face of the law to the wise who are sanctified by the Spirit and who are themselves made to shine through faith in Christ. After all, the law is a teacher that leads people to

[54] 2 Cor 3:6.

[55] Rom 10:4; 2 Cor 3:11.

[56] Dan 2:22.

Christ.[57] And if it is appointed to lead to someone besides itself, then it does not set its students before itself, but it leads them away to what is better and greater than itself. That is why, you know, the divinely inspired Paul says that he counts what is in the law to be rubbish "because of the surpassing value of knowing Christ."[58]

3:17 Now the Lord is the Spirit, and where the Spirit of the Lord is, there is freedom.

They must become spiritual, since there is no other possible way to contemplate Christ, who is the "end" of what was being "set aside," I mean the law. When that happens, the veil is in every way completely "removed," and they will see the holy Moses with a bare and unveiled face, no longer having the mask of the letter or the covering of the surface narrative. Those who are in this condition are the ones who in Christ have abundantly received the free revelation of the Spirit. And if wherever the Spirit is, there is complete "freedom," how could the Spirit not be free by nature? And if that is so, then he has left behind the limits of slavery. He is no longer originate, but should rightly be classified with the supreme free nature that shares in the power over all things. After all, the Spirit is of the Father, and he came to creation from the Father in Christ. **[338]**

3:18 And all of us, with unveiled faces, seeing the glory of the Lord as though reflected in a mirror, are being transformed into the same image from glory to glory; for this comes from the Lord, the Spirit.

Now Moses put on a veil, as you know, because the Israelites were not able to look at "the glory of his face."[59] That is because they were natural[60] and carnal and uninitiated in the faith. But we who are faithful, whose heart is enlightened by the illumination of the Spirit and who know how to see clearly with the mind's eye, gaze on the Lord "with unveiled faces." That is because he has spoken with us and appeared to us in glory and in the ultimate divine supremacy. We recognize him to be God and the "imprint" of the Father's "hypostasis."[61] And so we contemplate his divine and ineffable nature as in a mirror in the sense that the mind of the believers is refashioned, as it were, from study of the law to training in the gospel. It is transformed, so to speak, into spiritual knowledge, no longer putting up with shadows or types, but raised from the glory of the law to pass over to another glory, that which is in Christ through the Spirit. Therefore, we "are being transformed into the same image." When we change the types into the truth and from the shadow of the law we sketch the mystery of Christ in our thoughts, then we will find the same glory in that image. After all, if glory was given to the ministers of the law, then the glory of the holy priests who have been made competent by God to be ministers of a "new covenant, not of letter but of spirit,"[62] is even greater and incomparably surpasses the first glory. I presume it is quite clear and obvious to everyone who exists that those who make the complete transition from instruction in the law to exquisite knowledge of the gospel **[339]** should be understood to go from the first "glory," as it were, into another "glory" as they are reshaped, so to speak, into what is better. Indeed, the one who brings about this change in them is the Spirit, who sets us free from slavery to the law. In him we cry, "Abba! Father!"[63] as sons and free people. There is no other way to see the depth of what the law sketches except through the Holy Spirit alone.

[57]Cf. Gal 3:24.
[58]Phil 3:8.
[59]2 Cor 3:7.

[60]ψυχικοὶ.
[61]Heb 1:3.
[62]2 Cor 3:6.
[63]Rom 8:15.

He is the one who searches "even the depths of God."[64] We maintain that "depths of God" refers to the knowledge treasured up in the Holy Scriptures. The divinely inspired David, you know, prayed to God along these lines when he said, "Open my eyes, and I will understand the wondrous things from your law."[65] And the Savior himself considered a person wonderful who ascends from knowledge of the law to spiritual knowledge, that is, knowledge of the gospel. He said, "Every scribe who has been trained for the kingdom of heaven is like a rich man who brings out of his treasure what is new and what is old."[66] What is in the law is old, while what is in Christ is new. Now if any wish to understand our transformation into the same image "from glory to glory" in a different way, they should think of it like this: Those of us who know Christ are also reckoned among the children of God and are in every way in glory. But at the time of the resurrection, we are transformed "into the same image from glory to glory; for this comes from the Lord, the Spirit." Christ, who graced us with "the first installment of the Spirit,"[67] will supply the rest at that time and will refashion "the body of our humiliation that it may be conformed to the body of his glory."[68] **[340]**

Since the mystagogue says, "For this comes from the Lord, the Spirit," and, "Where the Spirit of the Lord is, there is freedom," we will not put up with the slander of the unholy heretics, who claim that the Spirit is numbered among originate beings. After all, if wherever the Spirit is, there is complete "freedom," how could the Spirit not be free by nature? And if that is so, then he transcends the rank of slavery. The Spirit is of the Father, and he came from the Father to creation in Christ.

[64]1 Cor 2:10.
[65]Ps 119:18 (Ps 118:18 LXX).
[66]Mt 13:52.
[67]2 Cor 1:21.
[68]Phil 3:21.

4:4 To keep them from seeing the light of the gospel of the glory of Christ, who is the image of God.

Since the holy proclamation shines like the sun and every faithful person beholds the "glory of Christ" in a mirror with an unveiled face, no one who thinks rightly will blame the ignorance of some on the divine proclamation. So why (if it is possible to know) do those whose minds are hardened by the devil's deception reject this knowledge, while those who are superior to the devil's perversity, who are wise and have good sense, abound in it? Well, let's say that this passage was recounting the story of some barbarians who were subject to the yoke of slavery, and someone else took pity on those who fell into this condition and released them from the hardship of their circumstances. But then they preferred being under the yoke to being free, and they further considered their misfortune to be inevitable. Tell me, would you blame the one who compassionately set before them the security of freedom? Or would you indict them for their foolishness instead? Along the same lines, the God of the universe has provided for those who want to believe in the Son that they should gaze on his glory with a naked and unveiled face. But **[341]** those who cling to the devil's worthless darkness and foolishly refuse to accept the light of the evangelical oracles have strayed far from this grace. "The light of the gospel of the glory of Christ, who is the image of God," would have shined on them as well. And he calls Satan the "god of this world," not because he is God by nature, but because some people think he is—those who do not know the one who is true God by nature. And the following point deserves another round of wonder. Paul speaks of the *theologia*, and he also clearly articulates the mystery of the *oikonomia* of the Only Begotten in the flesh.[69] Note that he explicitly refers to the apostolic proclamation as "the light of the gospel of the glory of *Christ*." Christ is said to be from God because he is his Son by nature. Yet at the time of his anointing he is said to have been anointed with the oil of gladness[70] by God the Father, even though he himself is the supplier of the Spirit. Therefore, once the Only Begotten Word of God has come to be in our form and has appeared as a man on the earth, then and only then is he correctly understood to be "Christ" and is called by that name. So the faith that is proclaimed to the world is not faith in one like us, a mere human being among others who also bear the Spirit. No, they proclaim that the Word of God has appeared in human form and that the Only Begotten is the firstborn among many brothers. What else could we understand "the light of the gospel of his glory" to be, **[342]** except that he is understood to be God and the image of the Father, not in the same way as we are, but essentially and by nature? Now we are surely not claiming that the Father himself, as if by some deficiency, is thought to have come into the flesh. The beauty of his image does not consist in that. Rather, it is fitting to think of it as follows: that the Word was God, and before the flesh he was the imprint and natural likeness of his begetter. Then, when he became like us, he still had the form of the Father, but he also had the humanity that came from his *oikonomia*. He is considered, then, to be one with his own flesh, and he is the "image" of the Father in this sense: in that he is both God and has been begotten from him by nature.

4:6 Who has shone in our hearts to give the light of the knowledge of the glory of God in the face of Jesus Christ.

The mystagogue makes it clear in this passage that faith is directed to God, even though it is brought about in the face of Christ. Both the Jews and the Greeks have been called to the knowledge of Christ. The latter are led from error and false worship to the true knowledge of God, while the former are led to a more precise knowledge of the law. For this reason even the divinely inspired Paul is found to place little value on the teachings of the law "because of the surpassing value of knowing Christ."[71] So since the mystagogues proclaim Christ, and those who believe in God believe in the one true God, how could Christ not be God? He is not a bastard or a so-called God, or (more precisely) of a different nature than the Father, but he is true God since he is from him by nature. The erring mind is full of spiritual darkness and demonic deception. But God promised to shine the "light" on us out of darkness. He said somewhere through the voice of Isaiah, "The people sitting in darkness have seen **[343]** a great light. Those who live in the land and shadow of death—on them the light will shine."[72] And the divinely inspired David adopts the persona of those in gloom and darkness when he says, "It is you who light my lamp, O Lord. My God, you light up my darkness."[73] Since the Father's promise to us has finally been fulfilled and the divine spiritual light has shone on us, we now know his glory "in the face of Christ." Now if Christ is not truly God by nature, have we seen the Father's glory in him? I hear God the Father clearly saying, "My glory will I give to no other."[74] But look, he has given it to the Son! Therefore, he is not another beside him (except insofar as he exists in his own hypostasis) so that the Father may not be exposed as lying when he places his own glory "in the face" of the Son. The fact that the Father is God by

[69]*Theologia* refers to discussion about God in his own essence, while *oikonomia* refers to discussion about God in the incarnation, or it can refer to the incarnation itself.

[70]Ps 45:7 (Ps 44:8 LXX).

[71]Phil 3:8.

[72]Is 9:2.

[73]Ps 18:27 (Ps 17:29 LXX).

[74]Is 42:8.

nature is made known in and through the Son After all, the Son is his face and image and the radiance of his hypostasis. The Son is revealed by the Father, and the Son in turn reveals the Father to us in himself. **[344]**

Book 3, Logos 1

4:7 In clay jars.

He refers to the ordinary style of his language as "clay jars." That is because the divine mysteries have not been handed down to us in pompous words, but in a style that is accessible to all so that all may learn and understand. What then, Paul? Was it not possible for the God who makes everyone wise to make the holy apostles exceedingly elegant with no trouble at all? Could he not give them far more refinement than they actually have, along with the ability to astonish those they meet with the sound of their words? Of course, Paul says, since God is the one who supplies wisdom. But he enclosed the divine treasure for us "in clay jars," that is, in a meager outward appearance. Why? "So that it may be made clear that this extraordinary power belongs to God and does not come from us." That is how they persuaded everyone to come to faith. Now if their own language had been dazzling, the faith of the called would in some cases seem not to have been a result of his power. But since they made their case with unadorned words, no one doubts that the "extraordinary power" in this case belongs to God.

Since we live in the world of the senses, we call the bodies that we wear "clay jars," meaning something like the following: because we are still wearing the flesh that hinders the contemplation of the truth, we have the knowledge of the Trinity—that "extraordinary" knowledge—"not of ourselves," but it is made known to us by the "power" of God. **[345]**

4:8-10 We are afflicted in every way, but not crushed.

Out of devotion to him, they manifestly endure even death itself. But even if it happens that they suffer this, they live anyway because they are going to be alive to God. As the word of wisdom says, "In the eyes of human beings they seemed to have died, and their departure was thought to be a disaster, and their going from us to be their destruction; but they are at peace, and their hope is full of immortality."[75] Paul then explains the meaning of this trouble when he says, "Always carrying in the body the death of Jesus, so that the life of Jesus may also be made visible in our bodies." We maintain that there are two kinds of death meant here. One is noetic and spiritual. The other is experienced by the bodily senses. His Only Begotten Word is God and came from God by nature. But he made the flesh from the ground his own, and he put on this mortal human body, having a rational soul. And what was his motive? He did it to kill sin in the flesh and to blunt the sting of the natural impulses[76] in the flesh that carry us off to foreign pleasures. Since the Word is God, it was not for himself that he succeeded at transcending our passions. After all, he knew no sin.[77] Rather, he transformed the entirety of human nature in himself into a holy and blameless life when he became a human being and came to be in our form. He has come to have "first place in everything"[78] so that by following in his footsteps we too may have his death in ourselves, that is, the neutralization of the power of sin in the flesh. **[346]** In this way we will also be able to take on blamelessness, resulting in life. One may take this phrase, "the death (and life) of Jesus," in another way

[75]Wis 3:2-4.
[76]ἐμφύτων κινημάτων.
[77]2 Cor 5:21.
[78]Col 1:18.

as well. He became obedient to God the Father, as it is written,[79] even to the point of death, and he laid down his life for the sheep.[80] Furthermore, he "died to sin once for all" (that is, for the sin of the world, since he gave himself as an atonement through faith), "but the life he lives, he lives to God."[81]

Now the mystagogues carry around this mortification in their bodies, which happens through suffering and extends even to the point of death, so that the "life of Jesus," as Paul says, "may be made visible in our bodies." For they too will live to God. They will live a holy, blameless, and blessed life. The sense of the previous passage proves that in the present passage he is thinking about his own death and life. It contains a description of the trials and sufferings that anyone must undergo who wants to complete the glorious course of an apostle. He confirms this view when he interprets what he said and immediately adds the following:

4:11 For while we live, we are always being given up to death for Jesus' sake . . .

With these words he shows that they would gladly endure the death of the flesh out of devotion to Christ. Their goal is not to look at present realities, but rather to look ahead to the future and to the reward for their [347] labors. They think nothing of the sweat of their struggles. Instead, they exult in the blessings from above because they are focused on the breadth of God's generosity. That is why they are "given up to death for Jesus' sake, so that the life of Jesus may be made visible in mortal flesh." And what is the "life of Jesus"? Immortality, sanctification, and great glory beyond that of this world. That is how it will seem to us when the judge descends from heaven for us. He will transform "the body of our humiliation that it may be conformed to the body of his glory, by the power that also enables him to make all things subject to himself."[82] "So death is at work in us, but life in you."[83] You see, the mystagogues of the world beneath the sun have imitated their Lord. They have laid down their lives so that we who once were wandering may obtain that life that comes from faith in Christ. That is why they address our Lord Jesus Christ through the voice of the psalmist and say, "Because of you we are being killed all day long, and accounted as sheep for the slaughter."[84]

Book 3, Logos 2

4:16 Therefore, we do not lose heart. Even though our outer nature is wasting away, our inner nature is being renewed day by day.

It is fitting and not without a touch of elegance to consider the passage at hand in relation to the experience common to just about everyone who undertakes to be godly: "For the flesh is opposed [348] to the Spirit, and the Spirit is opposed to the flesh; for these are opposed to each other," as it is written.[85] Now we maintain as an ironclad principle that when the flesh is degraded in some way and its impulses are weakened, that is when the other factor (that is, the mind of the spirit) is at its strongest. He adds the "therefore" as an explanation and a kind of recollection of the reason for the passage at hand. He had said that "while we live, we are being given up to death for Jesus' sake, so that the life of Jesus may be made visible"[86] in our hearts. He now says that since we have this hope and we exult in the future, "we do not lose heart" as we fix our gaze on the beauty of the coming glory. But if trouble should come, we

[79]Phil 2:18.
[80]Jn 10:15.
[81]Rom 6:10.
[82]Phil 3:21.
[83]2 Cor 4:12.
[84]Ps 44:22 (Ps 43:23 LXX).
[85]Gal 5:17.
[86]2 Cor 4:11.

bear it gallantly. That is because if we suffer as human beings and we endure some harm to our body, we will not be weakened by this. For "our inner nature is being renewed." It is a common story. When by the labors of asceticism "our outer nature is wasting away," that is when by necessity "our inner nature is being renewed day by day."[87] You could understand this passage in another way as well. As they proclaimed Jesus to both the Jews and the Greeks, they endured terrible and unbearable persecutions, and their bodies were injured by these tribulations. But the greater the tribulation, the greater and more abundant the reward of grace that would reasonably follow, I am sure. **[349]**

4:17-18 For this light momentary affliction that is beyond all measure is preparing us for an eternal weight of glory, because we look not at what can be seen but at what cannot be seen; for what can be seen is temporary, but what cannot be seen is eternal.

He strengthens the mind of those who want to be athletes by downplaying the struggles and exalting the crowns that belong to the victors. He does this by using the word "light" to describe the afflictions while using the word "weight" to describe the glory. He refers to the attacks experienced in this life as moderate because they are "momentary," even if they may be "beyond all measure." But he says they will result in an "eternal weight of glory," since the blessings of the coming age are beyond calculation. Therefore, we must not look at the temporary things that are seen but at the eternal things that are not seen.

5:1 For we know that if the earthly house of our tent is destroyed . . .

He refers to the tent (or rather our body) periphrastically as "the earthly house of our tent," as it is written in Job, "Those who live in houses of clay, of whom we also are formed from the same clay."[88] We know, he says, that when death destroys the "earthly house of our tent" (that is, our body), we will receive not long after (at the time of the resurrection) a habitation from heaven (that is, imperishability). And he says that this imperishability is from above for two reasons: first because it is given by God, and second because all who live in the city above (I mean the ranks of the holy angels) live in imperishable and indestructible bodies. The nature of angels, after all, is far removed from **[350]** this earthly coarseness. That is why he describes imperishability with the phrases "building from God" and "a house not made with hands" and indeed "eternal."

5:2 For in this tent we groan, longing to be clothed with our heavenly dwelling.

We "groan" for this reason: weighed down by perishability, we yearn to be clothed with the "heavenly dwelling" from above (that is, imperishability). Now we groan not because we want to get rid of what we are now, but rather because we want to be clothed with imperishability. We pray for the building "not made with hands," and "if we have put it on, we will not be found naked." Indeed, it is true that "a perishable body weighs down the soul."[89] And we have made this weighing down by perishability the occasion for our groaning, but we yearn to be clothed with the "heavenly dwelling" from above (that is, imperishability). Finally, what else does "being clothed" mean than that imperishability is surely wrapped around the body that we now have? Therefore, "we groan."

5:3-4 If we have put it on, we will not be found naked.

[87]Pusey notes that, according to Mai, the words "Now we maintain as an ironclad principle . . . renewed day by day" are attested by Severus of Antioch to come from the third book of Cyril's *Commentary on 2 Corinthians*. However, Pusey was unable to locate this text in Severus. For more information, see Pusey 5:484nn2–18.

[88]Job 4:19.

[89]Wis 9:15.

When he says "if," he is not expressing doubt, but he is making it clear and giving solid proof that when we wrap the heavenly dwelling from above around our current tent (that is, our earthly body), we will not be naked. So he uses "if" instead of "when," so that what he is saying is something like this: when we have put it on, we will not experience the loss of our first body, nor will we be naked of our current body. He makes that clear through what follows. "What is mortal will be swallowed up by **[351]** life." It does not disappear or go into complete nonexistence, but it is transformed into imperishability, just as it was created in the beginning. It is written that God took dust from the ground and formed the man.[90] In order that what is perishable might be swallowed up by life (since the flesh is perishable by nature), "he breathed into his face the breath of life, and the man became a living soul."[91] But death got between them through sin. Then, as the divinely inspired Paul himself says, it pleased God the Father to "recapitulate all things in Christ."[92] He came to renew us through the Spirit to what we were from the beginning. And he himself is the one who "prepared us for these things" as God and "has given us the Spirit as a guarantee." Therefore, the life-giving Spirit has been put into us by Christ as a kind of reliable pledge of the imperishability that will be given us at the end times of the world—now as firstfruits, but then the resurrection of the dead in full measure. Then—then!—perishability will be totally destroyed and we will go out, as the prophet says, and leap "as young calves released from their halters."[93] Indeed, we will jeer at perishability and say, "Where is your penalty, O Death? Where is your sting, O Hades?"[94] For sin and death will be put to an end, and Christ will rule over the saints in imperishability. And in order that what is perishable (that is, the flesh that is perishable by nature) may be "swallowed up by life," "God breathed into his face the breath of life, and the man became a living soul."[95] **[352]**

Book 4, Logos 1

5:5-21 Who has given us the Spirit as a guarantee.

Those who have the Spirit as a guarantee and who are rich with the hope of the resurrection lay hold of what they look forward to in the future. Grasping it as already present, they say, "So from now on we regard no one according to the flesh," since we are all spiritual and not subject to fleshly perishability. I think that he uses the word "flesh" in this passage to mean the perishability of the flesh. Since the Only Begotten has shone on us, we have been transformed after the pattern of the Word, who gives life to all things. Just as we were subject to the bonds of death when sin ruled over us, so also when the righteousness in Christ entered, we shook off perishability. Therefore, no one is in the flesh—that is, in the weakness of the flesh—which is what, among other things, perishability is reasonably understood to be. And after he says that he regards "no one according to the flesh," he suspects that some people have strange ideas, so he adds, "Even if we regarded Christ according to the flesh, we regard him so no longer." It is as if he had chosen to say, "The Word became flesh and lived in us,"[96] and he submitted to death according to the flesh for the life of **[353]** all, and that is how we once regarded him. But from now on, "we regard him so no longer." Even though he is in the flesh, he came back to life on the third day

[90]Gen 2:7.
[91]Gen 2:7.
[92]Eph 1:10.
[93]Mal 4:2.
[94]Hos 13:14.
[95]Gen 2:7.
[96]Jn 1:14.

and is with the Father in heaven. Therefore, we understand him to be above the flesh. Since he died once, "he will never die again; death no longer has dominion over him. The death he died, he died to sin, once for all; but the life he lives, he lives to God."[97] So if the captain of our life is in this condition, then we too, following in his footsteps, must surely be considered to be not in the flesh, but above the flesh. So the divinely inspired Paul is quite right when he says, "So if anyone is in Christ, there is a new creation: the old has passed away; see, the new has come!" "Old" refers to the statement, "Earth you are and to earth you will return."[98] It also refers to the statement in the book of Moses, "The human imagination is intently bent on evil from youth."[99] In addition, "old" refers to the contents of the law. He says that all of that has passed away since we have been justified by faith in Christ, and the power of the curse has been put to an end. He who trampled the power of death came back to life for us, and we know him as true God by nature. We worship him in spirit and in truth, as the Son serves as a mediator and gives to the world the blessing[100] from above and from God the Father. Because of this, you see, the divinely inspired Paul quite wisely says, "All this if from God, who reconciled us to himself through Christ." After all, the mystery of the *oikonomia* in the flesh and the renewal that came through it surely did not take place apart from the will of the Father. The mystagogue then adds to this that the Father reconciled us to himself "through Christ." The Greeks were at war with him through the error of **[354]** polytheism, and the Jews through their desire to latch on to the shadows of the law and their refusal to allow the true form of worship. For through him we have access,[101] and "no one comes to the Father," as he himself says, "except through me."[102] Therefore, "all this is from God, who reconciled us to himself through Christ, and has given us the ministry of reconciliation."

Next let us observe that when Christ gave them the ministry of reconciliation (since they were appointed by him to their apostolic office), it says that the one who gave this ministry is "God." For this reason, they proclaim him to be God and equal in glory with the Father, knowing that one lordship and authority belongs to both. So what sort of ministry is it? What is its definition? What is the manner of the reconciliation? He adds this information when he says, "In Christ God was reconciling the world to himself"—that is, God was the one who was reconciling the world to himself in Christ. By faith in Christ, he says, we have peace with God, or are reconciled. And the forgiveness of our transgressions, which God the Father grants to us, is the clear proof of this. The Son reaches out with authority as God and says to the paralytic, "Your sins are forgiven."[103] Therefore, in Christ (that is, in the *prosopon* of Christ), God "reconciles the world to himself, not counting **[355]** their trespasses against" the sinners. And since we have been ordained to the priesthood of the gospel message, he says, and the "message of reconciliation" has been given to us (since we are ministers of God), we must pray for those who believe; and to those who want to fall away, we must adopt the *prosopon*[104] of Christ himself, as it were, and say, "We entreat you on behalf of Christ, be reconciled to God" by believing in him, namely, the one

[97]Rom 6:9-10.
[98]Gen 3:19.
[99]Gen 8:21.
[100]"Blessing" is Cyril's most common name for the Eucharist, an evocation that is perhaps intended here.

[101]Eph 2:18.
[102]Jn 14:6.
[103]Mt 9:2.
[104]Here πρόσωπον refers to the character or persona of Christ. This usage illustrates why Cyril is opposed to describing the union of Christ's natures in terms of πρόσωπον. It is a phenomenological, not an ontological, association.

for whom we are "ambassadors." After all, Christ is the "gate" and he is the "way."[105]

Now it was likely that some would disregard the gospel proclamation and place no value on the truly acceptable time of salvation[106] and finally reject the faith. So the mystagogue devises something else for them that has the power to convert them and easily persuade them not to fall into indifference but rather to lay hold of the life in Christ. He says of God the Father, "For our sake he made him to be sin who knew no sin, so that in him we might become the righteousness of God." It is as if he were to say, "He arranged that he who has never sinned should suffer the punishment of the worst sinners so that he may render us righteous who have received faith in him." That is why he "endured the cross, disregarding its shame."[107] The one who was worth as much as all died for all. Now when he is said to have become "sin," you should not suppose that he has committed sin. After all, the Word is God; he does not know how to sin. Rather, you should understand it to mean that he has been given by God the Father for our sins. In fact, the animals slaughtered for sin in accordance with the law of Moses are referred to as "sin" in just the same way. For example, it is written in the prophets concerning those **[356]** ordained as priests, "They will feed on the sin of my people; they will set their hearts on their iniquities."[108] That is because the ministers in charge of the divine altars ate the sacrifices for sin in accordance with the law. Therefore, this wise thought has great power to convert those who want to neglect the faith: he who knew no sin was condemned and suspended from a cross with sinners for us so that "we might become the righteousness of God." For we have been justified by God the Father "not because of any works of righteousness that we had done, but according to the greatness of his mercy"[109] through faith in Christ.

10:1 I myself, Paul, appeal to you by the meekness and gentleness of Christ . . .

There were many Athenian wise men living among the Corinthians who considered the Savior's cross to be foolishness[110] and had the same opinion of the one who announced the message of the divinely inspired Scriptures. They called the blessed Paul himself a vagabond and a babbler,[111] together with the other saints. Others, of the circumcision party, were implanted among the believers. They praised circumcision and the sacrifices of the law, and they claimed that the blessed Paul abandoned them, thinking that he chose to make unholy war against the ancient oracles. So those in Corinth who were zealous for the faith were quite understandably stirred up against these people, and they wanted to lay hands on them as enemies of the divine proclamation. But this state of affairs was quite ugly and far removed from the gentleness that is fitting for the saints. "For the Lord's servant must not fight," as it is written, "but be kindly **[357]** to everyone, correcting opponents with gentleness."[112] Therefore, he commands them, saying, "I myself, Paul," a priest of the divine mysteries, a steward and apostle, one you should emulate, one who urges you to say with me, "For to me living is Christ and dying is gain"[113]—"I appeal to you by the meekness and gentleness of Christ," "who when he was abused did not return abuse; when he suffered, he did not threaten; but he entrusted himself to the one who judges justly."[114] He takes the opportunity

[105]Jn 10:9; 14:6.
[106]Cf. 2 Cor 6:2; Is 49:6.
[107]Heb 12:2.
[108]Hos 4:8.
[109]Titus 3:5.
[110]1 Cor 1:18.
[111]Acts 17:18.
[112]2 Tim 2:24-25.
[113]Phil 1:21.
[114]1 Pet 2:23.

to remind them of Christ's life to make them meek and gentle. "I myself, Paul," he says, am "humble when face-to-face with you," neither exultant nor eager for strife and contention. I am "bold when I am away," but I ask that now "when I am present I need not show boldness."[115] And I ask that your attitude be the same and that you take no audacious actions against those who think that we "walk according to the flesh,"[116] (that is, that we are living carnally in quarreling and jealousy). "For as long as there is jealousy and quarreling among you," he says, "are you not of the flesh, and behaving according to human inclinations?"[117] It is fitting, therefore, that those who want to follow the Savior's gentleness and who do not want to live carnally should be beyond the suspicion of these people. After all, if some do not believe, we should not subdue them by striking them with clubs, but we should wait for their willing conversion to God.[118]

10:3-6 Indeed, we live in the flesh, but we do not wage war according to the flesh; for the weapons of our warfare are not fleshly, but they have divine power.

Now those who know how to prove themselves in battle and counter those who make war against them in the flesh would quite reasonably possess a full complement of fleshly armor. They would have helmets and breastplates, shields and swords, and equipment that would enable them to conquer. But for us, our battle and our mode of warfare require spiritual armor. **[358]** Indeed, the divinely inspired Paul puts it very well. He says that those who consider themselves soldiers in Christ must be adorned with this sort of magnificent equipment. They put on righteousness as their breastplate[119] along with the helmet of salvation "and the sword of the Spirit, which is the word of God."[120] In addition to this, they take up the "shield of faith," by which all the fiery arrows of the evil one are extinguished.[121] Therefore, the weapons of the saints are not fleshly, but spiritual. They have "divine power," and they are capable of "destroying strongholds" (by which I mean the teachings of the Greeks and the heretics) and of showing their arguments to be unsound, utterly crude, and ignorantly constructed. And so we will put down such arguments "and every proud obstacle raised up against the knowledge of God." And we will take every thought prisoner "to obey Christ." That means we will tear down every proud thought of the godless that is raised up against God, and we will glorify him with appropriate language without imagining anything ignoble about him. We will also help the rest by escorting them on a correct and unerring road for their thoughts so that we may "punish every disobedience" once our own obedience is complete. After all, the one who will be "great in the kingdom of heaven"[122] is not the one who teaches only, but the one who chooses to supplement the lesson with the boast of good works.[123]

13:3-4 Since you desire proof. . . . For we are weak in him, but in dealing with you we will live in him by the power of God.

He threatens those who previously sinned in Corinth that unless they choose to do what is right and to live a holy life, he will not spare them "again."[124] The word "again" calls to mind

[115] 2 Cor 10:2.

[116] 2 Cor 10:2.

[117] 1 Cor 3:3.

[118] Early in Cyril's episcopacy, a Christian mob had killed the philosopher Hypatia. Perhaps that event is in the background here.

[119] Eph 6:14.

[120] Eph 6:17.

[121] Eph 6:16.

[122] Mt 5:19.

[123] Cyril seems to envision that his reader is charged with the task of teaching the faith.

[124] 2 Cor 13:2.

the trouble he already had with them. Because he wants to give a stern rebuke to the sinners, his language will be vehement as he attempts to persuade them from **[359]** what has already taken place as well as from what is expected to take place in the future. So he says, "Since you desire proof that Christ is speaking in me." You are probably expecting, he is saying, to see in what follows whether Christ is speaking in me and whether he finally engages in rebuke. But do not think, as some arrogant unbelievers now suppose, that he is weak. No, "he is powerful in you" (that is, in believers and those subject to him to whom he gives the care that they need), and he converts sinners. "He is powerful in you." That means that he acts as God and he shows the words of the saints to be true. And you will find my message to be powerful in every way, since I am not the one speaking, but Christ is speaking in me. When he mentions those who are so utterly silly as to imagine that Christ is actually weak because he underwent the cross and endured the insensibility (or rather godlessness) of the Jews, he gives a useful answer. At just the right time, he brings up the power of the mystery and recounts the voluntary emptying of the Only Begotten along with the incomparable supremacy of his glory that comes after it. [Yes, he admits, as those who are far from the faith think, "he was crucified in weakness," he suffered as a human being, and he willingly endured death in the flesh. But we must also know that in addition to that, once he had despoiled Hades and trampled on the power of death, he came back to life on the third day, not using human power, **[360]** but ineffable divine power. After all, the power to do all these things could belong only to God. The result was that he destroyed the power of death itself, and though his body was overcome by death, he crowned that body with the grace of imperishability. So he did willingly endure a brief weakness, at least according to the nature of the flesh. For example, he is said to hunger and thirst and grow weary and indeed die according to the *oikonomia*. However, he "lives by the power of God." And he did not receive the power to do all things from someone else, but he had it on his own and it was in him essentially. For he who suffered in the flesh for us is God by nature.

And because of this he said to the assembly of the Jews (since he did not refuse the weakness of the flesh that he took on, and he did not depart from the supreme power of his nature): "Destroy this temple, and in three days I will raise it up."[125] *And if Saint Paul is telling the truth that he heard God say, "My power is made perfect in weakness,"*[126] *how is it not be correct to say that in the first place Emmanuel was weak in the flesh and strong as God?*[127]

Therefore, if they are offended by the cross, let them marvel at the resurrection.][128] Since he is said to "live by the power of God," you should just as surely understand the Son himself to be the power of God.

[361] [We must say of him not only that he completely died, but also that he was wrapped in cloth, an act that decisively attests to the death of Emmanuel. Moreover, he was left in the grave, from which he came back to life, as I just said. Therefore, since he died in the body, he has completely convinced us that he has a body. And then, when the Word of God trampled on death, he proved that he is truly God by nature. Just as he acted in a human way when he endured death, so also he operated in a divine way when he conquered death.][129]

---

[125]Jn 2:19.

[126]2 Cor 12:9.

[127]The section in italics is translated from Syriac.

[128]Mai says the section in brackets ("Yes, he admits . . . resurrection") is cited by Severus of Antioch in his unedited apology against Julian, but Pusey was unable to confirm this. See Pusey 5:359n19.

[129]The section I have put in brackets comes from Cod. Vat. Syr. 100, and it is in Latin. See Pusey 5:361n1.

COMMENTARY ON THE EPISTLE TO THE HEBREWS (FRAGMENTS)[1]

[362]* A Fragment from the Preface

He has quite an erudite way of doing exegesis, and it is constructed with great subtlety and skill. He draws variously on the letter of the law, on spiritual conceptions, and on the multifaceted proclamation of the holy prophets. His goal is to provide the readers with complete, thorough teaching and to convince them that the words of Moses, which labor to give birth to the power of the truth, were types, while Christ himself is the truth. **[363]** Thus he shows that portrayal by type and shadow was utterly necessary for the ancients. On top of that, he shows us that even those who live gloriously by the law gain their renown and esteem in no other way than by faith in God, and that faith is the principal issue, as the holy fathers well know. He did not employ his usual opening and introduction since he was subject to suspicion and false accusation on the part of the Jewish believers. They charged that he joined them with Gentiles and taught everyone everywhere to place no value on the law and to despise the customs of their fathers as vain and to go down another path, as it were. This we learn from the Acts of the Apostles.[2] So he proceeds with the greatest discretion and safeguards their customs. He does not mention the grace of his apostolic office, but he goes right to the importance of remembering the fathers and the holy prophets, believing that by this his message will be more readily accepted by them. So he says,

1:1 He spoke to our fathers by the prophets.

God spoke to the ancients by the Spirit through the mouth of the saints and the voice of the prophets. For example, he spoke through one of them to rebuke the foolishness of the Jews: "Your fathers, where are they? And the prophets, do they live forever? But as for you, receive my laws and my statutes, which I command by my Spirit to my servants the prophets."[3] Now if the ancients had the grace of prophecy by the Spirit, it was not without the Word of God who is from the Father, since he speaks to the saints in the same way as his Spirit does. Certainly no one would say (at least no one with any sense) that the Holy Spirit acts as an assistant to us **[364]** and that he receives the knowledge or revelation about

*The numbers in bold brackets refer to the page numbers in P. E. Pusey, *Sancti Patris Nostri Cyrilli Archiepiscopi Alexandrini in D. Joannis Evangelium Accedunt Fragmenta Varia Necnon Tractatus ad Tiberium Diaconum Duo*, vol. 3 (Oxford, 1872; repr., Brussels: Culture et Civilisation, 1965). Though this is volume 3 of a subsection of Pusey's series, it is actually volume 5 of the entire series. Therefore, it is hereafter cited as "Pusey 5."

[1]These are as many fragments as Pusey found. Since then, a complete Armenian translation has been discovered. See Cyril of Alexandria, *Commentary on the Letter to Hebrews*, Armenian text compiled by Hakob Keoseyan, ed. Khachik Grigoryan (Yerevan, Armenia: Ankyunacar Publishing, 2020). A subsequent volume will contain both the Armenian text and an English translation: Cyril of Alexandria, *Commentary on the Letter to Hebrews*, Armenian text compiled by Hakob Keoseyan, trans. Khachik Grigoryan, ed. Diana Tsaghikyan (Yerevan, Armenia: Ankyunacar Publishing, forthcoming).

[2]Cf. Acts 21:21, 28.

[3]Zech 1:5-6.

the matter at hand from God the Word and in this way makes it known to us. If that is how it is, then he will be no different from the holy prophets. No, the Spirit is said to receive from him and make known to us[4] in the sense that the Spirit knows all things that are in the Word. So too, the Only Begotten spoke to the ancients "long ago" and "in various ways" through the Holy Spirit as he commanded them to sketch out the great and grand mystery of his incarnation. So we can hear him say through the prophets, "It was I who multiplied visions, and by means of the prophets I was represented."[5] And again, "I am the one who speaks. I am here, as springtime on the mountains, as the feet of one who brings a message of peace, as one who brings good tidings."[6] After all, at the consummation of the ages the Son himself has spoken to us directly, no longer through the mediation of the prophet and the voice of the saints. The Only Begotten, who has become like us, has given us his words directly. We maintain that the Father spoke "by his Son." He did not speak by some man who was appointed as a personal intermediary, who transmits to us not his own words but the words of someone else. No. He spoke with his own voice, which comes through the Son's mouth speaking to us (since the flesh belongs to the Only Begotten himself, not to someone else). He is God by nature, and he became man while remaining God. That is how he reveals God the Father's ineffable counsel to us. And that is why "his name will be called the Angel of the Great Counsel."[7]

So Paul is correct when he says that in the last days, God the Father has spoken to us "by his Son." He knew that Emmanuel was God and that the Word of God came to exist in human nature with us. He recognized him who is free **[365]** in the form of a slave. He confessed the fullness of him who emptied himself for our sakes. He gazed on the height of glory that belonged to him who lowered himself to humiliation for us, and who for that reason is said to be appointed as the "heir of all things,"[8] even though he rules over all things in that he is both considered to be and is God. Then he returns to his own riches even with his flesh. He certainly did not remain in our poverty. He did not become flesh so that he could throw away his own God-befitting riches and remain poor with us. No, he did it so that we who suffer from a lack of divine gifts may be made rich by his poverty.[9] You see, even though he is Son by nature and coeternal with the Father, when he underwent birth according to the flesh for us through the holy virgin, he said through David, "The Lord said to me, 'You are my Son; today I have begotten you.'"[10] He said this because he was restoring the source of sonship to us. Now the word "today" refers to the present time, which is when he became flesh, though he is by nature the Lord of all. You can see this because John has testified of him that he "came to what was his own,"[11] referring to his world as "what was his own." And the Son summoned the world to the glory of his kingdom, a glory that did not belong to it, when he said, "I have been appointed king by him,"[12] namely, by God the Father. He experienced these things so that he might be adopted as man (even though he is by nature God) and so open up a road through himself to participation in sonship for human nature. He also did this so that he might call those tyrannized by sin into the kingdom of heaven. Just as an inheritance passes from a father to all of his descendants, we possess calamity from Adam's transgression in that we bear the curse and death. And in the same way, Christ's glory will extend to the

[4]Cf. Jn 16:15.
[5]Hos 12:10 (LXX).
[6]Is 52:6-7.
[7]Is 9:6 (LXX).

[8]Heb 1:2.
[9]2 Cor 8:9.
[10]Ps 2:7.
[11]Jn 1:11.
[12]Ps 2:6.

entire human race as well. After all, what the Only Begotten received was for our benefit, certainly not his own. He has fullness because he is God by nature, and he lacks absolutely nothing. Rather, he himself enriches the entire creation with blessings from above. **[366]**

So as man he has been appointed as "heir of all things"[13] in accordance with the *oikonomia* in order to restore those on earth, who had been wickedly seized by the devil along with the evil powers, to be his own inheritance. Indeed, God the Father said to him, "Ask of me, and I will give you the nations as your inheritance," and so forth.[14] And when that is brought to completion, he speaks to his Father and refers to us as "those whom you have given me from the world. They were yours, and you gave them to me."[15] (Notice how when he ascends to the riches that he has by nature, he does so with his flesh as well.) Now if those in the world belonged to the Father, how could they be ascribed to the Word, who reigns with him? Well, he also said, "All mine are yours, and yours are mine; and I have been glorified in them."[16] So how is he commanded to ask, and how does he receive the nations as his inheritance[17] when he creates the ends of the earth as his own possession? When the Father and creator of all wanted to save humanity, which had foolishly skipped off from service to God, he sent the Only Begotten God, the Word, into the world to become flesh and live with humankind[18] as man, to proclaim release to the captives and recovery of sight to the blind, and to declare the acceptable year of the Lord.[19] Therefore, even though he is said to receive and to be appointed as an heir on account of his humanity, we will not forget about the *oikonomia*.[20] After all, how could he be poor at all except that he become poor (that is, human) for us while remaining God? The divinely inspired Paul persuades us to think this way when he adds the critical phrase "through whom he also created the ages."[21] So how could this be true as well? If the holy virgin bore Emmanuel for us in the last times of the age, how can Paul say that the ages were created by him? But he is quite right. The Word of God the Father, who was begotten before every age and time, **[367]** "in these last days"[22] is said to come into being in a fleshly way from a woman. The recentness of the *oikonomia* will do absolutely no harm to him who has God-befitting antiquity by nature, nor will the immense age of his existence destroy his glory. For it is written, "Christ Jesus is the same yesterday and today and forever."[23] Once he appeared in the flesh he testified to the immense age that he had in his divine nature. He will confirm this by saying to the Jews, "Truly, truly I tell you, before Abraham was, I am."[24] And the divinely inspired John the Evangelist said, "He who comes after me is ahead of me because he was before me."[25] Christ is rich and preeminent in all things.

1:3 He is the radiance of his glory.

Just as the Father is unchangeable and always remains what he is (namely, the Father and not

[13]Heb 1:2.
[14]Ps 2:8.
[15]Jn 17:6.
[16]Jn 17:10.
[17]Ps 2:8.
[18]Bar 3:37 (Bar 3:38 LXX).
[19]Is 61:1-2.

[20]The text from the beginning of the paragraph to this point ("So as man he has been appointed . . . *oikonomia*") is almost identical to Origen's comments on Ps 2:8 from his *Selecta in Psalmos* (PG 12.1108B). Perhaps Cyril is quoting Origen, or perhaps Origen's text was somehow inserted into the catena.
[21]Heb 1:2.
[22]Heb 1:2.
[23]Heb 13:8.
[24]Jn 8:58.
[25]Jn 1:15. In his *Commentary on John*, Cyril rejects the idea that Jn 1:15 is referring to Jesus' age, calling it an "overused" and "unconvincing" interpretation. Instead, he insists the verse refers to Jesus overtaking John in fame and honor (*Commentary on John* 1:15, trans. David R. Maxwell, 2 vols., Ancient Christian Texts [Downers Grove, IL: IVP Academic, 2013–2015], 1:66).

the Son), so also the Son stays in his own position, always remaining the Son and never being changed into the Father, so that even in this respect he is shown to be the "imprint" of the Father's hypostasis. One may see the beauty of the parent's surpassing excellence and glory conspicuous in him as well. He is "true God from true God" and "light from light,"[26] just as he is life from life. He surpasses all creation to the same extent that the Father himself is understood to do so. For he is unoriginate from unoriginate, and he is not numbered among those things that have been brought from nonbeing into being. The Word was in the beginning, and the Word was God.[27] How then could the claim of those who war against the Holy Scriptures be true when they say that he "was not"?[28] If he is originate as they claim, then he will surely be subject along with everyone else and will receive the yoke of slavery. **[368]** He will differ in no way from those who have come into being through him. But in fact he is God from God. He "bears all things by his powerful word," since "all things came into being through him, and without him not one thing came into being."[29] Again, he himself bears all things up unshaken forever.

We just said that God revealed himself to the ancients through Moses and the prophets. We, on the other hand, are "taught by God,"[30] as the prophet puts it. That is because we have the Word of God himself, who became a human being for us, as our teacher. He is the Creator of the ages, the radiance of the Father's glory, and the imprint of his hypostasis. We have already looked at each of these things in turn, but we will add the following.

The Word is the almighty power of God the Father. "He spoke and they were begotten. He commanded and they were created. He established them forever and ever. He issued his command and it will not be disregarded."[31] Since the nature of things that are brought into being does not have incorruptibility and certainly does not have the ability to remain the same forever (as this is a property of the nature that is supreme over all), he "bears all things by his powerful word." Because the Word is hypostatic[32] and is begotten of God the Father by nature, his word is almighty and active and can easily accomplish all things. Next he adds, "When he had made purification for sins, he sat down at the right hand of the Majesty on high, having become as much superior to angels as the name he has inherited is more excellent than theirs." After showing him to be the imprint of the Father's hypostasis and indeed the radiance of his glory, he proceeds logically to the *oikonomia* of the incarnation.[33] Through this we have been saved and enriched with the forgiveness of sins and sanctified through **[369]** his blood. As the most-wise Paul himself says, "In him we have redemption through his blood, the forgiveness of our trespasses."[34] And John writes as follows concerning God the Father: "If we walk in the light, we have fellowship with him, and the blood of Jesus Christ his Son cleanses us from all sin."[35] So we have been cleansed by the holy blood of Christ the Savior of us all, who "sat down at the right hand of the Majesty on high." When did that happen? When he "made purification" through his

[26]Here Cyril is arguing for the scriptural basis of phrases from the Nicene Creed.

[27]Jn 1:1.

[28]Arius had claimed that there was a time when the Word "was not."

[29]Jn 1:3.

[30]Is 54:13.

[31]Ps 148:5-6.

[32]ἐνυπόστατος. In modern Christology, this term is sometimes taken to mean "enhypostatic," i.e., existing in the hypostasis of another. Christ's human nature is called "enhypostatic" because it exists in the hypostasis of the Word. However, here it simply means "hypostatic," i.e., having its own hypostasis. This usage may be seen in Cyril's *Commentary On John* in his comments on Jn 1:1, where he says that the Spirit is "hypostatic" (ἐνυπόστατον) (Maxwell 1:14, see n59).

[33]ἐνανθρωπήσεως. Literally "inhumanization."

[34]Eph 1:7.

[35]1 Jn 1:7.

blood. That is when he is said to have sat down and to have become "superior to the angels" and to inherit a "name that is more excellent than theirs." That is because he is called the "Son." The "Word became flesh,"[36] though he is still the Word and the radiance of the Father's glory and the imprint of his hypostasis. And when he did so, he did not perform the labor (so to speak) of the *oikonomia* in the flesh for his own nature. He "endured the cross, disregarding its shame,"[37] and he also endured dishonor, violence, and spitting. But this was to free us by his own blood from every defilement and, once he made us pure, to unite us through himself to God the Father. "For through him we have access,"[38] and he himself is the "door"[39] and the "way."[40] Even though "the Word became flesh and dwelt in us"[41] and made his own the body that he assumed from the holy virgin, he was still in the glory and nature of his divinity and he did not depart from the supreme throne of God the Father. He was a man on the earth, but he also filled heaven and all things. For a little while, he was made lower than the angels,[42] at least according to the measure of his humanity. After all, human nature is inferior to the angels in glory. But even in this condition, he was "far above all rule and authority and power and dominion, and above every name that is named, not only in this age but also in the age to come."[43] Knowing this, the divinely inspired Paul writes, "For you know the **[370]** grace of our Lord Jesus Christ, that though he was rich, yet for our sakes he became poor, so that by his poverty we might become rich."[44]

1:4 Having become as much superior to the angels.

The word *angel* is a name indicating service and suggests to us the status of a household slave. The word *Son,* on the other hand, signifies the essential and natural being of the Father. Therefore, when he speaks of the Son being greater or more honorable, he is not making a comparison, lest anyone imagine that he is of the same kind as they are.[45] No, he uses the word *superior*[46] to communicate the difference between the Son's nature and those things that are originate. And we have proof of this from the Holy Scriptures where David sings, "A day in your courts is superior to thousand elsewhere."[47] And Solomon proclaims, "Wisdom is superior to precious stones."[48] Now how could wisdom not be of a different substance and nature than stones from the earth? And what kinship is there between the courts of heaven and houses on earth? Therefore, in the same way there is no kinship between the Son and the angels. And since there is no kinship, the word *superior* is not used to make a comparison but a distinction on account of the difference between his nature and theirs. In fact, the apostle himself explains the word *superior* when he applies it to this precise difference between the Son and originate creatures: he is the Son, while they are slaves. The one, as Son, is seated at the right hand of

[36]Jn 1:14.
[37]Heb 12:2.
[38]Eph 2:18.
[39]Jn 10:9.
[40]Jn 14:6.
[41]Jn 1:14. In his comments on this passage in the *Commentary on John,* Cyril makes clear that he understands John's words ἐν ἡμῖν to mean that the Word dwelt "in us," not (as most English translations render it) "among us" (Maxwell 1:63).
[42]Heb 2:9.
[43]Eph 1:21.
[44]2 Cor 8:9.
[45]In his *Commentary on John* Cyril articulates a principle used by the Arians that comparisons can only be made of two items of the same kind. There he endorses the principle and tries to turn it against the Arians. In the present passage, he is clearly employing it as well. See Cyril's *Commentary on John* 14:28 (Maxwell 2:203-7).
[46]κρείττων.
[47]Ps 84:10 (Ps 83:11 LXX).
[48]Prov 8:11.

the Father, while the others, as slaves, stand beside him and are sent and serve.

This is what is written. And it does not mean, O Arians, that the Son is originate. No, it means he is different from originate beings and belongs to the Father, since he is in his bosom.[49] Nor does the phrase *having become*, which is written here, mean that the Son is originate, as you imagine. Now if he said simply **[371]** "having become" and nothing more, the Arians would have a pretext for their argument. But since he already called him "Son" and showed him throughout the entire passage to be different than originate beings, he also did not insert the phrase *having become* by itself but joined the word *superior* to it. He did not think that this phrase changed anything. He does use the phrase *having become* (which is equivalent to "having come into being"), but he does so knowing that it refers to the obviously genuine Son, so he also says that he is "superior." When it comes to what is begotten,[50] it makes no difference if one were to say it came into being or was created. Originate beings,[51] on the other hand, since they are creatures, cannot be called begotten[52] unless they later participate in the begotten Son. Then they too may be called begotten, not because of their own nature but because of their participation in the Son, which takes place in the Spirit. The Holy Scriptures know this too, as when they say of originate beings, "All things came into being through him,"[53] and that in wisdom he made them all.[54] But when it comes to begotten sons they say, "Seven sons and three daughters came into being[55] for Job,"[56] and, "Abraham was a hundred years old when his son Isaac came into being."[57] So if the Son, who alone is from the substance of the Father as his own offspring, is different from originate beings, then the Arian pretext based on the words "having become" has been brought to nothing. Even if they are ashamed of this and are forced to repeat their argument that the words are spoken as a comparison and therefore the items compared are of the same kind so that the Son is of the same nature as the angels,[58] they will immediately be ashamed because they are uttering the position of Valentinus and Carpocrates.[59] One of these says that the angels belong to the same race as Christ, while the other says that angels created the world. So these people too, perhaps learning it from them, compare the Word of God to the angels. But those who imagine such things will be put to shame by the psalmist, who says, "Who among the sons of God can be compared with the Lord?"[60] He also says, "Who among the gods is like you, O Lord?"[61] **[372]** Let them hear, if they are willing to learn, that comparisons usually take place between items of the same kind, not items of different kinds, as everyone knows.

Therefore, no one would compare God with a human or a human with irrational animals or trees with stones due to the dissimilarity of the natures. Rather, God is an incomparable thing; a human is compared with another human, a tree is compared with a tree, and a rock with a rock. And no one would use the word *superior* in these comparisons. Rather, the term would be *more than* or *more numerous*. Thus Joseph is more beautiful than his brothers, and Rachel than Leah. And a star is not "superior" to another star, but it "differs in

[49]Jn 1:18.

[50]I follow Pusey's conjectural emendation γεν[ν]ητὸν rather than γενητὸν.

[51]γενητὰ.

[52]γεννητὰ.

[53]Jn 1:3.

[54]Ps 104:24 (Ps 103:24 LXX).

[55]ἐγένοντο.

[56]Job 1:2.

[57]ἐγένετο. Cf. Cyril's *Thesaurus de sancta et consubstantiali Trinitate* 20 (PG 75:342D).

[58]See n45 in this section.

[59]Two Gnostic leaders.

[60]Ps 89:6 (Ps 88:7 LXX).

[61]Ps 86:8 (Ps 85:8 LXX).

glory."[62] For items of different kinds, if someone wants to put them in juxtaposition with each other, that is when the word *superior* is used to indicate the distinction. It is used, for example, in the case of wisdom and stones. So if the apostle had said that the Son exceeded the angels by "as much *more*" or that he was "as much *greater*," then you would have a basis for your argument, since he would be comparing the Son to the angels. But as it is, he says the Son is "superior" and he differs by "as much" as the Son is distinct from slaves. By saying this, he shows that the Son is different from the nature of the angels. Again, by saying that he laid the foundation for all things, he shows that the Son is different from all originate beings. And since he is different and of a different substance from the nature of originate beings, what comparison or likeness could there be between his essence and originate beings? That is why the Son did not say, "My Father is *superior* to me,"[63] so that no one may suppose that he is foreign to the Father's nature. Rather, he used the word *greater*,[64] not in terms of size or time, but because of his begottenness from his Father. However, by saying that he is "greater," he also indicated the property of his nature. The apostle, on the other hand, chiefly wanted to distinguish the essence of the Word from originate beings, so he said, [373] "Having become as much *superior* to the angels." That is because he cannot be compared with them, or rather, he is different than they are. Focusing on the incarnation and the *oikonomia* that he carries out at that time, the apostle wanted to show that the Son is not like the former beings so that the grace that comes from him and through him may be superior to the ministry of the angels to the same degree that he differs in nature from those he sent out ahead of him. Tenants only collect the fruit, but the Son and master forgives debts and chooses the location for the vineyard.[65]

Now that is enough to put the enemies of the truth to shame. But because it says, "having become superior," they do not want to understand "become" as equivalent to "is" when applied to the Son[66] or to understand "become" as we have described it on the basis of the fact that his ministry has become "superior." Instead, they think that with this phrase the Son is being called originate. All right then, let them hear this: If the Son is one of the angels, then let the phrase *having become* apply both to him and to them and let there be no difference between their natures. Either let them be sons too or let him be an angel. And let them all together sit down at the right hand of the Father, or else let the Son stand with them all as a ministering spirit since he too is sent into a ministry like theirs. But since Paul distinguishes the Son from originate beings when he says, "For to which of the angels did he ever say, 'You are my Son; today I have begotten you'? Or again, 'I will be his Father, and he will be my Son'?" . . .

1:6 And again, when he brings the firstborn into the world.

He calls him "firstborn," not in the sense used by those who distort what is right [374] and classify him with creation, but because he is in all things preeminent. . . .[67]

. . . Marveling, they say, "Who is this that comes from Edom (that is, from the earth) from Bozrah (which in Greek means conflict

[62]1 Cor 15:41.

[63]Cf. Jn 14:28: "The Father is greater [μείζων] than I." Cyril's point is that John uses the word *greater* (μείζων), not *superior* (κρείττων).

[64]μείζων.

[65]Mt 21:33-34, 41.

[66]"Is" (ἔστιν) implies permanent existence, while "becoming" (γενόμενος) implies coming into being. The former is characteristic of God; the latter, of creatures. Cf. Cyril's discussion of Jn 1:6-7 in his *Commentary on John* (Maxwell 1:40-41).

[67]Pusey was unable to finish transcribing this scholion due to a fever.

or affliction) in garments stained crimson. Why are your robes red, and your garments like theirs who tread the wine press?"[68] Then they ask this questions as well: "What are these wounds in the middle of your hands?" And he answers, "These wounds I received in the house of my beloved."[69] Now no one should think that he was under any compulsion to bear the marks of the nails after the resurrection and to ascend to heaven with them. That is worth very careful consideration. He showed the marks of the nails and his side to unbelieving Thomas so that he might ultimately convince him to say from a ready mind, "My Lord and my God!"[70] In the same way, in my view, he appeared to the holy angels and showed them the character of his *oikonomia* in the flesh along with the signs of his suffering. He brought his crimson clothes and the very marks of the nails so that they might believe that the one who is truly God by nature has also become the Son of Man, taking his body from the holy virgin and emptying himself. He did this to present himself as an offering and sacrifice[71] for all as a pleasing aroma to God the Father and so to save the world under heaven. Therefore, the holy multitude of angels worships him. They do not decline to worship him because he was the firstborn and a man among many brothers. Instead, they were taught the *oikonomia* and they recognize that the Son is from God by nature even after he became flesh. **[375]**

1:8 To the Son he says, "Your throne, O God."

Is it not ignorant and audacious to meddle with that nature through which all things have been brought into being and which is older than all things? After all, they have come into being through it, and the Word of God is before every age. Yet these reckless people accuse him of being more recent, and they claim that he is originate. They do not realize that they are contradicted by the words of the Holy Spirit. Those who speak by the Spirit say that the ages were made through him.[72] But they insist that he who transcends both thought and speech is originate. They have no idea what they are saying. God the Father did not come into existence in time, but he always existed even in the beginning. Since this is so, it is absolutely necessary to think that the Son existed with him so that God may truly be the Father. If the Son is the Father's Word and wisdom and power and imprint and the radiance of his being, then let them enlighten us on this point: At what time was the Father irrational,[73] since the Son did not exist? When was the fount of wisdom without his wisdom? When was he separated from his power? When did the radiance of his glory not exist in God? How could his imprint not be with him and in him always? You see, if these things came into being in time, then he was not the Father before they came into being. He was irrational and without wisdom, lacking strength, and separated from his imprint and radiance. But I think it is godless to think this, and it is proof of the grossest impiety. The Father always was. **[376]** Therefore, the Son was as well, always existing with his begetter.

1:9 You have loved righteousness.

The divinely inspired David cried out in prayer to God the Father in heaven on behalf of all humanity: "Command your power, O God. Strengthen, O God, what you have done

[68]Is 63:1-2.

[69]Zech 13:6. Cf. Cyril's comments on Jn 20:26-27 in his *Commentary on John* (Maxwell 2:375). See also Cyril's *Epistula ad Acacium Scythopolitanum*, in *Acta Conciliorum Oecumenicorum* 1.1.4, ed. Eduard Schwartz (Berlin: de Gruyter, 1928), 46, section 18.

[70]Jn 20:28.

[71]Cf. Heb 10:5.

[72]Heb 1:2.

[73]ἄλογος. Since the word λόγος can mean "word" or "reason," saying that the Father is without the Word is the same as saying he is irrational.

among us!"[74] Now the Son is the power of the Father through whom he fixed the heavens and founded the earth. He is the one who accomplished the ordering of all things. He also created man in his image and likeness as a worker of righteousness, superior to corruptibility and death. But when death reigned through sin and we were subject to corruptibility and "all turned aside; together they became worthless,"[75] the Creator and Lord of all made provision for his creatures, as the situation demanded. God the Father was pleased to "recapitulate all things in Christ"[76] and to restore them to their original condition.

David expresses the deep mystery of the incarnation when he lifts his voice to the natural Son of God the Father and says, "You loved righteousness and hated wickedness. Therefore God, your God, has anointed you with the oil of gladness beyond your companions."[77] Now some think that these words do not apply to the Only Begotten, but that they were addressed only to the man who was begotten of the holy virgin. **[377]** There are many arguments to demonstrate the nonsense of those who think this. For example, he was not born as a regular man like us, devoid of the union with God, such that one could claim (as they do) that the God of the universe foreknew that he would love righteousness and hate wickedness by his own will alone. However, we could reasonably apply the psalmist's statement to the Only Begotten, who appeared in human form, if we carefully consider the prophecies of Isaiah about him. He said this: "Behold, the virgin shall be with child and shall bear a son, and they shall call his name Emmanuel. He shall eat butter and honey before he knows either to prefer evil or choose the good. For before the child knows good or evil, he rejects evil to choose the good."[78] He both loved righteousness and hated wickedness because he truly is righteousness and God. After all, if the child could not yet (in time) know what is blameworthy and approve what is not, how could he have rejected the evil to choose the good? But he was, as I said, God in the flesh, and so he could not be separated from the natural good properties in him. Now I do not approve of what I am about to say, but if the argument of these senseless people is correct, then let the separate one who is honored by the prosopic[79] union have his own virtue as well. But if they say that, I will reply: By what accomplishments will he be so great, even though he is by nature a human being, that he is deemed worthy to sit with God the Father on the divine thrones and bear the title Lord in natural equality with him? How does he have angels as worshipers who all serve him, even though the Scripture does not allow there to be a new god among us when it says, "Worship the Lord your God, and serve only him"?[80] Now perhaps they will run to their usual defense **[378]** and say that because of his union with God he will be clothed with the glory of the divine nature. Then admit that the union is true and stop equivocating on the matter! You divide the natures and assign each one its place. You say that each one is unconnected, and you discover (I know not how) only a union of *prosopa*.[81]

Now we maintain that the following statement was addressed to him who is the Son of God by nature based on the fact that he has become like us (that is, a human being): "You loved righteousness and hated wickedness. Therefore God, your God has anointed you with the oil of gladness beyond your

[74]Ps 69:28 (Ps 68:29 LXX).

[75]Rom 3:12.

[76]Eph 1:10.

[77]Ps 45:7 (Ps 44:8 LXX).

[78]Is 7:14-16.

[79]κατὰ πρόσωπον. Πρόσωπον means "person," but it can also mean "mask." In Cyril's view, a prosopic union is a union in appearance only. He is here attacking Antiochene Christology.

[80]Mt 4:10; Deut 6:13.

[81]τῶν προσώπων. See n79.

companions."[82] Since the first man trampled on the divine command and human nature succumbed to the propensity to sin, the Word of God, who is unchangeable by nature and holy and righteous and hating injustice became like us and was anointed a slave. He was enrolled under God the Father because of his human nature, even though he is God, and he is said to have been anointed by him through the Holy Spirit, though he did not receive this for himself. After all, as God he is holy by nature. No, he was leading us by grace through himself, as it were, and making us worthy of the Father's blessing, even though we offended him long ago both because of the transgression in Adam, and after that because of our own sin that tyrannizes us. "For it was no ambassador or angel" but the Lord himself who saved us.[83] Whoever thinks that the Word of God the Father received sanctification into his own nature has sailed off into an enormous sea of blasphemies. If we say that the anointing or sanctification referred to in this passage was done in the last times of the age, how would we not be forced even against our will to admit that he was not holy by nature, or at least that he was not holy in the beginning before the anointing or for that matter during the countless ages before he became **[379]** like us, since he had no share in sanctification? And if that is true, he was not free from sin.

Furthermore, how can the most-wise Paul say that the Son is the radiance of the Father's glory or similarly that he is the imprint of his hypostasis? An imprint, you see, completely impresses its shape on the archetype. So not even the Father himself is holy by nature. And then who would sanctify him? Therefore, we will say goodbye to the vomit of these people and confess that the Son is holy by nature just as, of course, the Father himself is. We further maintain that he was sanctified according to the flesh when he is said to have emptied himself by bearing the title of a man, in whom the sanctification dwells by participation from God and not by its own nature. And it is no surprise if the Word, who is God, lovingly appropriates the attributes of the human nature in the *oikonomia*. After all, how could he who wanted to undergo complete emptying turn around and reject its consequences? Therefore, if the Word of God the Father is considered on his own, he lacks no good thing and we maintain that he has the Holy Spirit as his own. But since, as I said, he became flesh, he anoints his temple[84] with his own Holy Spirit. The Father does what could be done through no one else in Israel except the Son alone. Therefore, the Son is said to receive the Spirit as man in the *oikonomia*. "How God anointed Jesus of Nazareth," it says, "with the Holy Spirit and with power."[85] As God he gives the Spirit to those worthy to receive him. For example, he breathed on the holy apostles and said, "Receive the Holy Spirit."[86] And the divinely inspired Peter addressed the people of the Jews and said of him, "Being therefore exalted at the right hand of God, and having received from the Father the promise of the Holy Spirit, he has poured out this that you both see and hear."[87] You hear in these words quite distinctly that he was exalted to the right hand of God and that he both received and **[380]** gave the Spirit. He was exalted, that is, after he had emptied himself. Just as he condescended to this willingly, so also he exalts himself along with his flesh, since he is the right hand of the Father through which all God-befitting works are accomplished. Accordingly, he exalts himself by the will of the Father when he breaks the bonds of death and says to the spirits below, "Come out!"[88] and sits down at the right hand of the Father.

[82]Ps 45:7 (Ps 44:8 LXX).
[83]Is 63:9.

[84]Cyril is referring to Jesus' body or his human nature. Cf. Jn 2:21.
[85]Acts 10:38.
[86]Jn 20:22.
[87]Acts 2:33.
[88]Is 49:9.

Now the natural Son was anointed by the oil of gladness when, after becoming like us, he called the Father his "God." And it is not strange at all to say this. He said somewhere to the holy apostles, "I am going to my Father and your Father, to my God and your God."[89] See, he clearly stated that his Father was his God on account of the human nature. And since we are called to adoption through him, he has the title brother to those who are slaves by nature, and he has given us his own Father. Now in our case, if we are called sons of the Father, we are still what we are (namely, human beings) and we are not unaware of the grace of him who honored us. So also in the case of him who is Son and Lord by nature, even if he should acknowledge the Father as his God on account of the flesh and his likeness to us, he does not stop being what he is. So we should not misunderstand words that are fitting because of his *oikonomia* in the flesh. Now come let us explain as best we can what it means when he is said to have been anointed "beyond his companions." When we are anointed by the Holy Spirit, those who are like us by nature are separate from him to the same extent that the nature of God is understood to be separate from every originate being. But when the Word of God, who became a man like us, anoints his own temple with his own Spirit, he does not pour in a partial energy, nor does he present his temple with a first installment as he does with us. No, he fills it up with sanctification and his own power and glory. That is why he said, "And for their sakes I sanctify myself, so that they also may be sanctified in truth."[90] **[381]**

The divinely inspired Paul leaves us in no doubt that even though he is said to have been anointed by the Father according to his human nature, he does not stop being what he was and is and will ever be, namely, God. Paul writes the following of the same person: "In the beginning, Lord, you founded the earth, and the heavens are the work of your hand; they will perish, but you remain; they will all wear out like clothing; like a cloak you will roll them up, and like clothing they will be changed. But you are the same, and your years will never end."[91]

Immediately then he adds the words: "But to which of the angels has he ever said, 'Sit at my right hand until I make your enemies a footstool for your feet'?"[92] I think that anyone with any sense would understand that the one seated with the Father is none other than he who was begotten of the holy virgin according to the flesh. And Emmanuel further confirms our position when he says to the teachers of the Jews, "'What do you think of the Christ? Whose son is he?' They say to him, 'The Son of David.'"[93] Then Christ replies, "How is it then that David by the Spirit calls him Lord, saying, 'The Lord said to my Lord: Sit at my right hand'?"[94] Understand, then, that he calls "Lord" the one anointed as man beyond his companions, and he says that "in the beginning" he founded the earth and made the heavens[95] and that he exists always.[96] That is because the Word of God the Father is eternal, while those things that came into being through him are not without beginning in their essence, since they have been called into being by God, who alone is said to "have immortality."[97] Nothing besides him is imperishable or indestructible. He goes on to add the clearest proof of the superiority that he has by nature: "To which of the angels did he say, 'Sit at my right hand'? Are they not all ministering spirits, sent to serve for the sake of

[89]Jn 20:17.
[90]Jn 17:19.

[91]Heb 1:10-12.
[92]Heb 1:13.
[93]Mt 22:42.
[94]Mt 22:43-44.
[95]Heb 1:10.
[96]Cf. Heb 1:11-12.
[97]1 Tim 6:16.

those who are to inherit salvation?"[98] After all, if *he* is seated on the divine thrones, **[382]** clothed in lordly honor even though he became the Son of David by taking a body from the holy virgin, while *they* stand beside him as the God and king of all, then who on earth could not see the difference between Christ and the angels? *He* is Son and God, while *they* boast a slave's station and their legitimacy is determined by their obedience before the highest glory. Now someone might ask, And what kind of argument will convince us to think that he who was begotten of the holy virgin in the last times of the age also founded the earth in the beginning and raised up the heavens? That person will get this reply from us: if you would just consider the power of the true union, not a union of *prosopa* by will or good pleasure, you will find that the human attributes became his own because of God's *oikonomia* and the attributes that are proper only to the Word are not foreign to the human nature when the Word is united to it. Since Emmanuel is the one and only true Son, we understand him to be both God and man.

2:8 Subjecting all things under his feet.

Raise your thoughts, he says, to the creation of humanity in the beginning and who the first man was. He closely examines how we were created by God in his image and likeness and how we were lavishly honored by receiving rule over the creatures of the earth. But since the head of our race (that is, Adam) broke the divine command and the human mind consequently fell sick with a severe propensity for transgression, we are stripped of glory and imperishability and the blessings we had in the beginning as we continue to live in the world. But we have been saved through Christ, and by his grace we have gained the means of recovering the gifts of long ago. The current passage covers the scope of this explanation. You see, the divinely inspired David was astonished **[383]** at his great kindness toward us. "What is man that you are mindful of him, or the son of man that you care for him?"[99] He is such a small, insignificant, earthly being. "You made him for a little while lower than the angels,"[100] since we are of course inferior to the nature and glory of the holy angels. Then the God of all deemed us worthy to crown with "honor and glory,"[101] and he made us resplendent. He appointed us as rulers over the creatures of the earth and installed us "over the works of his hands."[102]

Now the blessed David quite reasonably marveled at our condition, but the most-wise Paul, who is a master craftsman when it comes to spiritual meanings, elegantly guides the sense of the words to a mystical interpretation. He uses the words "coming world"[103] to describe the condition of the next age and our future recovery of the abundant supply of the gifts that had been given to us, which will take place at that time. For in Adam, as I said, we have fallen away from grace. The statement "Increase and multiply" and "subdue the earth"[104] was addressed to the first man representing human nature as a whole. "But now," Paul says, "we do not yet see everything in subjection to him." Therefore, we will look for another time for this reality when what God said to us will be true, since God cannot lie. That is what Paul means when he says that God has subjected the coming world not to angels, but he has given it to those on earth.[105]

How could anyone doubt that the mystagogue is speaking of the coming world that is for us? Those who renounce the present world persuade us to seek the future one, and they

[98]Heb 1:13-14.

[99]Heb 2:6.

[100]Ps 8:5 (Ps 8:6 LXX).

[101]Heb 2:7.

[102]Ps 8:6 (Ps 8:7 LXX).

[103]Heb 2:5.

[104]Gen 1:28.

[105]Heb 2:5.

advise us that we must press on "to the prize of the heavenly call"[106] and to thirst for what the saints hope for: that all things will be subjected to them and they will have dominion over the earth. The Savior himself reminded us of this when he said, "Blessed are the meek, for they will inherit the earth."[107] So who is the one through **[384]** whom God the Father's restoration of our condition takes place? Clearly, it is Christ. And we can express this fittingly through the lyre of the psalmist: "The Lord is the portion of my inheritance and of my cup. You are the one who restores my inheritance to me."[108] Through him we have gained the recovery of the good gifts that were given to our nature in the beginning, and we have this "prize"[109] as our possession. It is easy to see that this is how it is, since the divinely inspired Paul has written of him, "But we see Jesus, who for a little while was made lower than the angels, now crowned with glory and honor because of the suffering of death."[110]

You hear how the one enthroned with the Father and worshiped as God by the spirits in heaven is the highest of all. Thousands upon thousands of angels serve him, and ten thousand times ten thousand stand before him.[111] Next the mystagogue brings him down into our condition and tells of his self-emptying, immediately adding how many good things were accomplished by it for human nature. Consider, after all, that he was "for a little while made lower than the angels"[112] so that we might be enriched in him with blessings beyond our nature by the goodwill of God the Father. He raised us up with him and "seated us with him in the heavenly places in Christ."[113] Since Christ, the Savior of us all, is seated with us, this boast will extend to the entire human race. After all, how have we been enriched by his poverty if our condition did not improve when he who is above all creation became like us? Therefore, when he became human, he was made for a little while lower than the angels so that he might honor human nature and raise it up once again to its original condition by being crowned with "glory and honor"[114] in his human nature, even though as God he is the "Lord of glory."[115] Just as the transgression of Adam disgraced us, so also we have been glorified by the obedience of Christ on our behalf, who laid down his own life "so that he might be Lord of both the dead and the living."[116] **[385]**

How was he made less than the angels when he is worshiped by them? Well, he came down to the level of humanity, took a body that by nature was capable of dying into himself, and willingly suffered. And he is crowned with the ultimate glory on account of his suffering because through it he destroyed death and rendered corruptibility powerless, since he is incorruptibility and life. Now when the Son became flesh and died due to his voluntary emptying, superiority belonged to the angels, since they are both incorporeal and beyond death. But he who was made "for a little while lower than the angels" because of the limits of his humanity still has the superiority of his divinity and is worshiped by them. He takes his seat on the divine thrones, and they stand around them and continually sing their praises, calling him the Lord of the powers. **[386]**

2:9 So that by the grace of God he might taste death for everyone.

What it means that he "tasted" is clear to everyone, or at least I think it is. After he gave

[106]Phil 3:14.
[107]Mt 5:5.
[108]Ps 16:5 (Ps 15:5 LXX)
[109]Phil 3:14.
[110]Heb 2:9.
[111]Dan 7:10.
[112]Heb 2:9.
[113]Eph 2:6.
[114]Heb 2:9.
[115]1 Cor 2:8.
[116]Rom 14:9.

his body into death and in a fleshly way tasted the event, as it were, he came to life again and immediately trampled the power of death. So he who is said to have been for a little while made lower than the angels is himself the Word of God. He did not experience this lowering in his own nature, since he is always the same and remains what he is, immutable and unchangeable. But he experienced it humanly for us. Even though he was God by nature, he submitted to the limits of humanity according to the *oikonomia*. This belongs to the mystery concerning him, which deserves the highest wonder. Thus the prophet Habakkuk declared, "O Lord, I heard your report and was afraid; I considered your works and was in ecstasy."[117] And what happed was truly ecstasy beyond all wonder. But some people misunderstand the mystery itself (I know not how) and prattle on about it. In particular, in trying to explain the eighth Psalm they write, "Let us see, then, who the man is he is struck and amazed about—that the Only Begotten thought it worth being mindful of him and caring about him." After this they add the explicit claim that "the words, 'What is man that you are mindful of him, or the son of man that you care for him?'[118] do not refer to every man, but only to the Son." And they try to prove the truth of their statement by stating that the blessed Paul attributes the psalm to his person **[387]** when he says, "We see Jesus, who for a little while was made lower than the angels, now crowned with glory and honor because of the suffering of death." Then they divide the natures and say that when David marvels about the one deemed worthy of mindfulness and care, he is referring only to the man born of the holy virgin. And he is deemed worthy of things beyond his nature on the grounds that the Word of God is his benefactor.

[117]Hab 3:2.

[118]Heb 2:6.

It seems they are unaware that we do not understand Christ Jesus as a regular man by himself and separate, nor do we describe him that way. Rather, he is the Word of God incarnate. So that the explanation of these matters may proceed and be made clear before a world that needs it, come let us first of all take up the contemplation of this psalm. Since he was a prophet, the divinely inspired David knew that in accordance with the true divine promise, one would come "from the fruit of his loins according to the flesh."[119] Yet he was not unaware that he who would lower himself to our condition at the right time would still be God by nature. So he dialogues with him in the eighth Psalm and addresses him as man and God simultaneously, acknowledging the one who is from both as God. In this sense he says, "O Lord, our Lord, how majestic is your name in all the earth! Your magnificence was lifted above the heavens."[120] Where or before whom is Christ not majestic? How was his magnificence (or the brightness of his glory) not lifted above the heavens, if it is true that "at the name of Jesus every knee should bend, in heaven and on earth and under the earth, and every tongue should confess that Jesus Christ is Lord, to the glory of God the Father"?[121]

What comes next should reasonably demonstrate that the divinely inspired psalmist says these things of the Word who appeared in human form and was united to the flesh. **[388]** He said, "Out of the mouths of babes and infants you have ordained praise."[122] When he raised Lazarus from the dead, everyone marveled at him. He "found a young donkey and sat on it," at which point even children took the "branches of palm trees" and honored him with fitting worship and said, "Hosanna to the Son of David! Blessed is the

[119]Acts 2:30.

[120]Ps 8:1 (Ps 8:2 LXX).

[121]Phil 2:10-11.

[122]Ps 8:2 (Ps 8:3 LXX).

one who comes in the name of the Lord!"[123] When others rebuked them, Jesus said, "Have you never read, 'Out of the mouths of babes and infants you have ordained praise?'"[124] When David sees the Son, almost incarnate already and riding on a colt, he is understandably astonished at this as he considers the fact that he sees the Son lowering himself to such indignity even though he is God by nature. Next, the blessed David sees that there is no other reason for this emptying than us. We needed to be rescued from perishability and snatched from the tyrannical hands of sin (I mean the hands of the devil). Therefore, he deems the mystery of the *oikonomia* in the flesh worthy of all admiration. That is why he says, "Lord, what is man that you are mindful of him, or the son of man that you care for him?"[125] After all, what is human nature compared to God? How can I even say this? What is the human race? Could those on earth be thought to have as great a position (as the ranks of the holy angels, I mean)? But even though humanity is nothing at all both in its nature and number, the Creator did not ignore us. He was mindful of us and deemed us worthy of care, since we are perishable. When he first brought us into existence, he made us for a little while lower than the angels. But he crowned us with honor and glory. He established us as the works of his hands and put all things under our feet.

This is the point of the entire psalm, **[389]** and the divinely inspired Paul expounds it with outstanding philosophy. He skillfully brings our diseased condition into the renewal that takes place through Christ. In him there is a "new creation." The old has passed away and all things have become new.[126] The Holy Spirit makes the same point through one of the holy prophets: "Take courage, O Zion; do not let your hands grow weak. The Lord, your God, is in you.[127] He is strong to save you, and he will renew you in his love."[128]

Then Paul shows that we are stripped of the glory that was given to us long ago. That is why he says, "We do not yet see everything in subjection to him."[129] Now we who choose to think rightly certainly do not imagine that he says these things about one man. Rather, he represents all of humanity in one person and says that he regained participation in the glory that was given in ancient times. Now we must describe the construction of the entire passage and the outcome of its skillful composition. He shows that man has lost the glory because of the transgression of Adam in order to explain how to get it back, just as one might show the poverty of the human race in order then to point out the one through whom we have been enriched. You see, he immediately adds, "We see Jesus, who for a little while was made lower than the angels, now crowned with glory and honor because of the suffering of death." The Word of God, who is God by nature as we have often said, lowered himself to the point of emptying and shared our name, as a "man" who "for a little while was lower than the angels," so that he might become obedient to the Father "even to the point of death,"[130] and he might crown human nature with glory and honor, since he is crowned as one of us even though he is the "Lord of glory."[131]

[123]Mt 21:9.

[124]Mt 21:16.

[125]Ps 8:5.

[126]2 Cor 5:17.

[127]ἐν σοὶ. The NRSV translates ἐν σοὶ as "in your midst." I have translated it "in you" because I think it is likely that Cyril would take it to refer to the Word's presence in human nature through the hypostatic union. This is how he construes Jn 1:14, "The Word became flesh and dwelt in us [ἐν ἡμῖν]." See *Commentary on John* 1:14 (Maxwell 1:63). He makes a similar move in a comment on Lk 17:21, which is usually translated, "The kingdom of God is among you [ἐντὸς ὑμῶν]." Cyril, however, construes it as "within you," referring to the Spirit's presence in the believer through faith. See *Commentary on John* 7:39 (Maxwell 1:311).

[128]Zeph 3:16-17.

[129]Heb 2:8.

[130]Phil 2:8.

[131]1 Cor 2:8.

But if anyone says the Word of God deemed the man begotten of the holy virgin to be worthy of mindfulness and care, and that he was that man's benefactor and considered him worthy of honor that transcended his nature, such a person would drag, so to speak, the glory of the mystery down to the ground, **[390]** and would incur utter ridicule for that. Where is this Christ, who is a bare man? When do they think he was separate from the Word who is united to him? He is Emmanuel from his mother's womb. He did not become this at a later time. So how can they say that God the Word deemed him worthy of care and mindfulness? They would be caught red-handed separating and dividing him into parts and presenting Christ and the Son to us as stripped of the Word who is united to him. After all, the one who deems him worthy of care and mindfulness must be different from the one to whom he gives these things. In that case, how is there still "one Lord, one faith, one baptism"?[132] Even though there is a great difference between the natures, nevertheless the manner of union shows that there is one Son from both. Therefore, if we say that the Word of God deems him worthy of mindfulness, we are surely "worldly people devoid of the Spirit," as it is written,[133] since we are separating the one into two. But if he was in the beginning what he is now and he is Emmanuel from his mother's womb, then unless we accept the manner of the union, the Word would necessarily be mindful of himself and deem himself worthy of care and be the benefactor of himself. The force of these considerations will lead us to bizarre results. After all, the Word's body does not belong to anyone but the Word. Otherwise, who do the Holy Scriptures say emptied himself?

Now if they separate out on us the one begotten of the holy virgin and say that he underwent the emptying, how did the glorified one empty himself, since being deemed worthy of care and mindfulness and obtaining union with God is an honor and a glory that belongs to a human being like us? But if they should say that the emptying was done to the Only Begotten himself, then he did empty himself, since he suffered. After all, if suffering applies to someone, then emptying would apply to them even more. We have saved ourselves, however, if indeed the one begotten of the holy virgin is a man like us and not hypostatically united to the Word of **[391]** God, as they claim. In that case, how is Christ God, if he, along with us, was deemed worthy of mindfulness by God and gained a patron? This despite the fact that we approach him and pray to him as God, and ask him for an abundance of heavenly blessings as the one who divinely grants requests for all creation. **[392]**

2:14 Since, therefore, the children share flesh and blood, he himself likewise. [**393**]

I think that before we look at anything else, we must inquire carefully about what children the passage is talking about who "share flesh and blood," and who "likewise" shares the same. When the only begotten Word of God lowered himself to the level of humanity, even though he is God and Lord by nature and is seated with God the Father, he was thereby classified as a brother to those who have been called by faith to God's adoption. Then and only then did he say of us somewhere (fully preserving the exquisite craftsmanship of the *oikonomia*), "I will proclaim your name to my brothers,"[134] and somewhere else, "Here I am and the children whom God has given me."[135]

All things have been given to him by God the Father, and we have become his

[132]Eph 4:5.

[133]Jude 19.

[134]Heb 2:12.

[135]Heb 2:13.

inheritance, even though in ancient times we were the "portions for foxes," as David says.[136] That is because we miserable people were subject against our will to herds of demons. But Christ won and inherited us all by his own blood. Indeed, he spoke to God his heavenly Father of "those whom you have given me from the world. They were yours, and you gave them to me, and the glory that you have given me I have given them."[137] Although he is the Son by nature, he says that he shares this glory with us by grace on account of his humanity. He remained what he was and gave us his own glory. He sealed us by his own Spirit for adoption and in him "we cry, 'Abba! Father!'"[138] Therefore, we who are numbered among the children of God "share in flesh and blood"—that is, we are in blood and flesh and in perishable earthly bodies. For this reason, **[394]** the only begotten Word of God himself, who is life by nature, participated in the same things, and he did so precisely "likewise" so that he might destroy the one who has the power of death.

Since there was no other way that what was dominated by death and perishability and sin could be brought back to its original condition except through Christ alone, the blessed David pleaded for the mystery of the incarnation to be fulfilled at the appropriate time, saying, "Why, O Lord, do you stand far off? Why do you hide yourself in times of trouble?"[139] This is the sense in which he is called Emmanuel. No longer did the Word of God stand far off, but he came very near to us by appearing as a man. He "likewise" shared flesh and blood with us since the earthly race (that is, humanity) had been conquered by death and perishability, and it seemed good to the God of the universe, because of his kindness and love, to "recapitulate all things in Christ,"[140] so that death might finally be rendered powerless and yield for the first time to Christ, who won the victory for earthly bodies.

This—this!—is how the power of imperishability spreads to our entire race and how the divinely inspired Paul can be trustworthy when he writes, "For since death came through a human being, the resurrection of the dead has also come through a human being."[141] What had succumbed had to—had to!—be healed and destroy death through the very flesh that was under the power of sin. When the flesh offended in Adam on account of his transgression, it fell under the power of death. In the same way when it became pleasing in Christ on account of his obedience, it was freed from the snares and fear of death. As a result, we leap for joy and shout at them, "Where, O death, is your victory? Where, O Hades, is your sting?"[142] Since the only begotten Word of God is life **[395]** essentially, he united himself to mortal earthly flesh so that death might pounce on it like some wild beast and be defeated and rendered powerless. After all, it was impossible that life would yield to death. "For it is clear that he did not come to help angels, but the seed of Abraham. Therefore, he had to become like his brothers in every respect."[143] If the only begotten Word of God did not become man, but instead united the *prosopon* of a man to himself (as those people think who define the union as one of mere good pleasure or inclination of the will), how was he made "like his brothers in all things"? Would he not just be considered a brother—he who is beyond every originate being and who transcends creation with incomparable superiority (I mean superiority by nature)? How has he shared flesh and blood if they did not become his just as they are

[136]Ps 63:10 (Ps 62:11 LXX).
[137]Jn 17:6, 22.
[138]Rom 8:16.
[139]Ps 10:1 (Ps 9:22 LXX).
[140]Eph 1:10.
[141]1 Cor 15:21.
[142]1 Cor 15:55.
[143]Heb 2:16-17.

ours? Therefore, there is one Son and Lord by a hypostatic[144] union, since the Word was brought together with human nature that shares flesh and blood and was made "like his brothers in all things."

2:17–3:6 So that he might be a merciful and faithful high priest.

The divinely inspired Moses through type and shadow urged Israel on to divine knowledge and showed them the way of righteousness through the law. But he was "slow of speech and slow of tongue."[145] Therefore, at that time the God of the universe was known only to those throughout Judea,[146] and from Dan to Beersheba and from the river to the sea. These were the borders of the land of the Jews. His name was great and exceedingly well known. Seeing this, the prophet David sings somewhere and says to him about Israel, "You have brought a vine out of Egypt; you drove out the nations and planted it."[147] Then he adds, bounding Israel by the Euphrates River and the [**396**] Indian Sea to the south,[148] "It sent out its branches to the sea, and its shoots to the River."[149] Here you see that the proclamation of the all-wise Moses was restricted and hardly even extended to Gentiles. And to those who have been called, he adds temporary blessings that soon wither as a reward for obedience and a recompense for life in the law. (I mean that he everywhere refers to the promised land.) The law has justified no one, since no one is justified before God by the law and it is "impossible for the blood of bulls and goats to take away sins."[150] But our Lord Jesus Christ has become a "merciful and faithful high priest to make a sacrifice of atonement for the sins of the people." Because he became this "when he was tempted," he has helped those who are being tempted. He has called the world with a holy and "heavenly calling," and he has become a "merciful high priest" because he was not a servant of the law, which condemns. Rather, with forgiving grace and love he has justified us through faith and has granted a washing away of our ancient faults. He was always merciful by nature, but God's only begotten Word was appointed as a mediator between us and God through the incarnation so that just as he was always kind and merciful, so also he might be appointed high priest and have mercy on those on earth, acting in his characteristic and customary way, not separated from his own good attributes. And thus he might make the heavenly Father himself merciful to us. He also became "faithful" in accordance with the will of God the Father, presenting himself for us as a pleasing aroma and taking up the sins of us all "in his body to the tree," as it is written.[151] In this way he has helped those who are being tempted "because he himself suffered when he was tempted," for "by his wounds" we have been healed, as it is written. Now understand that in this passage the phrase "when he was tempted" stands for "when he suffered or bore the temptation of those who crucified him." By giving the body (in which he suffered) for all, [**397**] he freed us all from death, sin, and temptation. Therefore, he has helped those who are being tempted since one has died for all (and that one is worth more than all creation) "so that those who live might live no longer for themselves, but for him who died and was raised for them."[152]

[144]καθ' ὑπόστασιν.

[145]Ex 4:10.

[146]Cf. Ps 76:1 (Ps 75:2 LXX).

[147]Ps 80:8 (Ps 79:9 LXX).

[148]In an exposition of Joel 2:20 in his *Commentary on Joel*, Cyril identifies the "Indian Sea" as the body of water on the southeastern border of the vast desert south of Jerusalem (Pusey 1:328).

[149]Ps 80:11 (Ps 79:12 LXX). Cf. Deut 11:24.

[150]Heb 10:4.

[151]1 Pet 2:24.

[152]2 Cor 5:15.

The divinely inspired Paul confirms that Christ suffered in the flesh and so made us holy when he says to both Gentiles and Jews, "And you who were once estranged and hostile in mind, doing evil deeds, he has now reconciled in his fleshly body through death, so as to present you holy and blameless and irreproachable before him—provided that you continue securely established and steadfast in the faith without shifting from the hope promised by the gospel that you heard."[153] It was wise of him to say to those called to a living and enduring hope: "Therefore, brothers, holy partners in a heavenly calling, consider that Jesus, the apostle and high priest of our confession, was faithful to the one who appointed him, just as Moses also was faithful in his house." And he quite rightly refers to the calling through Christ as "heavenly" because the God of the universe will grant to those called through him not the temporary and fading blessings that the law of Moses gave to the ancients, but eternal blessings that are commensurate with those deemed worthy to receive them. So he has a possession that cannot be lost. We are also called "heavenly" in another sense, since Christ has become our leader and road and gate. Paul says, "Just as we have borne the image of the man of dust, we will also bear the image of the man of heaven."[154] And again, "The first man was from the earth, a man of dust; the second man is from heaven. As was the man of dust, so are those who are of the dust; and as is the man of heaven, so are those who are of heaven."[155] We have therefore become heavenly, since we are being transformed into Christ through the Spirit, who is from heaven. For that **[398]** reason, even while we walk on earth, we have our "citizenship in heaven."[156] We have not, like the ancients, come to "something that can be touched, a fire, and darkness, and gloom, and a tempest, and the sound of a trumpet, and a voice."[157] Rather, we have come to "Mount Zion and to the city of the living God, the heavenly Jerusalem, and to innumerable angels in festal gathering, and to the assembly of the firstborn who are enrolled in heaven, and to God the judge of all, and to the spirits of the righteous made perfect, and to Jesus, the mediator of a new covenant, and to the sprinkled blood that speaks a better word than the blood of Abel."[158] After all, the blood of Abel cried out against his fratricidal murderer, while the precious blood speaks better words than Abel's since it practically begs for the Father's mercy on the world, and we have been sprinkled by it for our justification.

Let us consider, then, that "Jesus, the apostle and high priest of our confession, was faithful to the one who appointed him" (that is, as an apostle and high priest). He became "faithful" even to the point of death and a cross, placing himself in the goodwill of the Father so that he might make us imitators of him. And so because of him we do not fear to undergo death if it should come at some time because of our reverence and obedience to God. The blessed Peter too will summon us to this when he says, "For to this you have been called, because Christ also suffered for you, leaving you an example, so that you should follow in his steps."[159] And the Savior himself says, "If any want to become my followers, let them deny themselves and take up their cross and follow me."[160]

Now the fact that he calls the Son "faithful" does no damage to his glory, since one may see that the word is utterly God-befitting since it is applied to God the Father himself. It is written that "God is faithful and there is no **[399]** unrighteousness in him; the Lord is

[153]Col 1:21-23.
[154]1 Cor 15:49.
[155]1 Cor 15:47-48.
[156]Phil 3:20.
[157]Heb 12:18-19.
[158]Heb 12:22-24.
[159]1 Pet 2:21.
[160]Mt 16:24.

righteous and holy."[161] And one of Christ's disciples said, "Therefore, let those suffering in accordance with God's will entrust themselves to a faithful Creator."[162] And indeed Paul said, "God is faithful; by him you were called into the fellowship of his Son."[163] What else does "faithful" mean in these passages except that he is steadfast, resolute, and worthy of faith in whatever he happens to say or decides to do? The Son became this when he sat down with the Father even in his humanity and when he endured the cross and death to accomplish the Father's will. Thus he said, "For I have come down from heaven, not to do my own will, but the will of him who sent me. And this is the will of him who sent me, that I should lose nothing of all that he has given me, but raise it up on the last day."[164] We have been given to the Son as Savior and life-giver, and this was the work he had from the Father. You see, the Father accomplishes everything he wills through the Son in a God-befitting way, since the Son is his power and wisdom. That is why the Son himself said, "But I have a testimony greater than John's. The works that the Father has given me to complete, the very works that I am doing, testify on my behalf that the Father has sent me."[165] And David sings somewhere, "O God, command your strength. Strengthen, O God, what you have wrought in us."[166]

Come let us examine carefully, if you please, what kind of priesthood the Son has and for whom he exercises it: whether it is a servile kind promoting the glory of another, or a kind that is perfectly fitting for the Son when it comes to his nature and not incompatible with the inner meaning of the incarnation. The ancient priests, in accordance with the law given by Moses, offered God worship in type and shadow. They offered the Son himself to the Father, [**400**] and they usually presented him as a pleasing aroma in a goat and a ram and a calf. You see, a young goat was slaughtered for sins in accordance with the faith of the Holy Scriptures, but in this there was a semblance of the truth. The most-wise Paul has written to us, "But when Christ came as a high priest of the good things to come, then through the greater and perfect tent (not made with hands, that is, not of this creation) he entered once for all into the Holy Place, not with the blood of goats and calves, but with his own blood, thus obtaining eternal redemption."[167] For the priests of the law, the power of the worship was effected by the blood of another since they worshiped with a "sketch and shadow" of the heavenly realities.[168] But for Christ this is not so. Far from it! He has saved the earth under heaven with his own blood, and he has "become a priest, not through a legal requirement concerning physical descent, but through the power of an indestructible life."[169] He has offered himself on our behalf since the worship in types is powerless for justification, and indeed it was "impossible for the blood of bulls and goats to take away sins."[170] Therefore a second covenant needed to be sought, since the first was not perfect in itself.[171] The Son, who is from the Father by nature, knew the Father's will, so he became a human being for us in order to bring and offer himself for us all as a sacrifice to him. And the blessed Paul, who does not lie, would be our witness to this. He said of him, "Consequently, when he came into the world, he said, 'Sacrifices and offerings you have not desired, but a body you have prepared for me; you have not asked for burnt offerings and sin offerings. Then I said: See, I have come

[161] Deut 32:4.
[162] 1 Pet 4:19.
[163] 1 Cor 1:9.
[164] Jn 6:38-39.
[165] Jn 5:36.
[166] Ps 68:28 (Ps 69:29 LXX).
[167] Heb 9:11-12.
[168] Heb 8:5.
[169] Heb 7:16.
[170] Heb 10:4.
[171] Heb 8:7.

to do your will, O God; it is written about me in the scroll of the book.'"[172] Who then is the one who comes into the world? How is he said to have entered in the first place? **[401]** Is it not because he was previously outside it and he left his home, as it were?

The Word of God, then, came into the world not spatially[173] but rather by nature when he appeared as part of the world. God the Father prepared a body for him that he might die in the flesh and so become a substitute for the life of all, in accordance with the Scriptures.[174] Therefore, he became the "mediator of a new covenant, so that those who are called may receive the promised eternal inheritance, because a death has occurred that redeems them from the transgressions under the first covenant."[175] So he is called the "high priest and apostle of our confession." He performed that task exceedingly well and brought us to the Father as a pleasing spiritual aroma and as people already purified, since we approach him confessing the creed of our faith. Since we are commanded to make confession of the pure faith and the consubstantial Trinity,[176] how is it not clear to all that he offers that confession not to someone else who ranks ahead of him and is superior by nature, but to himself with the Father and the Holy Spirit? Therefore, even after he has come to be in the flesh he is rightly understood to be God. After all, we are justified when we confess both that he has become flesh and that he remained the Word and he trampled the power of death for us, since he is life by nature as one who is from the life of the Father.

The blessed Paul offers even more proof that Emmanuel is God by nature and is truly the Son when he says that he has become "the apostle and high priest of our confession," faithful to the "one who appointed him, just as Moses was faithful in his house. Yet Jesus is worthy of more glory than Moses, just as the builder of a house has more honor than the house itself." Once again with these words I am struck with astonishment at the mystagogue. He skillfully sidesteps **[402]** Israel's headlong rush into unbridled behavior, or at least their belief that they had to oppose Christ. He engages in a laudatory description of Moses, calling him "faithful." Then he adroitly inserts the surpassing greatness of our Savior along with this. He says that Christ became the apostle and high priest and adds that he was faithful, just as of course Moses himself was. He expertly brings up Moses' name and having prefaced it with the praise for the Word himself, he immediately shows that Moses is inferior to the glory of Christ. He says that Christ receives more honor "just as the builder of the house has more honor than the house itself."

You can see how he exalts the Word of God, who has come to be in the flesh and is seen to be in the form of a slave in the *oikonomia*, placing him above the level of humanity and the limits of our servile condition. He says that he is the Creator of all things, and that means of Moses himself as well. And with these words he crowns him with the glory of lordship by nature. After all, if it is true that no creature can be the same in its essence as its creator, how could anyone doubt that the one who created Moses is greater in glory in every way? Observe as well that he says that the "apostle and high priest of our confession" has become "faithful to the one who appointed him" just as the priest Moses was, but he was deemed worthy of greater glory than Moses, "just as the builder of the house has more honor than the house itself." Then he shows that Jesus is God by adding, "Every house is built by someone, but the builder of all things

[172]Heb 10:5-7; Ps 40:6-8 (Ps 39:7-9 LXX).

[173]Following Pusey's emendation τοπικῶς. The text has τυπικῶς (as a type).

[174]Cf. 1 Pet 3:18; 4:1.

[175]Heb 9:15.

[176]The grammar of this sentence is unclear. Pusey notes that something seems to be missing.

is God." Therefore, even though Christ is a human being like one of us, we must separate out those attributes that he has only from the time of his birth in the flesh. When the only begotten Son, who is older than the ages themselves, became human by the good pleasure of God the Father, **[403]** he took the title Christ Jesus. This was a new name for him, you see, and it coincided with the time of the *oikonomia*. But even though he has become flesh, he still has his existence before all time, and we should confess that he is the Creator of all. "For there is one God, the Father, from whom are all things, and one Lord, Jesus Christ, through whom are all things."[177] And again, "Jesus Christ is the same yesterday and today and forever."[178] How could he be the same "yesterday" while being begotten in the last times of the age? It is because the immense age of the nature of the Word of God cannot be lost, as I said, but necessarily remains his even in the time of the very recent *oikonomia* in the flesh. Indeed, he once made a statement to Israel about their forefather Abraham, saying, "Your father Abraham rejoiced that he would see my day; he saw it and was glad."[179] But those who did not at all understand the mystery concerning him, but supposed that he was a mere human being like us and nothing more, ignorantly replied, "You are not yet fifty years old, and have you seen Abraham?"[180] And he said to them, "Truly I tell you, before Abraham was, I am."[181] He is therefore the maker and creator of Abraham himself, and Moses, and all things. And we absolutely must say that the Creator exists before his creatures and his archetypal beauty shines forth prior to those created in his image. Therefore, the glory of Christ incomparably exceeds the level of Moses, or rather, it exceeds all things that have been called into existence. Next the divinely inspired Paul tries to confirm from another angle that his statement about these matters is both wise and true. "Moses was," he says, "faithful in all God's house as a servant to testify to the things that would be spoken later. Christ, however, was faithful over God's house as a son, and we are his house." Now observe how he assigns the rank of household servant to the blessed Moses because of his legitimate service **[404]** when he says that he was faithful "in God's house to testify to the things that would be spoken later," that is, to be a minister of the words from God. Not so with Christ! He was not faithful in the house as a servant, but as the Son and master over the Father's house (that is, over us who have been justified by faith and sanctified by the Spirit). Moses tutored the ancients through the shadow of the law, and he received the reward of a genuine servant when God said to him, "But you, stand here by me."[182] But the reward is much greater in the case of Christ. He "sat down at the right hand of the Majesty on high,"[183] and he administered the Father's house as Son and Lord. He dwells in us as God through his own Spirit, while the all-wise Moses dwelt in no one. We have not become participants in Moses or any other saint for that matter, but we participate in Christ both through the Spirit and the Mystical Blessing.[184] God declared through one of the holy prophets, "I will live in them and walk among them, and I will be their God, and they shall by my people."[185] Yet now that the time for this to be fulfilled has arrived, Christ is the one who dwells in us according to the ancient promise in order to make us temples of the living God (that is, of him) and through him to unite us to God the Father. Indeed, he said to the holy apostles, "On that day you will know that I am

[177] 1 Cor 8:6.
[178] Heb 13:8.
[179] Jn 8:56.
[180] Jn 8:57.
[181] Jn 8:58.
[182] Deut 5:31.
[183] Heb 1:3.
[184] I.e., the Eucharist.
[185] 2 Cor 6:16; Lev 26:12.

in my Father, and you in me, and I in you."[186] For "anyone united to the Lord is one spirit with him," as it is written.[187] Again, he juxtaposes us with God the Father by saying, "I ask not only on behalf of these, but also on behalf of all who will believe in me through their word, that they may all be one. As you, Father, are in me and I am in you, may they also be one in us, so that the world may believe **[405]** that you have sent me. The glory that you have given me I have given them, so that they may be one, as we are one, I in them and you in me, that they may become completely one."[188]

Therefore, in Christ we have obtained the good of union with God the Father. And this glorious and resplendent honor surely remains in us if we maintain the "confidence and the pride that belong to hope" and also if we believe that the temple that comes from the holy virgin is not another Son, separate and apart from him who is from God the Father, but he "became flesh," as the Scriptures say, "and dwelt in us."[189] He did not stop being God, but Jesus Christ is one Son and one Lord.

4:12 Piercing until it divides.

Now the words "piercing until it divides soul and spirit" can be understood this way: the proclamation from God divides and separates the parts of the soul, making the soul of the hearers receptive and capable of taking it in. **[406]**

6:8 Ground that produces thorns.

The frivolous soul could reasonably be compared with worthless salted soil. It often receives seeds sown by those who work the ground, but it produces absolutely nothing. Paul teaches us the outcome that will take place for that soul that does not use the gift God gave it. He says that its "end is to be burned."[190] Do you want to see through events as well that what he says is true? Israel was once fruit-bearing ground, "a luxuriant vine," as it is written.[191] And the blessed prophets were like clouds, watering it with the words of God. They were eager to help it, but it "yielded thorns"[192] and became wild and overgrown. Therefore, it was given over to burning—that is, it was rendered completely useless and assigned to the fire.

9:4 Having a golden altar of incense . . .

There is a long discussion of the tabernacle and its contents. But we will summarize it briefly by saying that there were three areas of the tabernacle. The outer area was for everyone. After that was the first veil, which is also called a curtain[193] **[407]** because it is drawn. It separated out the courtyard where everyone entered in common and where they sacrificed at the bronze altar. The middle area behind the curtain was where the priests entered and performed their respective rites of worship. This place was called "holy."[194] It was a type of ancient worship in that blood sacrifices were performed there. But the inner area was called the Holy of Holies, which was a type of our mystery. The apostle calls the tent after the bronze altar but before the holy of holies the "first" tent.[195] It was in the middle, you see, separated from the courtyard by the curtain, and then after this middle tent the veil was placed. And beyond this was the tent called the holy of holies, which no one entered except the high priest alone, and he but once a year.[196] In this tent was stored the ark

[186]Jn 14:20.
[187]1 Cor 6:17.
[188]Jn 17:20-23.
[189]Jn 1:14.

[190]Heb 6:8.
[191]Hos 10:1.
[192]Is 5:4 (LXX).
[193]ἐπίσπαστρον. Cf. Ex 26:36 (LXX).
[194]Heb 9:2.
[195]Heb 9:2.
[196]Heb 9:7.

containing the tablets of the law as well as the jar of manna and Aaron's rod.[197] Actually, Kings says that only the tablets were placed in the ark.[198] Perhaps Paul added the staff and the jar from tradition.

9:5 Above it were the cherubim of glory overshadowing the mercy seat.

Observe how he makes the mercy seat an image of the Son, who became incarnate. That is when the Son became the mercy seat. In addition, he has the cherubim stand around in a circle, always facing him and looking at him. Furthermore, the prophet tells us that he beheld him "because he saw his glory and spoke about him."[199] "I saw the Lord of hosts," he says, "sitting on a throne, high and **[408]** lofty."[200] And the seraphim stood around him and praised the Lord on the throne, stretching out their wings. They were also positioned in the same way in the holy tabernacle, overshadowing the mercy seat with their wings. And if the golden cherubim could have cried out or spoken, they would have praised the only begotten Son, who is from God the Father by nature and who appeared in the form of a slave, as the Lord of hosts. **[409]**

9:19 And with various baptisms, regulations for the flesh imposed until the time comes to set things right.

The law has perfected no one when it comes to their conscience. Rather, it has introduced teachings about baptisms,[201] descriptions of sprinkling "for the purification of the flesh."[202] The power of the law's priesthood has basically ceased on this point. If anyone touched a dead body or a leper, or had a discharge, that person was baptized and thus was considered cleansed. These were "regulations for the flesh," that is, fleshly commands for the fleshly justification of those who were considered unclean according to the flesh. But we can see from the Holy Scriptures themselves that God did not allow those in Israel's bloodline to remain foolishly in the shadows of the law. He commanded them to sacrifice a lamb as a type of Christ and to eat it as they were ready to depart,[203] indicating that the types will not last forever but will run, as it were, toward the truth. **[410]**

10:29 And outraged the Spirit of grace.

Just as a soldier who throws down his shield and runs away from battle should not be honored by a second insignia but should be punished and reprimanded for cowardice, in the same way I think that one who outrages such an august and admirable grace should not be honored by receiving the Spirit again, since the first grace was rejected. Rather, that person should be subject to punishment. "Their faithlessness" will not "nullify the faithfulness of God."[204] And if some turn back and despise him, we will not put it down to the unreliability of divine grace. No, the judge of all will punish those who do not resist falling to such a level of godlessness that they have "trampled the Son of God" and "outraged the Spirit of grace" in whom they were "sanctified" and became "partakers in the divine nature."[205] **[411]**

10:35 It brings a great reward.

That is because through endurance and through not hesitating to put extraordinary

[197]Heb 9:4.
[198]1 Kings 8:9 (3 Kings 8:9 LXX).
[199]Jn 12:41, referring to Isaiah.
[200]Is 6:1.
[201]Heb 6:2.
[202]Heb 9:13.
[203]Ex 12:8, 11.
[204]Rom 3:3.
[205]1 Pet 1:4.

virtues into practice, but always thirsting after them, never being satisfied, and insatiably loving every good deed, they heap up approval for themselves by their actions. They have the same kind of desire that the lovers of wealth have, of whom it is written, "The lover of money will not be satisfied with money."[206] So if temporary earthly things that soon wither do not satisfy those people, should we not employ even more burning desire to obtain the things of God, which extend to limitless ages and hold unceasing contentment?

11:3 By faith we understand that the worlds were established by the word of God, so that what is seen was not made from things that are visible.

Faith is an extraordinarily great good. It contains the riches of removing sins and cleansing from all filth. It bestows betrothal to God. It is the way to sanctification and adoption. In sum, it is the matchmaker of every good thing. That is how the fathers gained their fame. That is how they had resplendent and renowned glory. Many of them fought bravely even against death itself, and they were crowned with an unfading crown of glory.

11:7 By faith Noah, warned by God about events as yet unseen, respected the warning and built an ark to save his household.

Since the entire earth had "corrupted its ways," as it is written,[207] and the human heart had inclined **[412]** "to evil from youth,"[208] God sent a flood over people throughout the entire earth, like one reclaiming some overgrown dry and barren garden. But he preserved one fertile plant in it, the virtuous Noah, so that through him the human race on earth might be saved again, as Noah was transformed into another beginning, as it were. "By faith Noah, warned, built an ark to save his household," "in which a few, that is, eight souls, were saved through water."[209] A general death sentence was declared against everyone on earth (that is, the earth was full of sin and provoked the Creator to a wrath that was not his will). But Noah, who was righteous, was saved with his whole household. That is because he believed God when he commanded him to build the ark. The whole earth was baptized, but the ark swam on top of the water since it had God, the Savior of all, as its pilot. And it contained a remnant of mankind, together with women and children. By faith he has the boast . . .[210]

11:17-19 By faith Abraham, when put to the test, offered up Isaac.[211]

I cannot avoid admiring this great deed. The blessed Abraham was an old man. He lamented his childlessness and prayed to God for an heir from his wife. And then when he received one and placed in him the entire hope of his family and had in him the fulfillment of God's promise, God commanded him to sacrifice him! What was the old man to do? I imagine he was in great despair. Nature compelled him to tender affection, but the divine command called him to obedience. He was attached to his child since that was all he had, but he also was afraid to offend God. The soul of that righteous man was just like a tall tree that practically staggers and is shaken as it is tossed to and fro by the blowing of the wind. **[413]** How then did he overcome the storm of testing? Paul, who knows the law better than anyone, teaches us

[206]Eccl 5:10 (Eccl 5:9 LXX).
[207]Gen 6:12.
[208]Gen 8:21.

[209]1 Pet 3:20.
[210]There is a lacuna in the codex here.
[211]Pusey includes this lemma from the catena, though he suspects it is from a homily of someone who is reading Cyril since, in Pusey's view, it uses language that is not characteristic of Cyril.

this when he says, "By faith, when put to the test, he offered up Isaac, considering the fact that God is able even to raise someone from the dead." What a solid faith! What steadfast reasoning fit for a saint! He ascribed to God the power to do all things. And what then? What goal did his faith reach? The Holy Scripture teaches us. "Abraham believed God," it says, "and it was reckoned to him as righteousness."[212]

12:2b Who instead of the joy that was set before him endured the cross, disregarding its shame.

Here we should keep in mind that it was certainly possible for him to enjoy the honors of his nature and exult in his incomparable divine superiority over all things. (That is what I think "the joy set before him" refers to.) But he emptied himself and descended into our condition so that he might endure death for all according to the flesh and then trample it through his resurrection from the dead, thus giving us access to the ability to return to life. His suffering was shameful and degrading, but when he raised his own temple, he cut a new path through death and overcame decay. As God from God (even though he appeared in the flesh), the Son did away with the disgrace of these experiences and the ugliness of their shame, and he was glorified because of his resurrection, even though before his resurrection he did not refuse the most dishonorable and ignoble death. **[414]**

12:2c He has taken his seat at the right hand of the throne of God.

When Daniel describes the divine prophetic vision for us, he places the Ancient of Days on the throne and surrounds him with thousands upon thousands of servants and ten thousand times ten thousand attendants.[213] And Isaiah says that he saw the Son in no less glory. "I saw the Lord of hosts," he said, "sitting on a throne, high and lofty, and the house was full of his glory. And seraphim stood around him."[214] Their cry contained a triple "holy" at the beginning, but it concluded with a single lordship.[215] So does it not look to you like the Son is placed in the same glory? After all, where there is the highest throne and the superiority is distributed equally and the heavenly powers stand in a circle—which demonstrates the servile position of originate beings and testifies to the glory of the lordship of the one seated—how could there be any room for doubt that the Son is glorified with the natural lordship of the Father? But even though he has equal glory and is seated together on the throne, as the Son with the Father and as God with God, he nevertheless seems almost to ascend to his original glory, which was so manifest and transcendent, when on account of the flesh and his *oikonomia* in the flesh he hears, "Sit at my right hand until I make your enemies a footstool under your feet."[216] Whatever the divine nature lulls to sleep and puts under itself is certainly put under the feet of our Savior, who does not act in a human way. The fact that he became flesh is not the reason he rules over unbelievers, you see. Rather, the only begotten Word of God raises the lowly condition of his humanity to the highest honor of the divine nature and places himself in the chair of the divinity even with his flesh, and so he rules over all, and not without the Father. All things take place equally through both. The Father acts, but he has **[415]** the activity and will for whatever he does through the Son and in the Spirit along with him.

[212]Rom 4:3.

[213]Dan 7:9-10.

[214]Is 6:1-2.

[215]Is 6:3: "Holy, holy, holy is the Lord of hosts."

[216]Ps 110:1 (Ps 109:1 LXX).

12:18-21 You have not come. . . . "I tremble with fear."

Now Paul calls to mind the story of the time when God came down to Sinai in the form of fire, and "the sound of a trumpet blasted."[217] The sight was overwhelming for those who saw it, and the sound of the trumpet was unbearable. So they said, "We will no longer see this great fire, and we will not hear the voice of the Lord our God."[218]

12:26 But now he has promised, "Yet once more I will shake not only the earth but also the heaven."[219]

Heaven knew the mystery, and so did the entire earth. In the history of the world, there were two conspicuous changes in our way of life. They are called two covenants, or two earthquakes due to the renown of the event. One was from idols to the law, and the other was from the law to the gospel. And we proclaim a third earthquake: a change from here to there, where our condition will no longer be moved or shaken.

12:28 Therefore, since we are receiving a kingdom that cannot be shaken, let us give thanks.

I would gladly say to those who think that the kingdom of Christ has come to an end:[220] Whose kingdom shall we say the apostle is thinking of here, which he says will be fixed firmly and will always be unshakeable? (That is what I think "cannot be shaken" means). Is he speaking of the kingdom of the Son in this passage, or the kingdom that will be given to the saints? If **[416]** they admit that the kingdom and superiority of the Son is superior to change, I think our opponents will be deeply embarrassed because of the random nonsense they have spewed. But if they omit the Son and say that the saints will have an unalterable reign, then right away they will appear to be superior to Christ himself since they gain an inheritance that surpasses his. That is because he gains a rule that can be lost, while they will gain everlasting joy and unshakeable glory. How could this uncivilized slander not be absolutely rejected? Having power and rule over all things would be fitting for no one other than Christ himself. And he possesses it not as an acquisition or a gift, as we do, but it follows from the inner reality of his natural lordship. We, on the other hand, will co-suffer and co-reign with him, as it is written.[221] Therefore, he is the Lord of his reign, while we are adopted and honored by participation. Christ reigns, but they will co-reign with him. How will they have this unshakeable honor and reign forever if the rule of Christ (in which we maintain they participate) will be shaken and come to an end? If the one who rules and supplies them with their reign will stop reigning himself, where will that leave them, since they are founded on such a gulf? How will they still participate in him if that which called them to glory is now weak? Is it not necessary that those who endure what he endures should sink down with him and whatever depends on him should sit in the deepest pits, since what supports them has dragged them down? You see, when the basis of their glory and the foundation of their honor collapses, then the hope of the others will surely go with it into ignominy and abasement. Therefore, the words "When he hands over the kingdom"[222] do not mean that he gets rid of it,

[217]Ex 19:16.

[218]Deut 18:16.

[219]Pusey notes that he retains this scholion, but not without doubt.

[220]Marcellus of Ancyra taught, on the basis of 1 Cor 15:24-28, that the Son would hand over everything to the Father and have nothing left for himself to rule. Cyril seems to be reacting to this view, or one like it, here. Cf. Cyril's comments on 1 Cor 15:28 above.

[221]2 Tim 2:12.

[222]1 Cor 15:24.

but that he takes it away from others and brings it to the Father. However, he himself will rule it along with the Father. [**417**]

13:8 Jesus Christ is the same yesterday and today and forever.

Some passages are fitting for God, such as, "I am in the Father and the Father is in me."[223] Others are fitting for a man, such as, "But now you are trying to kill me, a man who has told you the truth."[224] [Others are in the middle, and this is one of them. It says that Christ][225] is "yesterday and today and forever." Notice that the Spirit Bearer, who teaches the mystery concerning Christ from Christ himself, explicitly confesses that the Son has an unchangeable and unalterable nature. This is a thing that belongs only to God the Father and does not apply to anyone else among originate beings. So if only God the Father is unchangeable, and the Son has the same nature, always being what his begetter is, how could he be one of the originate beings? He alone competes with the one who produced him with respect to the ineffable nature of his essence. He alone is by nature what the Father is, save only that he is not the Father. In this passage the Spirit Bearer discloses that when the Word became a human being like us, he was not altered. He uses the word "yesterday" to refer to past time, "today" to refer to the present time, and "forever" to refer to the coming future time. But some people, since they take the words *yesterday* and *today* to refer to recent times, argue vehemently: how could one who is "yesterday and today" also be "forever"?[226] But we will turn the force of the question around to its opposite: How could the Word, who is "forever," take "yesterday and today" into himself if indeed Christ is one and not divided, as Paul says?[227] Clearly, Jesus Christ is "yesterday and today" in a bodily way and he is "forever" in a spiritual way.

13:9 Do not be carried away by all kinds of strange teachings.

Being "carried away" is used metaphorically of those who are driven mad, of those who are carried to and fro, of those [**418**] who bend like a reed to whatever pushes them and have no stability, even though Paul cries out, "Be steadfast, immovable!"[228] And the Lord himself levels the most severe accusation against those who are easily carried away and scattered, and he decrees punishment for those who have the disease of turning away. Here he said of some of them, "They have loved to wander, they have not restrained their feet; therefore, the Lord was not pleased with them."[229] After all, established and unwavering stability is useful for whatever you do, and it is safe and secure.

13:11 Of those animals whose blood is brought in . . .

There are many other things said about this passage, but I omit them here because of their number. Christ died according to the flesh so that he might purify us with his own blood.

13:12-13 Let us then go to him . . .

Let us then "bear his abuse," that is, the cross he bore for us. He himself said, "Whoever does not take up the cross and follow me is not worthy of me."[230] And we should understand "outside the gate" to mean "outside the world,"

[223]Jn 14:10.
[224]Jn 8:40.
[225]Pusey, following Mai, supplies the words in brackets, which have disappeared from the codex. See Pusey 5:417n5.
[226]Cf. Cyril, *Contra Nestorium* 3.3 (Pusey 6:152).
[227]1 Cor 1:13.
[228]1 Cor 15:58.
[229]Jer 14:10.
[230]Mt 10:38.

since the will to follow Christ takes us out of our worldly life. [419]

13:16 Doing good and sharing . . .

Look once again, I ask you, at how Paul here calls the Son God. He himself is the one who leads the whole creation to judgment. He repays "according to each one's deeds,"[231] and therefore receives those who treat their neighbor well, saying, "Come inherit the kingdom prepared for you, for I was hungry and you gave me food,"[232] and so forth. He is called God by the truthful voice of the saints. He receives the sacrifices of those who do well. He renders to each one the appropriate reward. He sends the chorus of the saints into the kingdom of heaven. So how could he not be God? [420]

Cyril, from the commentary on the epistle to the Hebrews.[233]

Even though the only begotten Word of God could perhaps be said to be united to the flesh hypostatically, we maintain that there was no pouring of the natures into one another. Rather, we understand the Word to be united to the flesh with each nature remaining what it is.

Cyril, from the second book of his comments on Hebrews.

"Claiming to be wise, they became fools," as it is written.[234] They separate the two natures from each other and show us that each one is, in turn, unconnected from the other when they say that the union takes place only among *prosopa*[235] and in mere agreement and identity of counsel and inclination of wills. I suppose that is just what is written in the Acts of the Apostles: [421] "Now the whole group of those who believed were of one heart and soul."[236] Each of the believers in terms of their own hypostasis was separate from the others, but insofar as there was identity of will and unity of faith, they are said to have one soul and heart. So do they too intend to confess the unity of *prosopa* in the same sense? And a little later he says,[237] And we deny that the nature of the Word of God is circumscribed in the human body, since God cannot be quantified. Then he adds, One may see in Christ a complete human nature in accordance with the constitution of his nature. Likewise, the Word who came from God is complete. Yet we will confess one Christ and Son from both, constructing the *oikonomia* not by a mere unity of *prosopa,* but gathering together the two natures into one reality in a manner that is ineffable and transcends reason, which only God himself knows. And we certainly do not say that some kind of pouring takes place between the natures so that the nature of the Word changes into the nature of the man, let's say, or that the human nature changes into the nature of the Word himself. No, each nature is understood to be and is within the definition of its own nature. And we say that the union takes place when the Word dwells bodily in the temple that comes from the virgin. And a little later: Therefore, if anyone says that the union is of mere *prosopa,* thus completely separating the natures from each other, they have been carried off the straight path. [422]

Cyril, from the same commentary.

Observe that in the two goats, the one Christ (that is, the incarnate God) both dies in a fleshly

[231]Rom 2:6.

[232]Mt 25:34-35.

[233]At this point, Pusey includes some comments drawn from the Mai catena, whose headings do not specify the verse on which Cyril is commenting.

[234]Rom 1:22.

[235]πρόσωπον can be translated "person," but more concretely it refers to a face or mask. Such a union would be a union in appearance only.

[236]Acts 4:32.

[237]This seems to be a remark of the catenist, introducing the next quote from Cyril.

way for our sins in order to sanctify the whole church by sprinkling with his blood, and at the same time he remains impassible in a divine way.

Cyril, from the commentary on the epistle to the Hebrews.

If he has perfected us through water and the Spirit, how could the same one not act in both a divine and human way at the same time, and as God and man in one?

Cyril, from the commentary on Hebrews, the second book.

Divinity and humanity came together with each other in an ineffable way that is beyond thought. Even though the two natures are different, as everyone knows, yet there is only one Son from both.

Cyril, from the commentary on the epistle to the Hebrews.

Although the natures of the things that combined into one (I mean the flesh and God) should be considered different and unequal to each other, yet there is only one Son from both. **[423]** And the temple united to the Word is animated with a rational soul like ours.

Cyril, from the commentary on the epistle to the Hebrews.

A mere human being like one of us did not have the ability to carry out the activity that belongs to life by nature. Therefore, when the very body of the Word, who became incarnate for us, tasted death for the salvation of all (even though he is life by nature), it did so "by the grace of God," as the most holy Paul himself says.[238] That way, no one would think that destroying death is an accomplishment of an earthly body. Rather, it is an accomplishment of the Word himself, who is united to it and is different from it by nature. **[424]**

Again he says in book two,[239] interpreting the epistle to the Hebrews:[240]

When we said that the Word became flesh, we meant that the Word communicated hypostatically[241] with the flesh in an ineffable manner. We cannot understand how. Then—then!—the *persona* of each hypostasis[242] (distinguished mentally) came together with the natures into a unity.

Later in the same work, in the fourth book:[243]

Therefore, he says, humankind began to bloom again as from the second root of Christ, the Savior of us all. It was reborn, as it were, into imperishability and overcame the power of the ancient charge that stood against it through the ages.

The same, from his commentary on the epistle to the Hebrews:[244]

But the law of sin would not have been put to death in us, nor would death, the greatest

[238]Heb 2:9.

[239]Facundus actually identifies the source as book three.

[240]This fragment is in Latin and comes from a citation by Facundus of Hermianae in defense of the Three Chapters; *Pro Defensione Trium Capitulorum* 11.7.14. Facundus is defending Diodore and Theodore by showing that Cyril can use "Nestorian"-sounding language as well. See *Facundus d'Hermiane: Défense des Trois Chapitres (Livres XI-XII)*, Sources Chrétiennes 499 (Paris: Les Éditions du Cerf, 2006), 104.

[241]*Secundum subsistentiam*. Presumably this is a translation of καθ' ὑπόστασιν.

[242]*Subsistentiae*. *Persona* is the standard Latin translation of πρόσωπον.

[243]This fragment is in Latin and comes from a citation by Facundus of Hermianae, *Pro Defensione Trium Capitulorum* 11.7.15 (Sources Chrétiennes 499:104-6).

[244]This fragment is in Latin and comes from *Variorum Patrum Epistolae: Ad variorum Patrum Epistolas concernentes Acta Ephesini & Chalcedonensis Concilii, nuperrime repertae in Bibliotheca celeberrimi Monasterii Cassinensis*, ed. Christianus Lupus (Venice, 1726), chap. 281, p. 379.

enemy of all people, have been destroyed if the nature in which it was condemned by the Word's own power had not truly been made the Word's own. After all, it was not possible for an ordinary human being like us to destroy the reign of death. But it was destroyed through Christ. Now it is clear to everyone that God is certainly greater than we are. Therefore, since he was a man, it was as God that he was much greater than we are. And the temple that received the "fullness of deity"[245] was holy. However, through the economic uniting, the temple is said and believed to be one with him who dwelt in it. Just as the Holy Spirit is in us and makes us the temple of God and shows us to be so, in the same way in the case of Christ himself we say that the Word of God dwells in the flesh as in a temple, and that as he dwells in it, he sanctifies it. Yet we maintain that although it is called a temple, nevertheless that which was assumed was his own so that it is considered to be one with him—not because it passed over into the divine nature, but because it went into a synthesis due to the economic uniting. For God was in the flesh for our sake. [425]

Because of this, he did not hesitate to say in his commentary on the epistle to the Hebrews:[246]

God the Word also rose again after he suffered in the flesh.

The same, from his book on the epistle to the Hebrews.[247]

He allowed his body to suffer death in the *oikonomia* "so that he might be Lord of both the dead and the living."[248] Since the body belonged to him who is Life, it immediately overcame corruption and returned to life. However, let us show reverence by attributing such an august achievement not to the nature of the flesh, but to the power of the Word.

This is what Saint Cyril teaches in the first book on the epistle to the Hebrews, writing the following:[249]

Now if you praise the Word of God as a man, then you are showing me that you despise him. But if you speak of the Word and remain silent about the other, you are showing that he was not in our condition. Of course, the nature of those things that are brought together with one another is different. But we believe that there is only one Son from the two, who is in the union in the *oikonomia*.[250] Now if we say that the union occurred in the will alone or in the *prosopon*,[251] I think we are depriving ourselves of the Word completely. Let's say someone comes and asks us if we believe the Word of God is united to many others in the same way, since they say he gave the glory of his person to the holy apostles when he said, "Whoever welcomes you welcomes me,"[252] and to the righteous and merciful, because they had shown mercy to them, "As much as you do to one of these little ones, you do to me."[253] Again, [426] we do not say that the Word is

[245]Col 2:9.

[246]This fragment is in Latin and comes from Alexander of Hierapolis's *Epistula ad Acacium* (PG 84:667A).

[247]This fragment is cited by Leontius of Byzantium in a catena that he provides to support his position in *Contra Aphthartodocetas*. It is excerpt 26. For the Greek text, see Brian E. Daley, ed., *Leontius of Byzantium: Complete Works*, Oxford Early Christian Texts (Oxford: Oxford University Press, 2017), 407. Pusey provides a Latin translation of it by Fabricius (Pusey 5:425). I have translated the Greek version.

[248]Rom 14:9.

[249]This fragment and those that follow are extant only in Syriac translation. The citations may have been taken from Severus of Antioch and then translated into Syriac, or they may come from from an anonymous Syriac collection. See Pusey 5:425n9.

[250]*Medbarānūtā* likely translates the Greek word οἰκονομία, which here refers to the incarnation.

[251]*Parṣūpā*. This is the Syriac equivalent of the Greek word πρόσωπον, which can mean "person" or "mask." A union of πρόσωπον, in Cyril's view, is a union in appearance only rather than an ontological one.

[252]Mt 10:40.

[253]Mt 25:40.

united to these others, but only to that temple who is from the holy virgin. The union, then, it is correct to confess, was brought about by the concurrence of the natures. It is not a union of mere *prosopa*.[254] That ignorant idea is not found in the doctrine of the church.

In the second book on the epistle to the Hebrews, he writes these things concerning this prosopic union:

Now if someone says that it is right to worship him and to praise him with the glory of the heavenly beings because, though he is a man like us, he has honor because of the union of will or mere *prosopon*, as it were, then that wretched person is deceived by the idea that there is an equal rank between these two. He crowns the servant and the Lord, the creature and the Creator, man and God. And after other comments: they are persuading us, if they will allow it, that these people uttered nonsense. They separate the Word himself from the man. It is construed as a mere verbal unity when he receives honor because of the prosopic union. I do not endorse this view, but let us say he has this special virtue, if you please. Then let them answer this since we have to ask a question: For which upright actions did he who is completely human become this, even though he was in the human nature? And how will he be worthy of the divine thrones?

And in the third book he demonstrates. . . . For he also writes . . .

The things that we have said are from the Holy Scriptures, but those people have not been careful enough regarding the true union. I say that it is hypostatic, but they invent the idea that the union is merely in the *prosopon* alone. They refuse to call the true Son Emmanuel. Since they reject any change of the natures, as it were, they maintain and insist that he is one and another.[255] **[427]**

From St. Cyril, from the fourth book on the epistle to the Hebrews.

He is therefore one Son and Lord in the hypostatic union, because the Word is united to the human nature and he shared in flesh and blood and for this reason became like his brothers in all things.[256]

Again, from the third book of Cyril's comments on the epistle to the Hebrews.

Paul, then, shows us an excerpt from a hymn.[257] First he gives the excerpt itself, and then on the basis of that excerpt he says, "Now we do not yet see everything subject to him."[258] They will never convince us, if we have a right will, to agree that Paul is saying these things about the one man, as though referring to that man united in one *prosopon*, or that Paul is saying that he was deprived of the possession of that glory which he was given from the beginning.

Again, from his commentary on the apostle's epistle to the Hebrews.

He is quite right when he explicitly tells those who want a reward to seize "the prize of a heavenly call."[259] When temptations come, we should not sleep or let down our soul's guard or worry, but fervently stretch out to pray to him who knows how to save and ask for deliverance from evil. For our kneeling is hard work and not without tears. A little later: Now

[254]*Parçūpā*.

[255]The rest of this fragment is missing.

[256]Heb 2:14, 17.

[257]The excerpt of the hymn is Ps 8:4-6, which is quoted in Heb 2:6-8.

[258]Heb 2:8.

[259]Phil 3:14.

the "good crop"[260] **[428]** is a pure soul. It has no thought like this: I love pleasure more than God; I have produced thorns that I should have avoided. That person is headed for destruction by fire, just like land that is similarly thorny.[261] God does not bestow rain from heaven or comfort through the Holy Spirit unless he deems the person worthy of compassion and care.

From Saint Cyril of Alexandria, from his commentary on the epistle to the Hebrews.

Expectation is hope for the outcome of things—the hope, that is, and the vigil. And so the creation longs for the revelation of the sons of God.[262] For there is no way for it to know about this kind of birth—how or where it takes place—except through the ineffable *oikonomia* of God, who transforms all things into what is excellent. I am talking here about the impending consummation. Just as it was in the beginning, he speaks and in this way he molds the sons of God from contemptibleness into glory, from weakness into strength, from corruption into incorruptibility. They—they!—have set their sights on lives of glory and goodness. They have purified themselves by following the evangelical laws. In the same way creation is completely transformed into what is excellent and into a condition that it would only be right and proper for you to boast about on that day. St. Peter, therefore, allowed for no doubt about this when he plainly said, "But the day of the Lord will come like a thief, and then the heavens will fall off their foundations, and the elements will be dissolved with fire, and the earth and everything on it will be burned up."[263] And after that he added, "But in accordance with his promise, we wait for new heavens and a new earth, where righteousness is at home."[264] And our Savior teaches us these things about the end of the age even more strongly when he tells the holy disciples: "Immediately after the suffering of those days, **[429]** the sun will be darkened and the moon will not give its light."[265] And the prophetic word confirms for us that all the stars will fall: "And the sky will be rolled up like a scroll, and all the stars will fall like leaves from the vine or like leaves fall from a fig tree."[266] And so this condition of creation will also belong to the glory of the saints, that is, a condition that is good and fitting.

260Heb 6:7.
261Heb 6:8.
262Rom 8:19.
2631 Pet 3:10.
2642 Pet 3:13.
265Mt 24:29.
266Is 34:4.

General Index

Scripture Index

ANCIENT CHRISTIAN TEXTS

SERIES EDITORS

Gerald L. Bray

Michael Glerup

Thomas C. Oden†

Ancient Christian Texts is a series of new translations, most of which are presented here in English for the first time. The series provides contemporary readers with the resources they need to study the key writings of the early church for themselves. The texts represented in the series are full-length commentaries or sermon series based on biblical books or extended scriptural passages.

This series extends the ecumenical project begun with the Ancient Christian Commentary on Scripture, promoting a vital link of communication between today's varied Christian traditions and their common ancient ancestors in the faith. On this shared ground, we gather to listen to the pastoral and theological insights of the church's leading theologians during its earliest centuries.

Many readers of the Ancient Christian Commentary on Scripture have wished to read the full-length works from which excerpts were selected. Several of those texts have not been available in English before or have existed only in cumbersome English in isolated libraries. The work begun by Thomas C. Oden and the Institute for Classical Christian Studies to make more of these texts available to the general reading public continues today.

The volumes, though not critical editions, provide notes where needed to acquaint general readers with the necessary background to understand what the ancient authors are saying. Preachers, pastors, students and teachers of Scripture will be refreshed and enriched here by the ancient wisdom of the church.